Raymond Williams

DATE DUE

RAYMOND WILLIAMS

Writing, Culture, Politics

Alan O'Connor

Basil Blackwell

First published 1989

Basil Blackwell Ltd
108 Cowley Road, Oxford, OX4 1JF, UK

Basil Blackwell Inc.
432 Park Avenue South, Suite 1503
New York, NY 10016, USA

British Library Cataloguing in Publication Data
O'Connor, Alan
Raymond Williams: writing, culture, politics
1. English literature. Williams, Raymond, 1921–88
Critical studies
I. Title
828'.91409

ISBN 0–631–16588–6
ISBN 0–631–16589–4 Pbk

Library of Congress Cataloging in Publication Data
O'Connor, Alan.
Raymond Williams, writing, culture, politics / Alan O'Connor,
p.   cm.
Bibliography: p.
Includes index.
ISBN 0–631–16588–6
ISBN 0–631–16589–4 (pbk.)
1. Williams, Raymond—Criticism and interpretation. I. Title.
PR6073.I4329Z85 1989   88–39920
828'.91409—dc 19   CIP

Typeset in 10.5 on 12pt Erhardt by Columns of Reading
Printed in Great Britain by T.J. Press (Padstow) Ltd, Padstow, Cornwall.

Contents

Foreword by
Terry Eagleton   vii

Preface   ix

1   Introduction: vocation
writer   1

2   Politics   6

3   Institutions   40

4   Keywords in culture
and society   49

5   The knowable community
in the English novel   68

6   Complex seeing in drama
and television   80

7   Marxism and theory   103

8   Conclusion: writing and
politics   120

A Raymond Williams
Bibliography   128

Index   177

Foreword

It is surprising that the work of Raymond Williams was not during his lifetime the subject of any single extensive study. For Williams was without doubt the most pervasively influential cultural thinker produced by post-war Britain, a writer who placed the very concept of culture back at the heart of social and political argument; and there is a case for going further and claiming that, when the historical record comes to be soberly reviewed, Williams will be accorded the status of the single most masterly, original cultural thinker in Britain of the twentieth century. By the time of his death in 1988, he was certainly the single most important intellectual within his home country of Wales, a society whose history and political destiny form the subtext, and sometimes the explicit concerns, of much of his work. But he was also by far the most commanding figure on the British left as a whole, with a wisdom, independence of thought and versatility of topic unparalleled by his fellow socialists. To find adequate comparisons for his achievement, one must look further afield to the Sartre of France or the Habermas of Germany, both of whom have been the subject of more than one major study during their own lifetimes. The closest living European counterpart to Williams is surely Pierre Bourdieu, whose work reflects something of the same variety of preoccupations coupled with the same unwavering political comment.

In this context, Alan O'Connor's wide-ranging, thoroughly researched survey of Williams's writings is especially to be welcomed. With impressive ambitiousness, it takes on the complete, complex range of Williams's thought and activity over a period of some forty or more years; and though it would be a rash commentator who tried to reduce this extraordinarily varied *oeuvre* to a single theoretical centre, O'Connor manages none the less to convey something of the differentiated unity of Williams's lifelong political and intellectual project. It is, then, a book written in the spirit of a man who insisted above all on relations, connections, complex affinities – on crossing the borders now jealously drawn between alternative discourses, cultures and social formations.

With admirable persistence, O'Connor has ransacked the archives and demonstrates an intimate familiarity with the hidden recesses of his subject's work, all the way from his very early writings as a Cambridge student to the television reviews of his middle age. O'Connor's method is not to provide separate studies of the major published texts, in the conventional academic manner, but to set those works in the context of Williams's long political career and of the social institutions – film, television, publishing, newspapers – with which he was engaged. Indeed one of the most rewarding chapters of the book is the tenaciously detailed review of Williams as political activist, from the Cambridge University Communist Party and the early years in the Workers' Educational Association to the rather better-known public interventions of his later life. There is also, in the introductory chapter, the fascinating outline of a psychobiography of Williams, concerned less with concepts than with recurrent images, formative fantasies, intensities of feeling. As a genuine labour of political love O'Connor's lucid, informative study constitutes a significant contribution to our understanding of this most adventurous and resourceful of modern thinkers.

Terry Eagleton,
Linacre College,
Oxford

Preface

Raymond Williams died on 26 January 1988. During his life he published some thirty books and many hundreds of articles. He also wrote novels and plays, took part in many television and radio programmes, and had two television documentaries based on his work. Three volumes of his essays and writing are now being prepared for publication. His unfinished book on *Modernism and the Avant Garde* will appear later. Joy Williams, who collaborated with him on many of his projects, and their daughter Merryn Williams are preparing a completed section of a historical novel for publication.

Williams was not only an important writer and thinker about culture and politics, literature and drama, television and communication. He was also a socialist writer and activist. He came from a Welsh working-class background, spent fifteen years teaching for the Workers' Educational Association, was a participant in the Campaign for Nuclear Disarmament (CND) and the New Left from the late 1950s, co-ordinated an important socialist manifesto in 1967 and 1968, welcomed the student/worker strikes of 1968, and in the 1970s and 1980s supported socialist, feminist, ecological, and peace movements. These political intentions are evident in all of his work, especially in his keen attention to what is *silenced* by the dominant cultural and political discourses.

Williams's writing in the post-war period had a kind of existentialist motif of blocked individual liberation. This co-existed with other themes: a very complex sense of the active making of community, an emphasis on language, and on the history of cultural forms. Williams's most important writing is organized about several tropes: the ways in which *keywords* operate through their semantic instability; the complex development of subjunctive discursive forms which Williams calls the 'knowable community' in the novel and 'complex seeing' in drama. This book is organized about these three themes of keywords, knowable community, and complex seeing.

The understanding of this multi-dimensional and, changing work is complicated by the fact that Williams's work has now had three generations of readers. There are those who were his contemporaries in the emergence of the New Left in the late 1950s;[1] there is a younger generation, including some of his students, who argued against ideas of experience and culture, in favour of the linguistic turn and structuralism in the late 1960s and early 1970s;[2] and there is now a third generation which recognises an affinity between Williams as writer and the emphasis on discourse and politics in Foucault, Said, Chakravorty Spivak, and de Lauretis.[3] In this kind of generation cycle, Williams encounters some of his best readers. Robert Christgau, rock critic for the *Village Voice*, insists in a 1985 article on Williams that: 'If inquiring college graduates (and dropouts) can read Milan Kundera and Roland Barthes and Dick Hebdidge and William Gass, they can damn well read Williams, a richer writer book by book or all in all, than any of them.'[4]

I would like to thank John O'Neill, Bryan Green, Ioan Davies, Philip Corrigan, and John Fekete for critical comments and Alan Yoshioka for help in preparing the manuscript. While revising the book I was supported by a fellowship from the Social Sciences and Humanities Research Council of Canada.

Notes

1 V. G. Kiernan, 'Culture and Society', *New Reasoner*, 9 (1959), pp. 74–83; E. P. Thompson, 'The Long Revolution', *New Left Review*, no. 9 and no. 10 (May/June and July/August 1961), pp. 24–33, 34–9; C. L. R. James, 'Marxism and the Intellectuals', reprinted in his *Spheres of Existence: Selected Writings* (London, Allison and Busby, 1980), pp. 113–30. For an example of quite a different kind of reception see Anthony Hartley. 'The Loaf and the Leaven', review of *Culture and Society*, by Raymond Williams, *Manchester Guardian*, 7 October 1958, p. 10; Hartley, 'Philistine to Philistine?' in *International Literary Annual 2*, edited by John Wain (London, John Calder, 1959), pp. 11–36; Hartley, 'The Intellectuals of England', *The Spectator*, 4 May 1962, pp. 557–81.
2 Stuart Hall, 'The Williams Interviews', *Screen Education*, no. 34 (1980), pp. 94–104; Stuart Hall, 'Cultural studies: two paradigms', *Media, Culture and Society*, 2 (1980), pp. 57–72; Terry Eagleton, 'Criticism and Politics: The Work of Raymond Williams', *New Left Review*, no. 95 (1976), pp. 3–23; Terry Eagleton, *The Function of Criticism: From The Spectator to Post-Structuralism* (London, Verso, 1984), pp. 108–15.
3 Michel Foucault, *Discipline and Punish: The Birth of the Prison*, tr. Alan Sheridan (New York, Vintage, 1979); Edward Said, *Orientalism* (New York, Vintage, 1979); Gayatri Chakravorty Spivak, *In Other Worlds: Essays in Cultural Politics* (New York and London, Routledge, 1988); Teresa de

Lauretis, *Alice Doesn't: Feminism, Semiotics, Cinema* (Bloomington, Indiana University Press, 1984).
4 Robert Christgau, 'Living in a Material World', *The Village Voice Literary Supplement*, no. 34 (April 1985), p. 1.

1

Introduction: vocation writer

'Fame', said Rilke, 'is the sum of misunderstanding which gathers about a new name.'[1] Raymond Williams is a case in point. The reputation is about working-class culture and the misunderstanding comes when activities and structures are taken to be a kind of plenitude: a contained oral culture, a Welsh countryside, a family kitchen. To point out that at quite a young age Williams wanted to be a writer is seldom enough to move beyond the fundamental misunderstanding. This ambition can easily enough be placed in the conventional category of a naïve working-class writer in which the main interest seems to be a kind of unmediated experience.[2] It will be as well to leave this kind of biographical model and start again in another way.

Between 1945 and 1951 there emerges in his writing the rhythms and characteristic intensity of feeling by which we still recognize Raymond Williams. The origin of this written rhythm and intensity is perhaps surprising. It emerges in the year after Williams's return from the Second World War. In 1945–6 he wrote a long essay on Ibsen. The essay starts by quoting from Rilke that fame is the sum of misunderstanding which gathers around a new name. It is a kind of writerly borrowing that is characteristic of Williams's prose.

Yet this writer, who has a highly developed sense of how words borrow their meaning from the history of their use, has insisted many times that in any cultural analysis it is necessary to start from the place where we live. There is a kind of astonishment in realizing that *childhood* is central to what have been key texts for Williams. This is not the early childhood of the Freudian psychodrama, but a kind of border country between delighted absorption and critical awareness. In the conclusion of *The Country and the City*, Williams describes how often the idea of the country is the idea of childhood: 'Not only the local memories, or the ideally shared communal memory, but the feel of childhood: of delighted absorption in our own world, from which, eventually, in the course of growing up, we are distanced and separated, so that it and the world become things we observe.'[3]

This theme recurs. Cobbett in the 1820s and 1830s is directly in touch with the rural England of his time but looking back to the happier country, the old England of his boyhood. Pasternak's *Doctor Zhivago* reaches a resolution in the ambiguous figure of the daughter of Yury and Lara, who is also the daughter of the revolution. There is a return to the youth of Isak Borg in Ingmar Bergman's *Wild Strawberries*. These are the subjects of exemplary texts by Williams.[4] They are also an index of the range of his writings: from a rural writer who became a popular radical, to a Russian poet who wrote a realist novel of the revolution, to a film-maker in the tradition of Ibsen and Strindberg.

There were few books in the house where Williams grew up. In one of his few autobiographical articles, he describes how, instead of the usual children's books, he read the Bible, the *Beekeeper's Manual*, a textbook from his father's English evening-class, *The Wonder Book of Why and What*, and a translation of Euripides' *Trojan Women* which his mother gave him for his birthday. Later, there was a one-volume Shakespeare, a set of Dickens, and a boyhood enthusiasm for Hazlitt. Williams says that he acquired the habit, which with some books he never lost, of over-and-over reading as if no other books existed.[5]

The over-and-over quality, the sheer density of the key terms of Williams's writing, should be no surprise. The central trope is not *making-strange* but that of doubling-over or *repetition*, or an interest in the density of experience along with a determination to return and give it shape. There is an insistence that experience, when examined again, has a kind of structure. There is an interest in the possibility of expressive images (the wild strawberries in Bergman's film) which concentrate meaningful experience. Communication is folded into communication: in *Wild Strawberries* the car moves through the country as the people in it talk and move through their dreams. Speech itself is founded on a gesture of body in tone, rhythm, mood, and atmosphere. It is founded, that is to say, on something like a dream.

Williams's reading of Ibsen, in the months immediately after the war, was like the childhood reading: over-and-over as if no other books existed. He says that he felt, as he was reading, that his life was being put in question. The experience of the war was appalling. There is a deep sense of unreality in Williams's description of that experience: of a lack of identity of oneself and the enemy. During the war Williams commanded a fighting unit of four tanks. In this situation one depended on vision because of the high level of engine noise. One can trace an interest in the theme of vision from Ibsen's *Brand* and *Peer Gynt*; also Canetti's *Die Bledung*, which Williams read at this time; to the phenomenology of perception in *The Long Revolution*; and to a 1960s essay on Brecht on 'complex seeing' which is a matter of returning and playing a previous scene over again to see how it could be different. There is little about the experience of war in Williams's novels until *Loyalties*, published forty years later, in which the central image is a pair of expensive German binoculars. The theme of blinding and vision makes problematic what is natural and what is fantasy. Out of exile and return there emerged, in the reading of Ibsen, the theme of *vocation*. For Williams it emerged through writing itself.

After the war Williams returned to Cambridge for the third year of his degree. As an ex-service person he was allowed to complete the English Tripos mainly by writing a 15,000-word thesis. In a disturbed personal condition after the experience of the war, Williams wrote his thesis on Ibsen. He became totally absorbed in the project: 'I really did feel as I was reading that my life was being put in question. I think most people would have the same sense when reading Freud, especially when he is near to the clinical experience of disorders and tragedies.'[6]

What Williams admires in Ibsen is not the social drama of *A Doll's House* but the fantasy world of *Peer Gynt*. It is significant that *Peer Gynt* was written outside the conventions of the theatre: it describes experience that was excluded from the dominant cultural form. It describes an emergent experience of leaving and return, vision and blinding, and play with time. Above all, it faces directly the problem of finding a vocation in a world that has been shaped by others. In order to write *Peer Gynt* it was necessary for Ibsen to withdraw from the theatre. It is a writer's drama, not written for performance.

The reason for the intense significance that Ibsen possessed for me then was that he was the author who spoke nearest to my own sense of my own condition at the time. Hence the particular emphasis I gave to the motif of coming to a tight spot where you stick fast. There is no going forward or backward. That was exactly my sensation.[7]

Ibsen gave Brand, in the play of that name, a religious vocation; but for Williams this is incidental: it could equally have been an artistic or political calling. Brand is the exile who has returned and seems to be a stranger to himself. He is unsure of his calling: 'Am I blind *now*, or was I then?' he asks (original emphasis).[8]

Drama is here a serious written form for the communication of particular experience. Ibsen abandons the character as the organizing theatrical convention. It is a matter of written form in relation to an emergent experience. Williams puts it this way: 'Ibsen needed a form which was more than the sum of the expressed relationships, also more than the action, since the lost – the alienated – quality, the life that might have been possible and is still deeply desired, is by definition not available as action'.[9] This emergent sense, this kind of connection of individual action to a social world, is more successfully present in *Peer*

Gynt than in *Brand*. This valuation of a romantic fantasy, called a
'caprice' by Ibsen himself, may surprise some readers of Williams.
According to Williams, the play is written as the quest of Peer Gynt for
his calling or vocation. There is a surprisingly modern sense of
selfhood. It seems to be both a fantasy and an *ensemble* of social
relations. Peer Gynt discovers this in Act Five when he returns home.
Williams admires this last act, which he says is a controlled pattern of
realized experience. The Strange Passenger and the Button Moulder
are not characters but dramatic images. One of Ibsen's own hobbies as
a boy was casting metal buttons. The image of the self is a metal button
which can be melted down and remade. Peer Gynt learns both the
reality and fantasy of the self through the experience of exile, war,
trading in human beings, and then through a return to carnival, local
tradition, community, and relationships with other people, when he is
confronted by the reappearance of this childhood Button Moulder. For
Ibsen, as for Williams, this is a matter of writing as an activity and as a
vocation.[10]

Notes

1 Quoted in Williams, *Drama from Ibsen to Eliot*, (Peregrine, 1964), p. 47.
2 There was an early confusion of Williams with Richard Hoggart, who also
   taught in adult education. For Williams on Hoggart see 'A note on Mr
   Hoggart's appendices', *Adult Education*, 21 (1948), pp. 96–8; 'Fiction and
   the Writing Public', *Essays in Criticism*, 7 (1957), pp. 422–8; 'The Uses of
   Literacy: Working Class Culture', *Universities and Left Review*, vol. 1, no. 2
   (1957), pp. 29–32; 'The reasonable Englishman', *Guardian*, 8 April 1982,
   p. 16; 'Affluence after anger', *The Nation*, 19 December 1966, pp. 676–7.
3 Williams, *The Country and the City* (Paladin, 1975), p. 357.
4 On Cobbett see Williams, *The Country and the City*, p. 19; on *Doctor
   Zhivago*, Williams, *Modern Tragedy* (Verso, 1979), pp. 167–73; on
   Bergman, Williams, *Drama in Performance* (Basic Books, 1968), pp.
   157–71.
5 Williams, in *Bookmarks*, ed. F. Raphael (Quartet, 1975), pp. 162–5.
6 Williams, *Politics and Letters* (New Left Books, 1979), p. 332.
7 Ibid., p. 62.
8 Henrik Ibsen, *Brand*, tr. F. E. Garrett (London, Dent, 1915), p. 101.
9 Williams, *Drama from Ibsen to Brecht* (Pelican, 1973), p. 57.
10 Marxism, more clearly than any other kind of thinking, has shown us that we are in
   fact aligned long before we realize that we are aligned. For we are born into a
   social situation, into social relationships, into a family, all of which have formed
   what we can later abstract as ourselves as individuals. Much of this formation
   occurs before we can be conscious of any individuality. Indeed the consciousness
   of individuality is often the consciousness of all those elements of our formation,
   yet this can never be complete. . . . So born into a social situation with all its
   specific perspectives, and into a language, the writer begins by being aligned. Yet

alignment goes deeper again, into the actual and available forms of writing. When I hear people talk about literature, describing what so-and-so did with the form – how did he handle the short novel? – I often think we should reverse the question and ask, how did the short novel handle him. (Williams, 'The Writer: commitment and alignment', *Marxism Today*, June 1980, p. 25).

2

Politics

Williams has written a surprising amount of direct political commentary but it is essential to understand how much remained unpublished including ordinary spoken discussion, unrecorded public talks, and unpublished writing. Williams has said that he regrets that it was much easier to publish literary criticism than political commentary in the 1950s.[1]

As an undergraduate Williams contributed to the *Cambridge University Journal* which, in fact, reads like many other undergraduate newspapers. It is difficult from its pages to get a sense of university politics in the 1940s, much less of Williams's own position. His first contribution to the newspaper makes the point that both the Cambridge English School and many progressive people insist on separating poetry, art, and spiritual values from progress. Against the dons, Williams makes the point that literature did not stop in 1920: literature is in history. But he then insists that 'In a materialist society the poet will have more freedom, less prejudice than ever before.'[2] There is a distance from the English faculty, but also from materialists who have no place for literature. A problem is stated but is not in any way solved.

Williams's working-class Welsh background and his experience of Cambridge University is described in *Politics and Letters* and in several of his essays which combine personal and theoretical reflection.[3] Williams was politically active as a teenager. He worked for Labour Party candidates in the 1935 and 1939 general elections and had experience as a public speaker. However, the usual maps of the 1930s do not hold for Williams. In particular his radicalism was based on his formative experience in a very particular working-class culture. His radicalism is therefore very different from that of 1930s intellectuals such as Auden and Orwell who did not have this direct experience and substituted an illusion of contact with the people of another country. Looking back, Williams sees the struggle against fascism in the 1930s as brave, urgent, and humane but at the same time a 'substantial confusion and failure'.[4] One of the achievements of the decade is to have published worker–writers such as Storm Jameson and B. L. Coombes. The dominant high-intellectual radicals do have to their credit a decade of opposition to fascism, imperialism, and war. However, their association of communism with the policies of the Soviet Union and their subsequent revulsion from Marxism were deeply damaging for the future of radical politics in their own country.

The academic year 1939–40 saw the strong continuation at Cambridge of a minority socialist movement and culture. By 1940–1 this was much more difficult. The war encroached more seriously on the university. Both the culture of the 1930s and the curriculum at Cambridge suddenly seemed less relevant. The *Cambridge University Journal* was under the control of the Socialist Club, which claimed 1,000 members or almost 20 per cent of the university membership. The Socialist Club was itself controlled by the Communist Party, which, as a strongly radical student, Williams joined in December 1939. Williams was appointed editor of the student newspaper for the third term of academic year 1939–40. As editor he wrote a weekly column of brief comments on student affairs. In November 1939 he made the interesting suggestion that the Arts Club, which was considering lunch-time ballet for following term, might do a critical analysis of propaganda 'from the cultural standpoint'.[5] It is interesting that under Williams's editorship a forum was established in the paper for representatives of the Socialists, Liberals, and Conservatives to debate political issues.

In his second year at Cambridge, Williams also did a considerable amount of writing for the Communist Party, including a pamplet written with Eric Hobsbawm which supported the Russian invasion of Finland. While this was written to instructions as a job of professional writing, Williams was also working as a committed member of the Party. He also worked on the production of an underground edition of the *Daily Worker* when it was banned in 1941.

As for literary work, Williams in 1941 also edited *Outlook: A Selection of Cambridge Writing* with Maurice Craig and Michael Orrom. The contributors were socialists but *Outlook* was not directly related to Party work. Williams's contribution is a short story called 'Sugar', which is about the need to make connections between local shortages and the world trade in the commodity.[6] The journal is in some ways an opposition to the dominant literary culture of the 1930s represented by *Left Review* and *New Writing*. Later in the 1940s he had stories published by Woodrow Wyatt and John Lehmann. However Williams resisted being drawn into this metropolitan literary world.

Workers' Educational Association

After two years as an undergraduate Williams was called up into the
Army and did not complete his degree until 1945–6. He did not often
write about the war. Although not a member of the Communist Party
during the war, Williams understood the fighting as a common struggle
with the Red Army.[7] His British Army officers did not share this radical
perspective. He seems to have been wholly sceptical of the opinion of
George Orwell and Tom Wintringham, who thought that the war effort
could be used to transform Britain into a socialist country.[8] Williams
was released early in October 1945 in order to resume his degree. This
was the year in which his work was mainly on Ibsen.

In the second edition of *Communications* Williams reflects on the
influences of working in different institutions.[9] He took a teaching job
with the Workers' Educational Association (WEA) between 1946 and
1961, when he shifted to university teaching at Cambridge. The
relation between the institution and the person is 'a continuing process,
in which the moments of choice and of direction are often subtle and
delicate, though the commitments they lead to are often profound.'[10]
Williams's books from *Reading and Criticism* to *Communications* belong
to a vibrant adult-education movement. Contemporary accounts of the
WEA make this clear.

There is a very interesting description by L. J. Barnes of a class he
taught in St Helens between 1940 and 1942. It was a neighbourhood
group of about fifteen persons. It was a three-year tutorial class and
would have elected its class secretary and chosen the subjects it wished
to study. It operated as a democratic voluntary organization. 'The
things these people insisted on discussing were issues of high politics
and high economics. . . . Week after week they went into all this with
great gusto and good humour. At the end of each meeting the tutor and
anyone else who felt the need adjourned to a pub for a pint.'[11] It was
not only a matter of taking a course: there was something that could
properly be called an educational movement which Barnes describes as
a product of the French Revolution and the Industrial Revolution.
These, according to Barnes, brought the masses into politics and led
them into discussing momentous issues. Although the WEA changed
rapidly through the 1950s, Williams's *Culture and Society* (written over
the period 1952–6) certainly fits with this educational movement.

Williams was part of a cohort of tutors hired in the immediate period
after the war. The WEA drew its teachers from the universities and
Williams was attached to the Oxford Delegacy for Extra-Mural
education. His first subjects were Current Affairs and Literature. The

WEA tutorial classes (Oxford delegacy)

Year	Total Classes	Lit. Classes
1918	15	2
1928	32	3
1938	46	5
1948	84	14
1958	115	33

Source: D. Butts, 'The Development of
Literature Teaching in the Oxford Tutorial
Classes'. *Rewley House Papers*, vol. 3, no. 7
(1959), p. 13.

first WEA Oxford tutorial class in literature began in 1917, although it was important as a university extension subject in 1895 (twenty-four out of a total of ninety-one courses in that year). The accompanying table shows the growth of classes in literature.

The rapid increase in literature classes after the war is in part due to increased numbers of women students and in part to the interests of the new group of tutors. Under the influence of Empson, Leavis, Murray, and Richards lecture courses (which had often covered an enormous amount of ground very rapidly) gave way to practical criticism and in-depth classwork on short passages of text. Williams's book *Reading and Criticism* was intended to provide a textbook for these new methods of teaching the subject. The method was extended to material outside the literary canon: film, advertisements, and the mass media. Butts, however, pointed out that Williams's teaching of Public Expression was not as new as he thought and had been a subject at least since 1919–20.[12] There were only ten tutorial classes on Culture and Environment, deriving from the Leavis's literary and sociological examination of the cultural scene.[13] Many of these may have been taught by Williams himself. This material contributed to *Communications*. Drama had long been a popular subject for WEA tutorial classes and the emphasis was often on drama in performance – as in Williams's book of that title.

The organizational structure of the WEA was also important. This local and democratic system survived in some parts of the country through the 1950s and beyond. Williams frequently gives this as an example of effective democratic organization. The WEA tradition was also one of exploring many approaches to a subject. Williams frequently uses R. H. Tawney's phrase that it is necessary to follow the argument where it leads.

There is a brief but useful discussion of the politics of the WEA in the interviews of *Politics and Letters*. Each district of the WEA was relatively autonomous and the political character of the organization varied in different parts of the country.[14] In Oxford the department was in the charge of Thomas Hodgkin, who, as Williams puts it, had 'a very strong and principled conception of how to develop a popular working-class education. He believed that essentially the people to do it were committed socialists.'[15] From the late 1940s this conception of workers' education and Hodgkin himself came under a sharp attack which Williams describes as a local form of the Cold War.

The debate continued into the 1950s. In an article in *The Highway*, Hodgkin criticized the drift to intellectual conformity. Although in this article he distances himself from the Communist Party, Hodgkin argues that the issue of the 'objectivity' of Marxist tutors was mistaken. A Marxist teacher is in the same situation as a Fabian or Christian teacher. Richard Hoggart and Henry Collins were among those who took part in the debate in the subsequent issues of *The Highway*.[16] The spokesperson for the other side was S. G. Raybould. He wanted courses related to the vocational needs of students: 'social workers, managers, administrators, police officers, co-operative employees.' He also argued for 'standards justifying university provision'.[17] By 1960 it was clear that this version of vocational and adult education had won the fight. The ideals of a working-class educational movement seemed, at least for the coming years, to be quite lost.

Williams looked back over these issues in 1961 in an article entitled 'The common good'. He argues that problems of the future adult education involve issues about the whole society. The question must be asked: 'For what are people being educated?'[18] Williams also argues the importance of the press, broadcasting, and television as educational communicators. It is necessary to move beyond the organizations of adult education to rethink many other experiences as part of a 'permanent education'. His book *Communications* is therefore a direct continuation of the WEA debates about the nature and purpose of education. Television, radio, and newspapers are, he insists, in the broadest sense *educational* institutions.

Politics and letters

The journal started by Williams with Wolf Mankowitz and Henry Collins involves several key debates of the late 1940s. Although the editors had met at Cambridge in 1945–6, the journal had a direct relationship with the adult-education movement. Wolf Mankowitz later became a well-known popular novelist and scriptwriter. Henry Collins, who had a central role in the work of the journal, was a member of the historians' group of the Communist Party. He later wrote a column on economic affairs for *Tribune* from 1964 until his death in December 1969.[19]

There were in fact two journals: *The Critic* and *Politics & Letters*. The former was intended to be a forum for critical judgements based on close readings of texts, and the latter was intended to set such judgements in a broader political framework. In Spring 1947 the first issue of *The Critic* appeared. By the second issue the address was no longer Mankowitz's in Essex: The Critic Press Ltd. had an office in Soho.[20] The first issue of *Politics & Letters* appeared in the Summer of 1947. In all there were two issues of *The Critic* and four of *Politics & Letters* (number 2–3 was a double issue). They were serious minority journals: the ideal reader was a politically involved adult-education tutor.

The editorial of the first issue of *Politics & Letters* set out a serious and fundamental programme involving an exploration of the relationship between organization and individual freedom. In the late 1940s this appeared as a conflict between government planning and individual values. This was a difficult ideological knot to untie. *Politics & Letters* was to deal with 'the deepest level of personality which is traditionally associated with literature and the arts'[21] and with the objective problems of the society. The terms were, of course, already occupied. It would be necessary to fight against the abstract values of the 'moralists' and their frequent personal indulgence. On the other hand it would be necessary to fight against the 'political' groups who were much too quick to attack contemporary art and literature as irrelevant, decadent, or idealist.

It would be wrong to give a summary account of the journals, especially since they set out to have an open editorial policy. In retrospect, however, it is clear that *Politics & Letters* is the more significant and that the central debate in the journal was about the relationship between politics and writing. This debate was given the title 'Critic and Leviathan' and the contributors to it were R. O. C. Winkler, Christopher Hill, F. R. Leavis, Lionel Elvin, and George Orwell. Other articles became part of the debate: a translation of Sartre on 'commitment' in literature, and Williams on a debate that was known at the time as 'the Soviet literary controversy'.[22]

This controversy gained in importance because the action of Zhdanov in the Soviet Union against several writers was seen by Cyril Connolly and others as an example of the kind of effect that socialism would have on Britain. It was also part of Cold War attitudes which were the frequent subject of Williams's wrath in *Politics & Letters*. The debate was about criticism made by the Central Committee of the Soviet Communist Party in August 1946 of the work of Zoschenko, a popular humorist, and the well-known poetess, Akhmatova. The Executive of the Union of Soviet Writers and Communist party authorities in Leningrad were also criticized.

In England the action was defended by John Lewis in *Modern Quarterly* (a Communist Party journal) and held up by Cyril Connolly in *Horizon* as an argument against socialism in general and the Soviet Union in particular. Williams goes through their arguments, pointing to contradictions and assumptions,[23] and he also takes their prose as evidence. However his main response is to read the short story at the centre of the controversy. It seems to him to be ordinary commercial humour and his more general criticism of the Soviet Union's cultural policy is its tendency to stabilize literary work at this fairly low level. Williams is making this literary argument against the merely political argument of John Lewis, who tended to see literary criticism as similar to criticism of inefficiency or poor management. However, Williams is also arguing against Connolly in *Horizon*, which magazine he takes as a symbol of a certain class-based life-style and self-indulgence. The issue, Williams argues, is not one of state control but of the conditions necessary to allow a writer to develop that sense of inwardness that is a necessary part of any serious social realism.

The 'Critic and Leviathan' debate was started by Winkler, who described a loss of community and individual response, arguing that this was the result of mechanization. The argument is much influenced by Leavis, but Winkler does not see Leavis's version of a minority English School in the university as an adequate solution to the problem. Christopher Hill responded by challenging Winkler to describe the values that he wanted to preserve and arguing that Winkler's account of industrialization was inadequate and better replaced by Marxist categories. F. R. Leavis responded to Hill by saying that one simply *knew* what these fundamental human values were: they could not be stated abstractly. Leavis was not interested in joining any political party. He had made his argument for educational work and for an English School and he stood by that.

With debates shaping up between the position of Leavis and that of the Communist Party, the editors made their comment. We can ask, they said, 'what forms of human organization are compatible with our experience of literature?'[24] The answer they gave was the sense of human *responsibility* in Martin Buber and D. H. Lawrence. They mean active caring, and also an openness to another person. This is an interesting answer since it turns the debate to the institution of humanity *in* literature.

George Orwell's response was quite different. Actual writers must take notice of the world crisis (which Orwell describes not in Cold War terms but as a matter of inequalities between industrialized nations and the Third World). However, they must do this as private citizens and not as writers. 'Whatever he does in the service of his party he should never write for it. . .'[25]

The contribution by Sartre, part of the argument of *What is Literature*, was not of course a direct response to the debate but it was directly relevant. However, there are political and theoretical differences between Sartre and Williams. As Perry Anderson has noted, the comparison which makes sense in the post-war years is with Sartre's colleague Merleau-Ponty.[26] Williams disagreed with Sartre's founding distinction between poetry and prose. The *Politics & Letters* editorial description of the institution of literature as human *responsibility* is a very different vocabulary from Sartre's existentialism.

There was an interest in *Politics & Letters* in actual cultural institutions: in radio, publishing, and state policy for communications and the arts. Williams wrote a note on 'The state and popular culture' in which he discusses policy for the Press, theatre, books, films, and advertising:

Democracy does not demand a cultural levelling-down, and the general record of the Labour movement, with the example of the Workers Education Association before them, ought to lead to sensible, discriminating aid. But so far there has been too much evidence of a strand on the untenable principles of cultural demagogy: the 'indeterminacy' of taste; the proof of value in commercial success; and the sticky populism which was given title by Mr. Priestley's *Let the People Sing*.[27]

Paper rationing, for example, was based on a percentage of pre-war consumption. No attempt was made to distinguish between valuable books and out-and-out trash. He is highly critical of the post-war Labour Government's insistence on seeing communications as a matter of organization rather than of values. The argument deals with very difficult issues through the practical experience of the workers' education formation.

CND and the New Left

As the 1950s turned into the 1960s new social movements took Williams's and others' independent intellectual work and brought it a much wider readership than it might otherwise have had. The effect of these movements was to end Williams's relative isolation since the collapse of *Politics & Letters* in 1948. In 1968 he mentioned in an article that he had been on every Easter march for the Campaign for Nuclear Disarmament (CND) since 1958.[28] Williams has also had a complex affiliation with the New Left.

In 1958 Williams contributed an essay to a collection called *Conviction* which was edited by Norman MacKenzie. This is not really a New Left book.[29] MacKenzie was a member of the editorial staff of the *New Statesman*. Others had connections with *Tribune* or were unaffiliated socialists. The average age of contributors was thirty-three (and apart from Iris Murdoch all were men). It was, in the words of Mervyn Jones, the generation that had grown up in the emergency. Williams agrees: the 1930s was not a time of serious thought. *Conviction* represents the conscript generation that is starting to produce original analysis. 'Our need is for thought', said Jones.[30]

The contributions are quite diverse. Peter Shore describes the rise of large corporations and the new class of managers. Brian Abel-Smith gives the results of his analysis of the Welfare State which demonstrate that it mainly benefits the middle classes. Hugh Thomas described his time in the Foreign Office; Peter Marris his time in Kenya; and Paul Johnson the effect on him of the violent suppression in Paris of the student and workers' demonstrations of 1952. Iris Murdoch describes the poverty of analytic philosophy and says that 'It is dangerous to starve the moral imagination of the young.'[31] Mervyn Jones describes a CND placard that said simply: 'STOP AND THINK'.

There is a remarkable similarity in tone in all the essays: an emergent generation finding its voice. The *form* of the contributions is also very similar. They are all in some way personal, perhaps close to new styles of investigative journalism. The writer's experience is there, but also a firm base of research, or information derived from work (in the Foreign Office, for example). The essays are addressed to a *general* reader rather than to left intellectuals or members of a movement such as the Left Book Club of the 1930s.

This kind of literary journalism very much suited Williams. 'Culture is ordinary' starts with a narrative of a bus journey in which many different kinds of culture are evident: conversation, advertisements, a library, a cinema, the countryside itself. Then Williams describes his experience at Cambridge: the actual work which was a direct continuation from his life in Wales, but no connection with what he calls the 'culture of the teashop'. It is an oppositional article which takes issue with conservative ideological arguments about culture: that democracy means a levelling down, that extended education *caused* the low level of newspaper journalism, and that democracy will not work because (it is implied) ordinary people do not deserve to have power or influence.[32]

Williams contributed to a special edition of *Tribune*, the left-Labour weekly, published for the 1959 Aldermaston march.[33] It was the second annual march organized by CND. The campaign gained wide support during the period 1958–61 and this issue marks one of the high points of a coalition between CND, the left of the Labour Party, and the cultural concerns of the emergent generation. The contributions to this special issue are very diverse: they certainly do not add up to anything like a coherent position. Michael Foot tried to describe what made Labour different from the Conservative Party. He set out these policies:

1 the need to extend the Welfare State in the light of new research showing the continued existence of real need;
2 defence of Labour's policy of nationalization of industry;
3 in foreign policy a commitment to dismantling imperialism (but nothing about relations with the United States);
4 declarations on H-bomb *tests* and policy in the Middle East and the Far East.

These policies represent a limited left-Labour position. Thus, for example, he asks for a declaration on H-bomb tests but says nothing about their continued manufacture. The remainder of the special section was taken up with cultural issues. Norman Birnbaum describes the lack of fundamental thinking in the universities and the weakness of Labour Clubs at a time when many students were looking for something to believe in. John Osborne launched an attack on the London theatre business and the majority of critics who supported its standards. Paul Rotha described the need for a Labour policy on film. He argued that it was not simply an economic issue: film had a broader contribution to make. He suggested the provision of production facilities for independent companies, a distribution organization, and a chain of cinemas run on non-commerical lines.

Williams's contribution 'Man on the run from himself' is a discussion of recent literature. He describes Amis, Wain, and Osborne as the end of an old movement rather than the beginning of a new one. Williams sees the 'angry young men' of the mid-1950s as continuing the frustration and despair of writers such as Orwell in the 1940s. Faced with a kind of social and political blockage these writers react as *outsiders*: man on the run from society or from himself.[34]

The overall situation was confused but exciting. In an article in 1960 for *Partisan Review*, Williams writes that 'I wish I knew enough about Britain to be able to say with any confidence what is really happening here. The difficulty, as usual, is that too much is being said by too few people. . . .'[35] He goes on to say that apart from the public facts he gets most of his impressions from the people to whom he lectures (still adult education classes). He describes the development of the New Left: the publication of *The Uses of Literacy*, *Culture and Society*, and *Conviction*. The journal *New Left Review* was launched in December 1959 by the amalgamation of *New Reasoner* and *Universities and Left Review* and New Left Clubs were springing up all over the country. There were interesting developments in the Free Cinema and in theatre the emergence of Arnold Wesker, John Braine, Shelagh Delaney, and others. Above all is CND which:

In the wonderfully successful marches from Aldermaston and in scores of crowded meetings, is bringing thousands of young people into politics, but politics of a new and independent kind which the traditional parties are hardly in touch with. It is all a glorious and lively muddle, changing in character continuously, full of serious differences within itself, but recognizable as a social mood absolutely different from that obtaining at the beginning of the 1950s.[36]

With this new popular mobilization and the new cultural movements, young people seem to have bypassed the deadening failure of nerve that marked the period 1945–55. The relation of all of this to the Labour Party is unclear, but it surely *had* to take account of the new mood and change – or else continue to decline. It was an exhilarating moment.

In an article for *The Nation* in the same year, Williams writes in much the same mood. The new generation looks to the Labour Party as its own movement, but rejects the strong Fabian influence of bureaucratic reform from above (the attitude that workers should be organized for their own good) and its unimaginative policy of ensuring a *minimum* standard. However, this new generation also rejects the Communist Party because it does not seem that its kind of discipline will result in genuine industrial democracy. The CND marches and the New Left Clubs were this new generation's politics. This moment of exhilaration was, however, short-lived. By 1962 Williams was writing in *Encounter* about his renewed sense of deadlock. The issues of the 1950s were still there under the surface. Actual tensions between the Soviet Union and the United States had increased: in part this is why CND was so strongly active. However, after 1961 the campaign declined in strength. There was a crisis at the *New Left Review* in which Williams and others were replaced on the editorial board and the editorial policy shifted to left-intellectual and theoretical interests. The broader connections of what had seemed to be a new kind of politics in the late 1950s and early 1960s were now broken.[37]

The Labour Party and *Communications*

Williams had been brought up as a Labour supporter. By the early 1960s he expected sharpening conflict and deadlock to continue for many years. The way out seemed to include a long march through the Labour Party. It would be necessary, he said in 1960, to get back to 'basic analysis, basic education, basic democratic organization'.[38] Williams's active involvement with the Party between 1961 and 1966 was on three levels: first, continued general support for the Party, which always included serious questioning of its organization and policies; second, activity in a constituency party organization; and third, a special interest in policy in the area of communications, the arts, and education.

William argues that the Labour Party drew on a moral argument against capitalism which surfaces again and again in the history of the working class. The mass mobilization of CND was a similar expression of these values. The dominant tradition within the Labour Party actually blocks the expression of these values. The tradition of a centralized organization and Fabian arguments for the provision of only minimum standards of living and education, effectively blocks the strong moral critique of actually existing social organization and the alternative of local democratic collectivity. Williams therefore rejects Labour Party arguments in the early 1960s which were expressed in terms of modernization. Arguments for modernization were in effect attempts to displace pre-political values of democratic control and collectivity. The issue, Williams said, is not how to modernize British industry; the issue is one of political power.

In an article in *Esprit* in 1964 and in a similar article that year for *The Nation*, Williams warns that the Labour Party's foreign policy is 'dangerous and obscure'. A year later, in a comment in *Views* he gives this first priority: Labour's long-term policies are being determined by its positions on international relations. Labour has no new policy for nuclear weapons. It consistently chooses the wrong side in national and social struggles in the Third World. Its policy of dependence on the United States is effectively setting real limits within which the government has then to operate.[39]

From 1961 to 1966 Williams was an active member of the Cambridgeshire Constituency Labour Party. It was an unusual time to join: many socialists entered the party in 1963 when it seemed possible that Harold Wilson's election to the leadership marked a new beginning. That he joined at that time may have been due to the fact that he and Joy Williams moved house when he took up work at

Cambridge University. It was also no doubt a decision against a repetition of the 1940s pattern of intellectuals abandoning active politics: a determination not to be an outsider. The Williams' decision is an early recognition that CND, the new cultural work, and the New Left Clubs were by themselves not enough to have a direct political effect. The political party organizations and the centres of political power had not been displaced by these new popular movements.

Joy and Raymond Williams edited a monthly paper for the Cambridgeshire constituency organization. They saw the party not as a machine (for contesting elections) but as a place for discussing ideas, for political education, and for self-education. It was a mixed experience:

At first it was very encouraging. At that level of the Labour Party people have a sense of natural loyalty to the Party, but there's an absolute famine of ideas, and there are so many unanswered questions. Initially, when we tried to make this little periodical a place where things could be discussed, people were interested. There was no problem of censorship or conformity to the line. But as it developed, we began to get the message back from the offices of the Party.[40]

There were Constituency Parties in which very active work went on. However, in this case the Party was using the traditional loyalty of its members to stifle new ideas. One man in particular had gone to a regional conference full of the ideas that they had been developing and had got the message that the Party was not pleased with that sort of thing.

The third aspect of Williams's relation with Labour is in the area of communication and culture. In 1962 Williams published two statements on cultural policy: a Fabian Society pamplet, *The Existing Alternatives in Communications*, and a Penguin Special titled *Communications*. The Penguin book is a consolidation of adult-education teaching on newspapers, magazines, and radio, and it also makes a general political argument about communication and democracy. The book ends with suggestions for teaching communications, with immediate and medium-term policy suggestions, and with an argument about long-term socialist goals. The Fabian pamphlet covers some of the same ground. It argues for the need for historical studies of communications. Contemporary communications are dominated by advertising and the accompanying reduction of every decision to a matter of buying and selling, and financial constraints make it impossible for a newspaper, magazine, or film to be started up outside this commercial network. Williams's immediate policy is to keep commercial interests out of communications as far as possible. In the long term he argues that the means of production (presses, studios, broadcasting networks, theatres) should be publicly owned but leased out to independent producers.

In 1964, with the likelihood of a Labour Government after the next general election, Williams wrote a more detailed policy document on communications which he published as the basis for a public discussion in *Views*.[41] The document was also circulated to unions, organizations, and interested individuals. Following two articles on Labour's communications policy by Jill Craigie in *Tribune*, Williams wrote a letter to the editor inviting a debate about the document published in *Views*[42] In February 1965 with a Labour Government in power, Jennie Lee published her White Paper *A Policy For the Arts*. Williams wrote a welcoming article about it for *Tribune*, but entered a warning note about its ambiguity about whether culture is the 'fine arts' or a whole way of living. The issue was whether the welcome but modest recommendations of the White Paper were the beginnings of a policy for popular cultural institutions and education, or the full extent of the government's understanding and intentions. It was the first flower of spring, said Williams. We are entitled to expect more than one flower after so much work in preparing the soil.[43]

The debate for which Williams had hoped does not seem to have happened – in print at any rate. About a year later Williams was again writing in *Tribune*[45] but about reports that the Labour Government was considering setting up commerical radio stations. This commercial provision of popular music programming was the complete opposite of Williams's argument for a priority on local communications.[45]

In October 1966 Williams was back in *Tribune* arguing against a powerful campaign which was attempting to get local radio into commercial hands, using the existence of the 'pirate' radio stations as evidence of an existing demand. A week later Hugh Jenkins described a plan for local stations which carried advertising but were supposed to be protected from any commerical influence by a new Television and Radio Authority.[46] Two weeks later Williams replied, showing that this plan in fact conceded almost everything to commercial interests. The proposal was based on insufficient research into alternatives. The advertising would get on the air and contribute to already enormous pressures to see the world only in terms of consumer choices. It was nonsense to imagine that it would have no effect on programming.[47] Whatever plans the Labour Government had in mind were evidently shelved.[48]

In the 1960s Williams was actively involved with campaigns of solidarity with the National Liberation Front in Vietnam. In Cambridge, Joy Williams was knocked down in an orderly demonstration against the

Unilateral Declaration of Independence (UDI) in Rhodesia by a group
of young men supporting Rhodesia's Smith regime. In April 1966,
when CND was still active but past its strength of the years 1957–61,
Williams published a very important article in *Sanity*, arguing for
fundamental democracy. The bomb is defended, he said, in defence of
democracy:

But the fact of the bomb is that it imposes, by its very character, the most
centralized and arbitrary kind of politics in the modern world. The decisions
about war and peace, even in the two world wars of this century, have been
made, in the democratic societies, by some kind of parliamentary process, and
because of their time-scale have been subject to some kind of parliamentary
and public challenge and discussion. The necessary timing of nuclear war
allows no such process. At extreme points of crisis, decisions have to be made
in a matter of hours or minutes. . . .[49]

Because there are no institutions by which the discussions about
nuclear weapons (and other issues) can have effect on a highly
centralized and bureaucratic government, it is necessary to march. An
educational and discussion movement is not enough.

In September of the same year Williams again published in *Sanity* on
the future of the left. He argued that it was necessary to defeat an
unusually ugly version of Toryism in the 1966 elections; but more
important, he supported Labour because he found so much in common
with the active constituency Labour members. He did not want to
repeat the kind of exile that intellectuals made for themselves in the
1940s. At the same time, Williams had a growing impatience with the
ruling-class style of the Labour Government.

The key to our future, I firmly believe, is the extension of politics beyond the
routines of the parliamentary process, as CND, more than any other movement
has already shown to be possible. Not all our campaigns will be of that size or
character, but what we have to do, in open practice, is to define politics
differently, in every kind of popular institution and demonstration, so that we
can go on changing consciousness (our own included) in ways that are
intrinsically of a participating, extending and therefore democratic kind.[50]

It will be necessary to keep this vision of popular democracy in mind to
understand Williams's final rejection of the Labour Party, only a few
weeks later in 1966.

The immediate occasion was the seamen's strike in 1966. The
dispute with the shipowners was made by the Wilson government into a
test of its new incomes policy. This policy was in turn linked with an
economic crisis caused by overseas military spending and the export of

capital which followed the Labour victory in the elections. Wilson refused to devalue the pound because he feared that such a move by a Labour Government would bring a crisis of confidence and even demands for a new general election.[51] However, the acceptance of international financial aid brought with it conditions, including the implementation of a wages freeze.

Making the seamen's dispute into the ground where this policy would be implemented was doubly unfair. At Cambridge there was a meeting of the Centre for Socialist Education where one of the seamen presented his case. The seamen's union had been under conservative and bureaucratic leadership for many years. When this blockage was eventually overcome by the workers, their conditions and wages had dropped well below national standards. There was a very clear case for making them a special case in any incomes policy. What made the Wilson action even more unbearable was the award of substantial increases to professional groups, doctors, judges, top civil servants, Members of Parliament, and Government Ministers. Williams's response was short and sharp. In an article in July 1966 he declared his break with the Party. We should not be surprised to see the New Left move on, he said, perhaps to a closer association with the Communist Party.

The issue was more than Wilson's attack on the seamen's union. Williams came back to the importance of Labour's international relations. Acceptance of NATO and the American alliance meant not only acceptance of nuclear weapons, but also silence on the Vietnam War. The problems facing Britain could not be solved by clever negotiations, by Wilson or anyone else. What was at stake was the whole system of US-dominated economic and political relations. When Williams made this argument in September 1966 the initial organization for the May Day Manifesto was in place to develop an understanding of this new system of international capitalism.

Against this system, Williams put the ideal of fundamental democracy. The problem was also what he called the ruling-class style of the Wilson government. The images he described were 'the backs of cars sweeping through the gates of Chequers; the three-second public smiles at the front door in Downing Street'.[52] As Williams had discovered in the issue of commercial radio, the real decisions were being taken by this supposedly socialist government, behind closed doors and at big dinners: 'I have since read Harold Wilson's speech at the Guildhall dinner on the tenth anniversay of I.T.V. It affected me like the description of the dinner at the end of George Orwell's *Animal Farm*.'[53] Since then the government had made no attempt even to modify the commercial domination of communications. Indeed, after another dinner Wilson was reported to have made a promise of immunity to Lord Thompson from the Monopolies Commission if he wanted to take over the *Sunday Citizen*. Williams's response to this kind of decision-making was that it was beyond parody and even beyond anger. 'We shall have to leave the Labour Government to its dinners and its friends, and make the changes for ourselves, in quite different ways.'[54]

May Day Manifesto

Very soon after Williams's rejection of the Labour Government in 1966 there was a meeting out of which came a working group which produced a radical analysis and political position in opposition to the Labour Party. This was published in 1967 as the *New Left May Day Manifesto*.[55] The *Manifesto* was an attempt to create a coalition of left groups, and Williams personally played an important mediating role. The coalition included people from the Communist Party, left Catholics, left Labour, *New Left Review*, and a large number of left teachers and writers. It was an attempt to develop an independent socialist position, but may have appeared to be moderate to the existing Fourth International, Maoist, and anarchist groupings of the late 1960s.[56]

It was important to Williams that the process was different from the centralized control that operated in the Labour Party. Three editors were appointed: Williams, E. P. Thompson, and Stuart Hall. This original group was expanded and the *Manifesto* published in 1967. Meetings were held in different parts of the country to discuss it and a *May Day Bulletin* established. This achievement, said Williams, of a 'self-organizing, self-financed socialist intellectual organization' was itself worth recording.[57]

The *Manifesto* itself made a complex argument. It started from everyday life: the facts of poverty, health, housing, work. The central argument was that a new form of capitalism was developing (against the accepted theory in the Labour Party that capitalism was being replaced by a different economic system) in which international corporations played a dominant role. The central fact of this new form of capitalism is the political and economic hegemony of the United States. The single most important issue was whether this hegemony is accepted or fought against. For the 1968 expanded edition of the *Manifesto*, published as a Penguin Special, these positions were argued in some technical detail. Michael Barrett Brown, especially, seems to have brought technical expertise on international economics.

The prose is recognizably that of Williams. The 1968 edition starts with May Day itself which 'for many hundreds of years has been a people's holiday: a celebration of growth on the land. For the last eighty years, coming out of this history, May Day has been an international festival – a demonstration and commitment – of the labour movement.' There is a paradox that the Labour Party in Britain is now set against that history and commitment. The prose is full of these tensions. 'This is now a dangerous gap: between the name and reality; between vision and power; between our human meanings and the deadening language of a false political system.'[59]

An increasingly educated society, with this history of a labour movement to draw upon, was being blocked by a centralized and manipulative politics which executed its purposes in the name of the labour movement. The complex analysis of the *Manifesto* would attempt to show how and why that happened. The analysis of communications is only one section of a much longer analysis. In another sense it is a general theoretical statement. 'For any actual people, including the most exposed, direct experience of the society is fragmentary and discontinuous. To get a sense of what is happening, at any given time, we depend on a system of extended communications.'[59] This is, again, the insistence that communication is not secondary but is part of the society to be understood and analysed. It is impossible to separate understanding and experience. The overwhelming majority of the systems of extended communications are not a common source of exchange and understanding. They are in capitalist hands and are organized within its priorities.

The attempted coalition based on the analysis of the *Manifesto* was organized in the National Convention of the Left, which Williams chaired. The coalition fell apart over the issue of the 1970 general election. The issue was support or opposition to the Labour Party. The Communist Party was committed to running its own candidates. Williams argued for opposition to Labour. Left-wing supporters of Labour and those who felt that it was necessary to support the Party even though they disagreed with its positions quitted the coalition and it collapsed.[60]

1968

The detailed and sometimes difficult argument of the *Manifesto* seems a long way from the popular demonstrations of the late 1960s. There seems to be little of the new cultural forms of encounter and personal affirmation. However, Williams did not experience such a gap. In a talk for BBC Radio Williams argued that there was no separation between analysis such as that of the *May Day Manifesto* and politics in the streets.

Anybody who participates in these movements knows of this link and these interactions, between theory and practice, between idea and mood. Anybody who takes the trouble to talk to a regular participant with some readiness to listen, rather than simply to ask the usual questions about long hair and violence, can in fact discover this. Yet even people who are normally well-informed go on saying: to the demonstrators, that what they need is some theory, some serious political position; to the theoreticians, that it is all very well, but rather remote and abstract.[61]

The connections have indeed left their published traces. The manifesto itself was translated into several languages and reprinted in part in the United States in *The New Left Reader* (1969). There were also European connections. Those involved in the *Manifesto* in 1968 moved back and forth between England and Paris.[62]

In 1969, Williams reviewed Stephen Spender's *The Year of the Young Rebels*.[63] It is a careful, serious review of a book which reports on the universities of New York, Paris, Prague, Berlin. The problem is the usual one of reportage: that it is written by someone who has visited rather than someone whose life is there. Beyond the mood of sympathy with the students' rebellion there is a lack of description of the ordinary workings of the universities and the structural problems that led to the moments of rebellion. This is a matter of organization and also a revaluation of the purpose of learning. Beyond this Williams is critical of the weakness of Spender's assumptions about the nature of advanced capitalist society. The *May Day Manifesto* has as its purpose to challenge and replace these notions about 'consumer society' and 'mass communications'.

By 1970 an obviously tired Williams described the difficulties of building a united left that might at least survive the seventies: 'Every month, it seems, we have to begin all over again.' The difficulties stem from the displaced, mediated reality of the new capitalism. The one hope was that young people did not accept this as any actual reality. 'I am no longer young in that sense, but it is worth saying that these young people are the only generation I can bear. All they can do, perhaps, in these next few months is shout at the puppets, mock the wonderland, take their casualties. I can't say anything easy.'[64] In the decade that followed, Williams produced some of his most important books: *The Country and the City* (1973), *Marxism and Literature* (1977). Before turning to consider Williams's work at Cambridge there are several issues which should be mentioned. These are his positions on censorship and on Britain's entry into the European Economic Community (EEC) – the so-called Common Market.

Williams had practical experience of government restrictions on publishing when *The Daily Worker* was banned in 1941. Twenty years later he was one of a large number of expert witnesses in the trial of Penguin Books for publishing *Lady Chatterley's Lover* in an inexpensive paperback edition.[65] By the early 1970s public arguments about pornography seemed to Williams to have reached a dangerous stage. Positions were being taken on the basis of little evidence and little serious thought.[66]

In response to a question, Williams seemed in 1963 to think favourably about joining the EEC. His culture had always been European: opposed to conservatives in England and Germany, and aligned with radicals in France and Italy. Perhaps joining the Common Market might break the two-party deadlock in England.[67] Asked the same question in 1971, Williams identified the EEC as a mode of capitalist integration and modernization: he was not interested in joining that. He was however interested in closer connections with European socialists. The alternative of increased dependence on the United States would be very damaging for the future of British society.[68]

Cambridge

After Williams's early retirement in 1983 as Professor of Drama at Cambridge University, Stephen Heath wrote that: 'In the university I have always thought him a writer and an intellectual before a teacher.'[69] At least three of Williams's books have a direct relation to his work at Cambridge. *The English Novel* is a record of his lectures on the English novel. *The Country and the City* originated in opposition to the way country house poetry was taught at Cambridge. The argument of *Modern Tragedy* comes from a similar opposition. Williams's reception at Cambridge when he returned to teach in 1961 was an icy essay in *The Cambridge Review* in which he is described as part of a group of 'English radicals, lapsed Stalinists, academic Socialists and intellectual Trotskyites . . . from the extra-mural boards, the community centres and certain Northern universities. . .'[70]

There is a description of the workings of the English Faculty at Cambridge in Williams's 1984 essay on Leavis. In particular he describes his own work as secretary of a committee to decide on a new examination paper on the novel which had been proposed for Part II of the Tripos. With difficulty Leavis was persuaded to be a member of the committee, to which he made sensible and helpful contributions. There was a major difficulty about the scope of the paper: whether it should include some European fiction or only English novels. Leavis took the second position and insisted on it, even though he was obviously in a minority. Williams as secretary was mainly interested in getting the committee's decision. A compromise was reached, which later turned out to be unworkable. What we have here is very clearly the ordinary difficulty of democratic decision-making. It is a process that Williams respects; for Leavis it was something else. Though he was often helpful at meetings, writes Williams, he both hated and projected the repeated experience of being in a minority. Speaking later with Leavis he said: 'But isn't that the problem, working in any institution? So long as I can teach as I want, I have to accept a framework built by a majority I don't agree with.' 'No, you don't have to accept it.' 'Accepting as you have. To continue the work. To put these other ideas in.'[71] However, Leavis could not accept this as a general position: that it is not a matter of throwing one's personal weight behind an argument, but a matter of democracy in an institution and of finding a way of living within it, especially if one is in a minority.

There are many occasions when intellectual work becomes a political intervention. In 1969 Williams wrote a review for *The Cambridge Review* which started: 'Marcuse has been called the philosopher of student revolt.' There follows a detailed discussion of two essays from Herbert Marcuse's *Negations*. Williams is almost wholly critical of Marcuse's attempt in 'Aggressiveness in advanced industrial society' to combine Marx and Freud. It does not seem to him that this can work. But, he continues: 'I respect Marcuse very much as a man. In these last years, especially, under severe pressure he seems to me to have acted and spoken with an exemplary and quite uncommon dignity, intelligence and force. I find myself standing with him, or wishing to stand with him, in repeated political battles, and in the conflicts within the universities.'[72] Williams then goes on to discuss an early essay, 'The affirmative character of culture', and to recognize therein some of the themes of *Culture and Society*.

Meanwhile, politics entered Cambridge in a much more direct way. At a public meeting in London in 1971, Williams described carefully how he interviewed a candidate for a research degree on Lukács, on *History and Class Consciousness* in its political context. The candidate was Rudi Dutschke, the West German student leader who had been shot and now intended to rest and convalesce in England. Dutschke was accepted, after an unusually prolonged admissions procedure, as a student at Cambridge. He was admitted to England by the Conservative Government of Edward Heath on condition that he should not engage in political activity. Following secret police surveillance which included the tapping of telephones, Dutschke was expelled from the country by a secret tribunal because he had communicated with political activists. The evidence adduced by the tribunal, said Williams, as a threat to national security was 'all of a kind which could be adduced against many of us: in our work and contacts inside the university, to say nothing of any more general public life.'[73] It was an issue of civil liberties.

Writing two weeks later in *The Nation*, Williams saw the Dutschke affair as evidence of sharpening strain and tension within a more general crisis which included the government's attempt to control and discipline the trade unions. The post-war consensus was only a covering for deep unresolved tensions within managed capitalism. The consensus has broken into a minority radicalism and a majority that seems to assent to a new authoritarian style of government in the name of the 'national interest'.[74]

In 1981 Williams was involved in a public debate over the refusal of the English Faculty at Cambridge to confirm the tenure of Colin MacCabe. The effect of this would end his appointment at Cambridge. This was reported in the national press as a conflict of French 'structuralism' against English literature. Williams argued it was MacCabe's work which actually continued the tradition of Cambridge English. MacCabe lost and in addition Williams and Frank Kermonde were both voted off the appointments committee.[75] Williams's own academic work is itself an argument for organizational change within the university: in particular, an argument for the establishment of a School of Humanities.[76]

Arts Council

Williams was appointed a member of the Arts Council for a three-year term from 1976–8. There are twenty members of the Council which in 1976 had a budget of just under £30 million. Williams was appointed by Hugh Jenkins, the Labour Government Minister responsible, who agreed that substantial reform was needed in the workings of the Council. The organization, meanwhile, was under pressure from several different directions. The 1975–6 Annual Report was entitled 'The arts in hard times', and that of the following year 'Value for money'. Pressures of a different kind had resulted in the inclusion of

Community Arts as a separate category in the Council's activities and budget. Meanwhile, there were the usual criticisms of particular events and shows which received financial support from the Council. The Institute of Contemporary Arts in particular had been subject to a 'moral' campaign in the Press and much of the criticism directed at the Arts Council.[77]

Williams's main interest was in reform of the Council itself. Writing later about his experience he said that he concluded within six months that substantial internal reform was not possible.[78] He stayed mainly in order to contribute to public discussion with detailed knowledge of the problems. Attacks on the Council from the left and the right tend to divert attention from its major structural problems. The first problem is the power exerted by the government's control of the overall budget. A second set of problems is what Williams called 'administered consensus by co-option'. Members of the Council and its many committees are appointed after a hazy process of consultation among the Minister of State, the Chairman of the Council, and its senior administrators. The Council operates by a process of consensus rather than open debate followed by a vote. These factors operate effectively to contain any fundamental debate about issues such as the definition of 'the arts'. Even more important, issues about the Press, broadcasting, and the cinema are completely outside the mandate of the Arts Council. There is a need, Williams argues, for a Department of Communications and the Arts to develop a coherent overall policy.

In a later lecture Williams describes contradictions in its mandate which the Arts Council inherited from its founder, John Maynard Keynes. Its purposes included state patronage of the existing arts; a kind of economic pump-priming of arts which were supposed to be self-supporting; an intervention to take the arts out of the market economy; and the expansion and transformation of a serious and popular culture. Williams's own support goes to the fourth of these, which means real and actual change. He notes that there is no coherent public cultural policy in Britain, and indeed that there are powerful groups who are determined that there should never be one.[79]

In 1984 the Institute of Contemporary Arts held a conference on 'Culture and the state'. It is interesting that the German contributions especially include discussions of state policy towards film and broadcasting in their discussion of arts policy. Williams's own contribution to the conference again makes a case for something different from direct state sponsorship, as in Eastern Europe, or overwhelming commercial control. He distinguishes several different senses of the state in relation to culture. There is, first, the display of state power in the use of public ceremony and the arts. Second, there is

the use of the arts for national business: tourism, business entertainment, prestige sponsorship by business. Third, there is the state as a
patron of existing activity; and finally, the policy of extending access and
the artistic forms. The development of the fourth policy is in practice
not easy. Williams suggests possibilities for regional organization and
self-managing companies, where necessary using commonly owned
facilities.[80]

Wales

There seems to be little of Wales in Williams's best known books of the
late 1950s and early 1960s, except for the important case of his Welsh
novels starting with *Border Country*. By the 1970s the place where he
was born is there in essays, talks, and reviews. The images he used in
his 1975 talk for the BBC on Welsh culture are used again in the
novels: the folk museum at St Fagans in *The Volunteers*; touching the
handle of a shovel from the past in *Loyalties*. The themes of culture and
a passion for education are part of the history of Welsh culture. In this
talk, Williams's thoughts go back to learning history at school. He then
moves forward to a complex and changing culture.[81]

The themes of complexity, culture, and education recur in a talk by
Williams on the Welsh experience of the 1926 General Strike. He
describes the multiple articulation of those who, like his father, were
industrial workers and also connected to a rural network of activities
and support. The complexity of 1926 includes those like this; but also
those in the same places and elsewhere who supported the government
against the strike. The process of 1926, during the strike, was also one
of learning and new forms of complex decision-making. This broad
'educational' process grew in strength as the strike continued.[82]

The alternative

In the years after 1979 and the election of the Thatcher Conservative
Government there were important discussions and debates about the
future of the left. The seriousness and liveliness of these debates,
especially in magazines such as *New Socialist* and *Marxism Today*, is
itself a sign of hope. Williams's contributions to these debates is based
on his political experience of previous decades. Thus, for example, he
firmly rejected a coalition with the Social Democrat–Liberal Alliance,
his reason being that this would set aside the meaning of socialist

politics. The worst effects of the Thatcher government may be removed but fundamental problems of British capitalism remain. Williams therefore adds to the debates about the future of the left in Britain the need for institutions of discussion, research, and debate. Such a need has always been important for Williams's notion of politics.

There is an emergent analysis in Williams as early as the 1960s that there is a possibility of an authoritarian populist government in Britain. The analysis that began to emerge in his political writing is of a crisis of British capitalism that is completely unresolved in the post-war years; these deep structural problems are superficially covered over in the 1950s; and the consensus finally breaks around 1966 or 1967. Signs of the emergence of a radical left included in 1967 the *May Day Manifesto*, and of the hard right, the first major speech by Enoch Powell on race and immigration in the same year. The break to the right was not confined to the Conservative Party. The first signs of populist authoritarianism were there in Wilson's conduct as Labour Prime Minister during the 1966 seamen's strike. The crisis of socialism in Britain did not come in one day in 1979. It is much more serious and a much longer crisis.[83]

An important debate about the history of the working class and socialism took place in the pages of *Marxism Today*. In 1978 Eric Hobsbawm argued in his Marx Memorial Lecture that the basis for the Labour movement, in particular the composition of the work-force, had been eroding rapidly since the early 1950s. This gave rise to a wide-ranging debate collected in the book, *The Forward March of Labour Halted?*. Williams's contribution is not so much to question the detail of Hobsbawm's historical analysis as the theoretical presupposition that these historical factors are more important than moral and practical arguments for a different kind of society. Where Hobsbawn sees (for example) the composition of the work-force as a basis for the labour movement, Williams looks at the potential of broad educational and cultural movements for popular democracy.[84] This theme is central in Williams's political writing of the late 1970s and 1980s. He understands campaigns for nuclear disarmament, the women's movements, and ecological organizations as political movements which are also forums for discussion and the production of alternative bodies of knowledge and organizational skill.

Barbara Taylor's *Eve and the New Jerusalem* is important not only for its historical study of relations between feminism and socialism in the nineteenth century, but also for a revivial of interest in Robert Owen's kind of socialism, which has a direct connection with the present movements for decentralized and democratic practical institutions. In a review of *Eve and the New Jerusalem*, Williams makes this connection and then stresses the diversity that Taylor finds in the women's movements of the 1830s and 1840s. Then, as now, there was also a wide diversity of responses from men and from women.[85]

There is a similar openness and questioning, which is equally unresolved, in a review by Williams about Edward Carpenter. Like Robert Owen, he is a figure who was set aside in the orthodox history of socialism. Yet Carpenter shares many of our present concerns: 'His characteristically early concern with the industrial environment (as in his clean-air campaign in Sheffield); his work as a popular educator, taking some of the first university extension classes in astronomy and general science; his complex and active relations with different socialist tendencies, with anarchism, with the movements against war: all these deserve recognition.'[86] The recognition was in part blocked because of the difficulty even socialists had with Carpenter's homosexuality. The revivial of interest in his life and his writing is due to both the modern feminist and gay movements. There is especially the example of his attempt (as in Robert Owen's experimental communities) to develop new kinds of household and practical local economy. Although Terry Eagleton had written his dissertation on Carpenter,[87] Williams still found it difficult to see the person behind all the work. Here, as in Taylor's book, issues of sexuality have no easy answer in socialism. What is important is to keep the questions and the discussions open.

Another important movement that is a resource of fundamental democracy is concerned with issues of ecology. Properly understood this goes well beyond issues of the control of particular problems (acid rain, lead in the atmosphere, deforestation) to a complete questioning of the priorities of industrial and agricultural production. With his background in the country, it is perhaps understandable that Williams should be personally interested in the emphasis of 'Green' politics. Yet the complexity of Williams's emphasis goes well beyond only a personal feeling for the country. Williams approaches these issues through the books of Rudolf Bahro, which also raise historical and theoretical problems of communism. Bahro's *The Alternative in Eastern Europe* is a detailed examination and critique of 'actually existing socialism' from the principle that communism is both necessary and possible.

The problem is then to explain 'actually existing socialism' in Eastern Europe and the Soviet Union. In an essay on Bahro's *The Alternative*, Williams rejects an explanation in terms of a process of industrialization common to East and West. Explanations in terms of a technical dynamo are unconvincing since an adequate social system ought to be able to include technological change in a non-disruptive way. There is some weight in the argument that actually existing socialism has been determined by the forms of capitalism outside its borders. The fundamental explanation lies however, in its history of *minority* control of the means of production: the appropriation and expropriation of skills, effective knowledge, and powers of practical decision.[88]

Bahro's description of resistance to a system of minority control in Eastern Europe in terms of the 'surplus consciousness' of educated persons in all strata (but especially technological workers) is remarkably close to Williams's emphasis on culture and extended education in *The Long Revolution*. This surplus consciousness is defined by Bahro as that which is not required for the reproduction of the society. Yet, says Williams, it must not be considered as a quantity or a unilinear direction. Bahro is at his best when he is describing in detail the uses of this surplus: it is at times only compensation, at other times an emancipatory consciousness.

Much of Bahro's emphasis is on local democratic institutions. It is also necessary, says Williams, to describe a structure of interconnections and planning for these institutions. This is the case even when we understand that the answer to the question of what a society is to produce is that it produces *a whole way of life*. Williams finds a structural problem in Bahro's argument that the technical intelligentsia might in the West be the leading edge of a transformation to communism. The cultural revolution that Bahro describes must in the West include (for example) women who are absolutely excluded from the central processes. The experience of the technical intelligentsia (mainly at work) is also hardly relevant for other issues, about locality and housing for example. In conclusion, says Williams, it must be recognized that 'human emancipation is intrinsically, and as a matter of principle, more diverse than *any* philosophical definition of emancipatory transformation.' (original emphasis)[89]

What Williams accepts from Bahro is the interest in *institutions* of democracy. He places much less emphasis on the notions of 'rich individuality' and 'genuine communality' which Bahro develops from the early Marx and also from Fromm. When Bahro describes a renovated Communist Party, he seems to have in mind mainly the example of Czechoslovakia in 1968. Williams, on the other hand, gives institutional examples of what he means by fundamental democracy: that the channels of communication should be operated as common carriers for independently produced programmes; that there should be *two independent planning groups* for necessary overall planning.

This is not to say that Williams does not accept the need to create a potential alternative hegemony. For him as for Bahro this is absolutely necessary. Bahro's imaginative League of Communists is to be the agency of this alternative. He describes the League as a *collective intellectual* 'which anticipates in itself something of the human progress for which it is working.'[90] Bahro does not mean intellectuals as a social strata, but every person who questions his or her own situation. The proposal clearly has much in common with Williams's own interest in working for intellectual/educational forums: the WEA, New Left Clubs, May Day Manifesto groups, the Socialist Society. His only criticism of Bahro here is that he underestimates the diversity and differences that will arise.[91] Williams's point is that there has always been, for example, this diversity among the working class. Any movement(s) for an alternative hegemony, any League of Communists must recognize this, even encourage it. Here and in a review of a later book by Bahro there is a recognition by Williams that the new ideas and movements are a fundamental redefinition of the socialist project.[92] However, Williams questions any argument that the concept of the revolutionary proletariat has failed: the effects of the Thatcher government, for example, are still unknown and it is difficult to say that new kinds of working-class organizations will not emerge.[93] There are now more questions and uncertainties than ever. Even more there is a need for popular institutions of discussion, information, and decision.

Notes

1 Williams, *Politics and Letters* (New Left Books, 1979), p. 84. John Berger comments in *Permanent Red: Essays in Seeing* (London, Writers and Readers, 1981) that he also found it easier to publish art criticism than political writing in the 1950s.
2 Williams, 'Profundities for Poets: The Muse in Utopia', *Cambridge University Journal*, 3 February 1940, p. 7.
3 For the relationship between Wales and Cambridge see Williams, *Politics and Letters*, pp. 21–54: Williams, 'Culture is ordinary', in *Conviction*, ed. N. MacKenzie (MacGibbon 1958), pp. 74–92; Williams, 'An Introduction to Reading in Culture and Society', in *Literature and Environment*, ed. F. Inglis (Chatto and Windus, 1971), pp. 125–40; Williams, in *Bookmarks*, ed. F. Raphael (Quartet, 1975), 162–5; Williams, in *My Cambridge*, ed. R. Hayman (Robson Books, 1977), pp. 55–70.
4 Williams, 'The Left in the Thirties', *Guardian*, 22 March 1968, p. 9. In 'Affluence After Anger', *The Nation*, 19 December 1966, Williams argues that as a decade of general social change the 1950s is more important than the 1930s.
5 Williams, 'Commentary: Union Turns Left – but how', *Cambridge University Journal*, 9 November 1940, p. 2.
6 Williams, 'Sugar', in *Outlook*, ed. R. Williams *et al.* (Cambridge, 1941), pp. 7–14.
7 Williams, *Politics and Letters*, p. 53.
8 See David Fernbach, 'Tom Wintringham and Socialist Defence', *History*

Workshop Journal, no. 14 (Autumn 1982), pp. 63–91; Williams, *Orwell* (Fontana, 1984), pp. 62–8.

9   Williams, *Politics and Letters*, p. 67.

10 Also Williams, *Communications*, 2nd edn. (Penguin, 1968), pp. 13–14.

11 L. J. Barnes, 'Adult Education: Ends or Means?', *The Listener*, 31 January 1957, pp. 178–9.

12 D. Butts, 'The Development of Literature Teaching in the Oxford Tutorial Classes', *Rewley House Papers*, vol. 3, no. 7 (1959), pp. 13–19.

13 Ibid., p. 16.

14 Williams, *Politics and Letters*, pp. 78–83; also John Lowe, *Adult Education in England and Wales: A Critical Survey* (London, Michael Joseph, 1970), p. 116.

15 Williams, *Politics and Letters*, p. 80; see also Roger Fieldhouse, 'The problems of Objectivity: Social Purpose and Ideological Commitment in English University Adult Education', in *University Adult Education in England and the USA: A Reappraisal of the Liberal Tradition*, ed. Richard Taylor, Kathleen Rockhouse and Roger Fieldhouse (London, Croom Helm, 1985), pp. 29–51; Roger Fieldhouse, *Adult Education and the Cold War* (forthcoming). For historical background see Geoff Brown, 'Independence and incorporation: the Labour College movement and the Workers' Educational Association before the Second World War', in *Adult Education for a Change*, ed. Jane L. Thompson (London, Hutchinson, 1980), pp. 109–25; Anne Philips and Tim Putman, 'Education for Emancipation: The Movement for Independent Working Class Education 1908–1928', in *Capital and Class*, no. 10 (Spring 1980), pp. 18–42; Andy Miles, 'Workers' Education: the Communist Party and the Plebs League in the 1920s', *History Workshop*, no. 18 (Autumn 1984), pp. 102–14; Sheila Rowbotham, 'Travellers in a strange country: responses of working class students to the University Extension Movement – 1873–1910', *History Workshop Journal*, no. 12 (1981), pp. 62–95; Jonathan Ree, *Proletarian Philosophers: Problems in Socialist Culture in Britain 1900–1940* (Oxford, Clarendon Press, 1984). Also Raymond Williams, review of *The Central Labour College*, by William W. Craik, *Guardian*, 1 January 1965, p. 6.

16 Thomas Hodgkin, 'Objectivity, Ideologies and the Present Political Situation', *The Highway*, vol. 42 (January 1951), pp. 79–81; Richard Hoggart, 'What Shall the WEA Do?', *The Highway*, vol. 44 (November 1952), pp. 46–53; Henry Collins, 'Working Class Education and University Standards', *The Highway*, vol. 44 (January 1953), pp. 131–3. Williams's contribution is 'Figures and Shadows', *The Highway* (February 1954), pp. 169–72.

17 S. G. Raybould, 'University Extension and the WEA', *The Highway*, (January 1957), p. 70. Raybould also mentions the influence of US trade-union educationalists in Britain in 'Adult Education in Transition', *Political Quarterly*, 28 (1958), pp. 243–53. See also John Sewell, 'Let's Get this Straight', *The Highway*, vol. 39 (January 1948), pp. 55–6.

18 Williams, 'The Common Good', *Adult Education*, vol. 34, no. 4 (November

1961), pp. 192–99; also Williams, 'Going on Learning', *New Statesman*, 30 May 1959.

19   For Henry Collins, see Eric Hobsbawm, 'The Historians' Group of the Communist Party', in *Rebels and Their Causes*, ed. Maurice Cornford (Atlantic Highlands, Humanities Press, 1979), pp. 21–47; and Collins's articles in *Tribune* from 1964 to December 1969.

20   Ken Worpole comments on Mankowitz and the Soho location in his *Dockers and Detectives* (London, Verso 1983), p. 114.

21   The Editors, 'For Continuity in Change', *Politics & Letters*, no. 1 (1947), p. 3.

22   R. O. Winkler, 'Critic and Leviathan', *Politics & Letters*, no. 1 (1947), pp. 32–9; Christopher Hill, 'A Comment', *Politics & Letters*, no. 1 (1947) pp. 40–2; F. R. Leavis, 'Literary Criticism and Politics', *Politics & Letters*, nos 2/3 (1947–8), pp. 58–61. Lionel Elvin, 'David and Goliath', *Politics & Letters*, nos 2/3 (1947–8), pp. 61–5.

23   Williams, 'The Soviet Literary Controversy in Retrospect', *Politics & Letters* no. 1 (1947), pp. 21–31; Connolly, 'Comment', *Horizon*, vol. 14 (October 1946), pp. 205–14; Lewis, 'Editorial', *The Modern Quarterly*, vol. 2 (Winter 1946–7), pp. 3–15. For general overviews see George Bisztray, *Marxist Models of Literary Realism* (New York, Columbia University Press, 1978) and Jurgen Ruhle, *Literature and Revolution: A Critical Study of the Writer and Communism in the Twentieth Century*, tr. Jean Steinberg (New York, Frederick A Praewger, 1969).

24   The Editors, 'Culture and Crisis', *Politics & Letters*, nos 2/3 (1947–8), pp. 5–8.

25   Orwell, 'Critic and Leviathan: A Comment', *Politics & Letters*, no. 4 (1948), pp. 36–40. Reprinted as 'Writers and Leviathan', in *The Collected Essays Journalism and Letters of George Orwell*, vol. 4, (Harmondsworth, Penguin, 1970), pp. 463–70. Orwell also offered *Politics & Letters* his essay 'George Gissing', which appears in the same volume, but by then *Politics & Letters* had closed.

26   Sartre, 'Commitment in Literature', *Politics & Letters*, no. 2/3 (1948), pp. 24–33. See also Sartre, *What is Literature*, tr. Bernard Frechtman (New York, Harper and Row, 1965). Perry Anderson makes the connection between Williams and Merleau-Ponty in 'Problems of Socialist Strategy', in *Towards Socialism*, ed. Perry Anderson and Robin Blackburn (London, Fontana, 1965), p. 289. For Williams on Sartre see his review of R. D. Cumming's anthology, 'The Need for Sartre', *Guardian*, 29 November 1968, p. 11; Williams, 'Who are the intellectuals', *Guardian*, 25 April 1974, p. 17; 'Goodbye to Sartre', *New Society*, 21 June 1984, pp. 470–71; 'The Writer: commitment and Alignment', *Marxism Today*, June 1980, pp. 22–3.

27   Williams [Michael Pope], 'The State and Popular Culture: A Note', *Politics & Letters*, vol. 1, no. 4 (1948), p. 72.

28   Williams, 'Socialism's crisis of theory', *The Nation*, 26 February 1968, pp. 274–6.

29 Norman MacKenzie (ed.), *Conviction* (London, MacGibbon and Kee, 1958); by comparison *Out of Apathy* (1960) was a New Left book.
30 MacKenzie (ed.), *Conviction*, p. 186.
31 Ibid., p. 228.
32 Williams, 'Culture is Ordinary', in *Conviction*, pp. 74–92.
33 *Tribune*, 27 March 1959.
34 Williams, 'Man on the Run from Himself', *Tribune*, 27 March 1959. Williams always distanced himself from the so-called 'angry young men'. He comments on Dennis Potter in Williams, 'The Common Good', p. 196. See also Williams, 'The New Party Line?', a review of *The Outsider*, by Colin Wilson, *Essays in Criticism*, 7 (1957), pp. 68–76.
35 Williams, 'The New British Left', *Partisan Review*, 27 (1960), pp. 341–7. On this period see David Widgery, *The Left in Britain: 1956–1968* (Harmondsworth, Peregrine, 1976); reviewed by Williams, 'Only Yesterday', *Guardian*, 12 February 1976, p. 12; and John Saville 'How Not to Reappraise the New Left', in *The Socialist Register 1976*, ed. Ralph Miliband and John Saville (London, Merlin Press, 1976), pp. 111–27. Also, Williams, 'An Experimental Tendency', review of *The New Left*, ed. Maurice Cranston, *The Listener*, 3 December 1970. On Williams and the New Left see Bernard Anthony David Bryant, 'The New Left in Britain: The Dialectic of Rationality and Participation', Ph.D. dissertation, London School of Economics, 1981.
36 Williams, 'The New British Left,' p. 341.
37 Williams, 'Socialism's Crisis of Theory', *The Nation*, 26 February 1968, pp. 274–6; Williams, 'The Future of Marxism', *Twentieth Century*, (July 1961), pp. 128–42; Williams, 'The Deadlock', *Encounter*, vol. 18, no. 1 (January 1962), pp. 14–15.
38 Williams, *Monthly Review*, (1960), p. 333.
39 Williams, 'La gauche britannique', *Esprit*, 32 (1964), pp. 581–92; Williams. 'The British Elections', *The Nation*, 28 September 1964, pp. 154–7; Williams, 'Labour in Britain: Other Views', *Views*, no. 7 (1965), pp. 13–15. For comments on Fabian socialism see Williams, 'Virtuous Circle', *The Listener*, 30 November 1961, pp. 933–4.
40 Williams, 'The Labour Party and Beyond', *Revolutionary Socialism*, no. 5 (1980), pp. 3–4.
41 Williams. 'Labour in Britain'.
42 Jill Craigie, 'What Will Labour Do About Mass Communications?' *Tribune*, August 1964; Williams, 'Culture and Labour', letter to the editor, *Tribune*, 14 August 1964, p. 2.
43 Williams, 'We are starting to use our own voices!', *Tribune*, 5 March 1965, pp. 1, 6.
44 'Just What is Labour's Policy for Radio?' *Tribune*, 18 Feb 1966, p. 8.
45 He mentions a pamphlet by Rachel Powell of the Centre for Contemporary Cultural Studies which describes the possibilities for genuine local radio services.
46 Williams, 'What Happens After the "Pirates" Walk the Plank?', *Tribune*, 7 October 1966, p. 9; Hugh Jenkins, *Tribune*, 14 October 1966, p. 9.

47 Williams, ' "Bemused Liberalism" from Hugh Jenkins', *Tribune*, 21 October 1966, p. 6.
48 The commercial radio lobby eventually had its way in 1972 under a Conservative Government. This could have been prevented if Labour had taken the initiative to set up genuinely local radio stations in the 1960s. See Local Radio Workshop, *Capital: Local Radio and Private Profit* (London, Comedia, 1983); Robert Jenkins, *Tony Benn: A Political Biography* (London, Writers and Readers, 1980), pp. 107–8.
49 Williams, 'Why I am Marching: You Can't Have it Both Ways – The Bomb *and* Democracy', *Sanity*, April 1965.
50 Williams, 'What is the Future of the Left', *Sanity*, April 1965, p. 9.
51 Williams, 'Significance of the seamen's strike', *The Nation*, 4 July 1966, pp. 18–19. On the Wilson government see *The Crossman Diaries*, ed. Anthony Howard (London, Methuen, 1979); Ken Coates, 'Socialists and the Labour Party', *The Socialist Register 1973*, ed. Ralph Miliband and John Saville (London, Merlin 1973), pp. 155–78; David Coates, *The Labour Party and the Struggle for Socialism* (London, Cambridge University Press, 1975).
52 Williams, 'You Can't Have it Both Ways', p. 6
53 Ibid., p. 6.
54 Williams, *Communications*, 2nd edn (Penguin, 1968), pp. 184–5.
55 Stuart Hall, Raymond Williams, Edward Thompson (eds), *New Left May Day Manifesto* (London, 1967)
56 There were seventy signatures on the *Manifesto* (p. 45). See also National Convention of the Left, *April 1969 Report and Proposals* (London, mimeo, 1969), p. 12, for details of the National Convention of the Left meeting of 25–29 April 1969. A total of 622 people attended, of whom 246 were delegates from organizations. Those listed include *Slant* magazine, of which Terry Eagleton was editor. For Eagleton's critical remarks on the May Day Manifesto movement see his *Criticism and Ideology* (London, New Left Books, 1976), p. 35.
57 Raymond Williams (ed.), *May Day Manifesto* (Harmondsworth, Penguin, 1968), p. 10.
58 Ibid., p.13.
59 Ibid., pp. 39–40.
60 Williams, 'Great Britain: Saying "No" to the Labour Party', *The Nation*, 15 June 1970, pp. 710–12.
61 Williams, 'Why do I demonstrate?, *The Listener*, 25 April 1968, p. 522.
62 *The New Left Reader*, ed. Carl Oglesby (New York, Grove Press 1969); Williams, *Politics and Letters*, p. 375.
63 Williams, 'Spender on Students,' *Guardian*, 17 April 1969, p. 9.
64 Williams, 'Great Britain: Saying "No" to the Labour Party', p. 712. For images of students on television see Williams, 'Based on Reality', *The Listener*, 12 June 1969, pp. 838–9; Williams, 'Between Us and Chaos', *The Listener*, 24 September 1970, pp. 432–3.
65 *The Trial of Lady Chatterley*, ed. C. H. Rolph (Baltimore, Penguin, 1961), pp. 133–5.

66 Williams, 'Stand up for what?', *Guardian*, 28 September 1972, p. 16.

67 Williams, 'Going into Europe', *Encounter*, 20 (March 1963), p. 68.

68 Williams, 'Going into Europe – Again? *Encounter*, 36 (June 1971), p. 13. Also, Williams, 'The Referendum Choice', *New Statesman*, 30 May 1975, p. 719. For criticism of Williams see Tom Nairn, 'The Left Against Europe', special issue of *New Left Review*, 75 (September/October 1972), pp. 106–8.

69 Stephen Heath, 'Modern English Man', *Times Higher Educational Supplement*, 20 July 1948, p. 17.

70 Maurice Cowling, *The Cambridge Review*, 82 (27 May 1961), p. 546

71 Williams, 'Seeing a man running', in *The Leavises*, ed. D. Thompson (Cambridge University Press, 1984), pp. 118–19.

72 Williams, 'On Reading Marcuse', *Cambridge Review* (30 May 1969), p. 366. Reprinted in *The Cambridge Mind*, ed. Eric Homberger, William Janeway, Simon Schama (Boston, Toronto, Little, Brown and Company, 1970).

73 Williams, 'Dutschke and Cambridge', *Cambridge Review*, (29 January 1971), p. 94.

74 Williams, 'Downhill to Dutschke', *The Nation*, 15 Feb. 1971, pp. 210–12.

75 Francis Mulhern, 'The Cambridge Affair', *Marxism Today* (March 1981); Colin MacCabe, 'Class of 68', in his *Theoretical Essays: Film, Linguistics, Literature* (Manchester, Manchester University Press, 1985), pp. 17–31; Williams, 'Their bark may well be lost, if it is not tempest tossed,' *Guardian*, 24 Jan. 1981, p. 11.

76 Williams, in his *Writing in Society* (London, Verso, 1984).

77 *Community Arts: The Report of the Community Arts Working Party* (London, The Arts Council, 1974). See also Roy Shaw, Secretary General of the Arts Council, in the *Guardian Weekly*, 15 October 1978, p. 20. C. B. Cox claimed in 1981 that the consensus of the Council had become impossible because of conflict between traditionalists who assume the autonomy of individual works of art and agitprop groups who declare that the traditional arts are elitist. See his 'Lecture' in *The Arts Council: Politics and Policies* (London, The Arts Council, 1981), p. 4.

78 Williams, 'The Arts Council', *Political Quarterly*, 50 (1979), pp. 157–71.

79 Williams, 'Lecture', in *The Arts Council: Politics and Policies* (London, The Arts Council, 1981), pp. 9–16.

80 Williams, 'State Culture and Beyond', in *Culture and the State*, ed. L. Appignanesi (London, Institute of Contemporary Arts, 1984), pp. 3–5.

81 Williams, 'Welsh Culture', talk given on BBC Radio 3, 27 September 1975, in *Culture and Politics: Plaid Cymru's Challenge to Wales* (Cardiff: Plaid Cymru, 1975). See also 'Nationalisms and Popular Socialism: Phil Cooke talks to Raymond Williams', *Radical Wales*, no. 2 (Spring 1984), pp. 7–8; Williams, 'The Welsh Industrial Novel', in his *Problems in Materialism and Culture* (Verso, 1980), pp. 213–29.

82 Williams, 'The Social Significance of 1926', *Llafur*, vol. 2, no. 2 (Spring 1977), pp. 5–8.

83 See Williams's articles in *The Nation* after 1966. More generally, Williams,

'You're a Marxist, Aren't You?', in *The Concept of Socialism*, ed. Bhikhu Parekh (London, Croom Helm, 1975), pp. 231–42.

84 *The Forward March of Labour Halted?* (London, Verso, 1981).

85 Williams, 'The new morality', *Guardian*, 17 March 1983, p. 16.

86 Williams, 'The Little Green Book', *Guardian*, 20 November 1980, p. 18.

87 T. F. Eagleton, 'Nature and Spirit: a study of Edward Carpenter in his intellectual context', Ph.D., Cambridge University, 1968–9.

88 Raymond Williams, 'Beyond Actually Existing Socialism', in his *Problems in Materialism and Culture* (London, Verso, 1980), pp. 252–73.

89 Williams, 'Beyond Actually Existing Socialism.' p. 261.

90 Ibid., p. 262.

91 Rudolf Bahro, *The Alternative in Eastern Europe*, tr. David Fernbach (London, Verso, 1978), pp. 366–7.

92 Williams, 'The Red and the Green', *London Review of Books*, 3–16 February 1983, p. 3.

93 Meanwhile, Williams was writing his own *Alternative*. His *Towards 2000* is discussed in Chapter 8.

3

Institutions

If we imagine Williams writing in the 1940s and 1950s as part of the post-war formation of workers' education tutors, this imagination must then include some discussion of small magazines, newspapers, radio, and film in Britain after 1945. The central issue is the conditions on which a minority culture will be extended to a majority and thereby transformed. Williams argues that, with some notable exceptions, the working class in England did not develop its own culture (novels, plays, poetry, art) but did develop a culture of democratic institutions such as co-operatives, trade unions, and collective decision-making. How do the institutions of critical writing, publishing, broadcasting, and cinema measure by the standard of a democratic culture?

There is no systematic theory of the state in Williams. The central term in his analysis of the modern capitalist state in Britain is *management*. His example is the wartime relationship between an officer and his men.[1] The underlying idea is an attempt to deal with the contradictions of power by a culture of personnel relations. This attempt to 'handle' people and committees is not only part of a culture of inequality but is quickly seen as such by those upon whom it is worked. Other examples of the role of culture in maintaining political hegemony might include the culture of those co-opted on to such state bodies as the Arts Council – a culture which allows such bodies to operate in hidden and predemocratic ways. This contrasts with the rather different, highly centralized, and bureaucratic state aparatus of a country such as France.

During the war the state in Britain became more involved in the regulation of conditions for cultural production. The new journal *Politics & Letters* was possible in part because of the continuation of paper rationing and the general shortage of reading materials in the immediate post-war years. Harold Wilson at the Board of Trade was responsible for this kind of regulation. Writing in 1948, Williams was highly critical of Wilson's timid attempts to control advertising and his understanding of culture in only organizational terms. Wilson's position was that content could not be taken into account because it was a matter of 'taste'.[2] Williams's main point is that leaving the production of culture mainly to commercial organizations is itself a form of control of oppositional culture.

Mankowitz, Collins, and Williams hoped to sell between 1,500 and 2,000 copies of *Politics & Letters*. There were also plans for The Critic Press to publish books. By 1948 the project had collapsed. Williams's allocation of rationed paper as an ex-service person gave the project only a temporary advantage. The journals were quarterly whereas John Lehmann and George Orwell argue convincingly that to have any real effect such journals had to appear monthly. *The Critic* and *Politics & Letters* cost two shillings and sixpence at a time when Penguin books cost one shilling and sixpence. Cyril Connolly's monthly journal *Horizon* closed in 1949, having consistently failed to get 10,000 subscribers at one shilling a month. John Lehmann's *Penguin New Writing* ceased publication with issue number 40 in 1950. The reasons given were increasing production costs and a decline in periodical readership after the war. Left to the commercial market such literary magazines found it increasingly difficult to survive.

There was a cultural as well as an economic dynamic at work here. It seemed that the age of the general literary review was over. In 1947–8 the *Little Reviews Anthology* listed over seventy magazines. At the beginning of the 1950s nearly all had disappeared. The functions of the general literary review, as Stuart Laing argues, were split 'between small poetry magazines, academic journals and the literary sections of the weeklies or 'quality' press'.[3] When Williams started to publish again after the collapse of the *Politics & Letters* project, these were the kinds of places in which he was published.

Film

State policy for film is an important case because film production is expensive and requires sponsorship of some kind. It is also important because film was a highly popular and majority cultural form. The documentary film movement of the pre-war period was sponsored by state institutions: the Empire Marketing Board and later by the Post Office. The key figure in this movement is John Grierson, who made education and democracy central terms of the argument for his work. He argued, somewhat in the tradition of the Workers' Educational Association, for an alternative kind of education. The isolated person in the library and the traditional kind of university work were unnecessarily restricted forms of learning. Grierson himself had experience of this:

I have gone through the farce of teaching *A Midsummer Night's Dream* to evening-school brush workers, and Plato to tired labourers. . . . It is an anaemic conception. It lacks what seems to me respect for the labourer as such and for the man that is in him and for the part he can play in his own community. It does not create an image in his mind of what he, himself, on his own doorstep, and out of his own rich human character, could do and enjoy within the community. It is education with its roots in the air.[4]

While Grierson did not think that the age of the book was over, he insisted on the importance of new cultural forms such as film. He accepted the argument of Walter Lippmann in the 1920s that the world was becoming increasingly complex and that education had to pass on more than facts. Film was important because strictly speaking film does not communicate ideas. Film communicates a dramatized pattern, a pattern of relationships. 'We have become more and more citizens of a community which we do not see', Grierson argued.[5] Film, especially documentary film, could help us see.

Williams's interest in working in film in the late 1940s was a continuation of an interest that was developed in the Socialist Club at Cambridge. Films were an important part of the club's activities. They were organized by Williams's friend Michael Orrom. The example of the early Russian film was a shaping force even if the main concerns of British documentary films in the 1930s were social problems such as housing, work, food, and health. Williams describes the tension between form and content in this way:

The early Soviet film always seemed to me the major work that took up the original naturalist project of the secular, the contemporary, the socially extensive. But it had broadened its movement out into the public and historical action of new concepts to the process of production. In that respect, the Soviet film of the twenties was crucially superior to, say, the Italian neo-realism of the forties and the fifties. I was sympathetic to the new social material it presented, of which there were many decent examples after the war. But its form seemed to be a step backward, much like the later English drama of working-class experience of which I've spoken. The conceptual innovations of Eisenstein's cinema, which can be related to Brecht's complex seeing, are missing.[6]

Williams's point is similar to the lesson that Grierson took from the early Soviet film – the need for a sense of relativity as against the old absolutes of a dominant power. Grierson argued that documentary film must record important shapes and movements. Losing patience with the inability of British politicians to understand the nature of fascism in the 1930s, Grierson argued that 'The important shapes are obviously those more directly related to the national and international management of industrial, economic and human forces.'[7]

One of Williams's projects in 1946 was to make a documentary history of the Agricultural and Industrial Revolutions, which he was to make with Paul Rotha. The Central Office of Information, which financed such films, was not interested in such an ambitious scheme and suggested something suitable for a short introduction to a film about post-war reconstruction.[8] These were years of internal and external difficulties for the documentary movement. Among these was the failure of the post-war Labour government to continue funding. Williams argues that the Labour Government could not see the cultural importance of continuing the documentary film tradition.

Radio

Producers of British radio programming in the 1940s also experienced a tension between what they described as minority and majority audiences. During the war the Forces Programme was added to the existing Home Service. The Forces Service became the Light Programme in July 1945 and in September 1946 it was joined by the Third Programme with its 'high cultural level'. This meant music, drama, and serious talks. This post-war division brought to a climax the separation into popular and serious programming which had already started to emerge in the 1930s. The intention of the BBC was that the ratio of listeners between the Home, Light and Third Services would be 40, 50 and 10 per cent respectively. The Third Programme, however, started with less that 5 per cent of radio listeners and this fell to under 1 per cent.[9]

The BBC had realized in the late 1930s that the audience for serious talks was stratified. An internal memorandum written in 1938 divides the audience into three parts: first, the 'intelligent and well-informed' who needed to be catered for only occasionally; second, the 'intelligent and not so well-informed' who were the most important audience; and third, the largest part of radio listeners were described as 'not-so-intelligent and mostly uninformed' and not interested in serious talks from the BBC. The large sales of Pelican non-fiction paperbacks, Left Book Club books, and the success of *Picture Post* were taken as evidence that the intermediate group had considerable potential as listeners for serious radio talks.[10]

Williams gave talks on Ibsen for the Third Programme in December 1949 and May 1950. For university audiences the publication of the talk in *The Listener* was as important as the broadcast itself. When Williams's talk appeared in 1949, *The Listener* had reached its peak circulation: 151,350 copies for that year. While greater than the circulation of a literary magazine, it was still much less than the 7,765,361 copies of *Radio Times* in the same year.[11]

Book publishing

Williams's first book, *Reading and Criticism*, was intended for use in adult-education classes and was published in 1950 by Frederick Muller. From 1962, Williams was General Editor of the New Thinkers Library published by C. A. Watts. The original Thinkers Library was associated with movements for popular adult education. Most of Williams's books have been published by mainstream but 'progressive' companies: Chatto & Windus in hardcover and Penguin in paperback.

By the 1960s there was a major transformation of the British publishing industry. Michael Lane described the transformation as one from 'traditional' values and organization to 'modern' publishing.[12] For the traditional publisher, culture is understood as a single tradition. It is elitist, born in the creativity of the lone artist, and highly moralistic. The modern publisher, on the other hand, is frankly interested in publishing as a business. There is less of an idea of a single cultural tradition and publishers recognize similarities between their work and other media such as film and broadcasting.

Chatto & Windus published a distinguished list of progressive novelists and critics, including William Empson, Richard Hoggart, Aldous Huxley, F. R. Leavis, Wilfred Owen, and Lytton Strachey. In 1953 Chatto ceased to be a private partnership and became a limited company, and by the late 1950s it was involved in educational and technical publishing. In the late 1960s the company acquired a children's books division and also became involved in university publishing. In order to forestall a takeover Chatto amalgamated with Jonathan Cape in 1969. Williams's main publisher was therefore affected by the crisis of English publishing after the 1960s, yet managed by a series of astute business moves to retain some of its 'traditional' identity.[13]

Penguin Books was founded in 1935 and mixed its founder's entrepreneurial spirit with a progressive educational philosophy. In 1956, W. E. Williams of Penguin Books, who was also associated with the WEA, insisted that Penguin is not a mass market publisher: 'The Penguin market, despite its ten million sales, is not a mass market. Its books, especially outside crime and detection, are deliberately designed to appeal to a readership which probably does not exceed one-tenth of the population.'[14] The image is of the 'Penguin Educator' – the extension of minority culture to a broader but still limited readership. In later years Penguin Books came to be seen as a British institution somewhat similar to the BBC. The fundamental terms in which culture was offered were never really questioned. In 1956, for example, W. E. Williams commented that there were about sixty titles in the Penguin Classics series. He doubted that there were many more titles in the classical literature of the world. 'How can Penguin Classics expand', he asked, 'without diminishing the present rigorous standard of selection?'[15]

Newspapers and magazines

Williams has a reputation, well beyond university circles, as a book reviewer for the *Manchester Guardian*. He started to write on a regular basis for the newspaper in 1959. In the 1950s it had 20,000 local working-class readers – about one-sixth of its total. *Guardian* readers were strongly interested in literature and books and the paper had a reputation for not restricting the freedom of its writers. Its working-class readership declined in the 1960s when the paper moved to London, mainly under advertising pressure to become a 'national' newspaper.[16]

Although he wrote well of *Tribune*, the London-based left-Labour weekly, on the occasion of its twenty-first anniversary, Williams did not often write for the paper.[17] Most of these contributions were connected with Labour policy for culture and the arts in the 1960s. He had a similar relationship in the 1960s with *Sanity*, the magazine of the Campaign for Nuclear Disarmament.

Williams was a member of the large editorial board of the *New Left Review*. It was a magazine written for trade unionists, activists in CND, and for a new left generation interested in culture and politics. In 1963, a new editorial board turned it into a more systematic theoretical journal. E. P. Thompson writes:

Since taking on editorial control in 1963 Perry Anderson and his colleagues have conducted the review with system, conviction and decision. There was, however, a fracture in the passage from one tradition to another, which was never exposed to principled discussion. It was a very English transition: that is (according to one's viewpoint) gentlemanly and tolerant or otiose and manipulative.[18]

Williams gives a somewhat different account: that the magazine would
have collapsed and it was better to hand it over to a new group.[19] One
way of considering the issues involved is to think of the difference
between a left magazine that is intended for a general readership and a
theoretical journal that is intended for a more restricted readership.
Part of Thompson's polemic is that the difficult issues underlying such
a choice were never discussed. The project of the ejected *New Left*
editorial board continued to some extent in *Views*, a quarterly which
published eleven issues from 1963 to 1966. Williams published political
commentary in the American radical weekly, *The Nation*. He also
published in British weeklies such as *New Society* and *The Listener*.

In 1980, Williams was one of a panel of international figures who
were asked to write on the role of literary magazines in their country for
a special issues of the *Times Literary Supplement* on little magazines and
literary journals.[20] Williams's response was to insist that his country is
Wales. He was highly critical of London–English or (more recently)
London–New York metropolitan literary cultures, arguing for a large
number, hundreds, of alternative magazines which would encourage
'unknown writers' and screen writing by principles different from those
of the dominant metropolitan journals. He mentions as examples the
Lifetimes pamphlets, the Centreprise publications, and the Writers and
Readers Co-operative. Williams wrote for new small-circulation
magazines in recent years, as well as for left magazines with relatively
large circulations such as *New Socialist* and *Marxism Today*.

It is wholly idealist to consider Williams's work over a lifetime
without such histories of cultural institutions.[21] The problem in the
post-war years was the absence or weakness of institutions for workers'
education, film-making, publishing, and journalism. The institutions
which continued through from the 1930s – the Workers' Educational
Association, Penguin Books, and the sponsored documentary movement
– had an ambiguous though sometimes radical role. The BBC and the
Guardian were clearly much more restricted. If there was some free
space within the WEA, Penguin and the documentary movement, it
seemed to exist because of individuals in key positions such as Hodgkin
in the Oxford Delegacy of the WEA, Paul Rotha in film after the war,
and the ambiguous radicalism of Allen Lane in Penguin and John
Grierson in documentary film. The space for radical work in cultural
institutions was closed rapidly by direct political pressure in the Cold
War years, but it was just as often controlled by the withdrawal or
refusal of economic support. It should be quite clear that if the post-
war Labour Government had supported popular publishing and
institutions such as the documentary film movement, Williams's life as a
professional writer would have been very different.

Notes

1 Williams. *The Long Revolution*, (Penguin, 1965), pp. 333–4.
2 [Michael Pope], 'The State and Popular Culture', *Politics & Letters*, vol. 1, no. 4 (1948). One of the many paradoxes of Wilson's position is that meanwhile other branches of the state continued to censor the content of books and films on the grounds of morality and matters of state policy.
3 Stuart Laing, 'The production of literature', in *Society and Literature*, ed. Alan Sinfield (London, Methuen, 1983), pp. 121–71.
4 Forsyth Hardy (ed.), *Grierson on Documentary* (London, Faber and Faber, 1966), p. 92.
5 Ibid., p. 175
6 Williams, *Politics and Letters*, (New Left Books, 1979) p. 232.
7 Hardy, *Grierson on Documentary*, p. 117.
8 Williams, *Politics and Letters*, p. 71; Paul Rotha, *Documentary Diary: An Informal History of the British Documentary Film, 1928–1939* (New York, Hill and Wang, 1973); Elizabeth Sussex, *The Rise and Fall of British Documentary: The Story of the Film Movement Founded by John Grierson* (Berkeley, University of California, 1975); Robert Colls and Philip Dodd, 'Representing the Nation: British Documentary Film, 1930–45', *Screen*, 26 (January/February 1985), pp. 21–33; Stuart Hood, 'John Grierson and the Documentary Film Movement', in *British Cinema History*, ed. James Curran and Vincent Porter (London, Weidenfeld and Nicolson, 1983), pp. 99–112.
9 Asa Briggs, *The History of Broadcasting in the United Kingdom: Sound and Vision*, vol. 4 (Oxford, Oxford University Press, 1979), pp. 65–6, 81–2, 551–8.
10 David Cardiff, 'The Serious and the Popular: aspects of the evolution of style in the radio talk 1928–1939', *Media, Culture and Society*, 2 (1980), pp. 29–47; Paddy Scannell and David Cardiff, 'Serving the Nation: Public Service Broadcasting Before the War', in *Popular Culture: Past and Present*, ed. Bernard Waites, Tony Bennett and Graham Martin (London, Croom Helm and The Open University Press, 1982), pp. 161–88.
11 Asa Briggs, *History*, vol. 4, p. 569.
12 Michael Lane, *Books and Publishers: Commerce Against Culture in Postwar Britain* (Lexington and Toronto, Lexington Books, 1970).
13 Oliver Warner, *Chatto and Windus: A Brief Account of the Firm's Origin, History and Development* (London, Chatto and Windus, 1973).
14 Williams Emrys Williams, *The Penguin Story: 1935–1956* (Harmondsworth, Penguin, 1956), p. 58. For the founder of Penguin Books see J. E. Morpungo, *Allen Lane: King Penguin: A Biography* (London, Hutchinson, 1979). One of the few studies not produced from within the company is Evelyn Green, *Penguin Books: The Pictorial Cover 1960–1980* (Manchester Polytechnic, 1981).
15 W. E. Williams, *The Penguin Story*, p. 59.
16 David Ayerst, *Guardian: Biography of a Newspaper* (London, Collins, 1971).

17 Williams, 'Tribune's Majority', *New Statesman*, 24 January 1959, p. 124.
18 E. P. Thomson, 'An Open Letter to Leszek Kolakowski', in his *The Poverty of Theory and Other Essays* (New York and London, Monthly Review Press, 1978), p. 312.
19 Williams, *Politics and Letters*, pp. 365–6. Also Williams's review of *Socialist Register 1973* in which Thompson's essay first appeared, *Guardian*, 14 February 1974.
20 Williams, 'The role of the literary magazine', *Times Literary Supplement*, 6 June 1980, p. 637. Williams also writes on periodicals in 'London Letter: The New British Left', *Partisan Review*, 27 (1960), pp. 341-7; Grammar of Dissent', *The Nation*, 188 (1959), pp. 174–5; Williams, 'Editorial Commentary', *Essays in Criticism*, 4 (1954), pp. 341–4.
21 Nicholas Garnham, 'Contribution to a political economy of mass-communication', *Media, Culture and Society*, 1 (1979), pp. 123–46.

4

Keywords in culture and society

It is apparent that 'keywords' has been an important part of Williams's work for the past four decades. It is an historical method, a type of investigation, and a way of writing. Williams describes in the introduction to *Keywords* his sense of strangeness on returning to Cambridge in October 1945, which he and an old friend expressed by saying that students seemed no longer to speak the language of the 1930s. Williams adds that he had found a similar difference when he came to Cambridge in 1939 from a working-class family. It seemed that a different language was being spoken.[1]

Keywords as a book evidently had a long history. It started as an appendix to *Culture and Society* which Chatto & Windus insisted be dropped in order to shorten the book. Williams offered to expand it as a series of articles for *Tribune*, which was not interested in the idea.[2] The project has a foundation in Williams's adult-education teaching. By the time it was eventually assembled as a book, Williams had enough material on some words to make scholarly articles or even monographs on the more complex words. However, he preferred to stick to a popular paperback format. The 1976 edition sold well and in 1983 a second expanded edition appeared.[3]

Although the issue of keywords is among the most important features of Williams's work, this is not generally recognized. Terry Eagleton apparently describes it in a wholly negative way as the 'ritualising of a cluster of key terms to the point where they seem less public concepts than private inventions.'[4] Some reviewers of Williams's *Marxism and Literature* and *Towards 2000* have commented on the use of keywords as a method of investigation and an organization of argument. These are generally brief comments and the implications are not explored further.[5]

The importance of keywords in Williams's writing is evident in many of his publications in the 1970s and after. His 1980 article 'The Politics of Nuclear Disarmament' may be taken as an example.[6] In this necessarily complex argument, Williams asked if E. P. Thompson was right to argue that nuclear weapons had produced a new type of social order which Thompson called exterminism. Williams also asked what a specifically socialist contribution might be to activity against the arms race. The central part of Williams's article is organized about 'the question of the current real meanings of the leading terms of the general argument, notably "deterrence", "multilateralism" and "unilateralism"'[7] Thus, 'deterrence' is both a military strategy and an ideology. As a military strategy it is often justifiable. The crucial dividing line, argues Williams, is to put it bluntly, 'between deterrence from military attack, which is still widely and understandably supported, and on the other hand the deterrence of communism *per se*'.[8] The reasonable desire of people to be protected from attack is colonized and exploited by a right-wing strategy which in the early 1980s spoke of destroying communism in the Soviet Union, China, and the new socialist and communist countries.

The book *Keywords* is composed of many short essays on the history and use of over a hundred words. Each entry starts by mentioning common-sense multiple meanings of the word. Williams provides an historical sketch of the ways in which the word has been used. He then often makes an argument about uses of the word and concludes, often with a touch of irony or an invented word-play. A simple reading of the book is that it explains the uses of these words. It has an educational function: to give readers confidence in the use of difficult words. This extra edge of consciousness has political importance in a society in which access to education is unequally distributed.

Beyond this necessary level of teaching, there is an encouragement to the reader to question the uses of words in the same way that Williams questions the use of nuclear weapons as 'deterrence'. Not all of these words will be as obviously political. Williams's own interest in the study of words derives from the post-war use of the word 'culture' within the university. As it was used in spoken argument and then elaborated in T. S. Eliot's *Notes Towards the Definition of Culture*, it represented a position which Williams wished to oppose. This is a very good example of a general debate whose terms were set by a distinguished and specialized but (from Williams's viewpoint) highly questionable formation. Any educational book should encourage readers to be critical about the material presented and *Keywords* certainly does this.

From the introduction to *Keywords* it is clear that Williams is aware of the difficult theoretical issues which the book raises. Although there are several schools of German and French historical philology, *Keywords* is an unusual book in English. Furthermore, because the origin of the project is personal and oppositional it fits no recognizable theoretical foundation.

One possible comparison is with William Empson's *The Structure of Complex Words* (1951). Empson's book is part of a debate with I. A.

Richards about the value of an approach in terms of *words* rather than stretches of spoken or written argument. Richards argued that only in logical thinking which recognizes that the definition of a term is different from statements about an already defined term can the analyst usefully attend to the meanings of single words. In the fluid state of ordinary discourse the words cannot be said to have any meaning.[9] Empson disagrees. For him words are effective precisely because they have several senses, emotions, and intentions. Complex words have a structure of sense in a writer or cultural formation: 'Granting that you must first know the spirit of the author or the period, I think that to write down the equations of the key words which carried it is really the quick and natural way to sum it up.'[10]

Probably the closest to Empson's method is Williams's essay, 'David Hume: Reasoning and Experience' (1964). The main theme of this essay is to describe Hume's discovery through his writing of a kind of scepticism which also affirms. Williams is as often interested in whole stretches of Hume's writing as he is in the use of particular words. As well as describing the *conventions* of Hume's writing there is an examination of certain keywords. 'Society' for Hume is both the common system of life and the activity of a particular class of persons. Hume sometimes uses 'society' in the sense of a restricted *company* of friends. Williams reports that:

I have made a rough count in the *Enquiry*, and taking 'company of his friends' as sense A, and 'system of common life' as sense B, find twenty-five uses of A as against 110 senses of B, but also, at some critical points in the argument, sixteen uses which are really A/B. His further uses of 'political society' (four), 'civil society' (three), 'human society' (nine), 'general society' (one), 'family society' (one), add further complications.[11]

This mechanism of sense A and sense B, and the unanalysed A/B (Empson would say A is B) and the selection of complex words seems close to the method of *The Structure of Complex Words*. One can see a somewhat different intention, since Williams's point is that 'society' as a particular class of persons (sense B) is in fact a ruling class.

It has been pointed out by Norris in his study of Empson that the English eighteenth century is central for *Complex Words*. There is a fundamental assumption of the primacy of common-sense intelligence: that structures of meaning are communicable in terms of the secular values of the humanist enlightenment. This can be seen even in the selection of keywords which Empson discusses in *Complex Words*: wit, sense, fool, dog, honest man, and then 'an honest dog of a fellow'.[12] The selection is based on a kind of genial common sense. This ethic of mutuality undermines what Norris calls a sense of tragic values.[13] In his discussion of 'folly' Empson describes structures of meaning in Shakespeare and Erasmus in terms of the fool as clown, or implications of foolishness in reason. Empson mentions but does not care to make connections between these meanings and another sense of folly: the tragic sense of contradictions and the depths that lie under your feet.[14] This is not the case in Williams's adopted use. Williams's sense of the past and the future that lie 'under your feet' has some of the reason and humanism of *Complex Words*. There is however another side to Williams: a tragic residual sadness in the central character of his novel *Border Country*; a tragic sense of revolution in *Modern Tragedy* as necessary and as disruptive and violent.

The difference between the two world views is evident in Empson's quite hostile review in 1977 of *Keywords*. There seems to be an underlying assumption on Empson's part that most use of language is unproblematic, that the workings of the mind readily solve most cases of ambiguous words, but there are some more difficult 'tricks' of words which require careful unravelling. Empson thinks that Williams has a theory which makes our minds more feeble than they have to be if they are to go through their usual performance with language. Williams's introduction

offers very little hope from the technique he provides. For example: 'to understand the complexities of the meanings of *class* contributes virtually nothing to the resolution . . . of actual class disputes'; 'what can really be contributed is not resolution but perhaps, at times, just that extra edge of consciousness' – meaning perhaps that an enlightened orator might swing votes by understanding the psychology of his audience. It is a dark picture as a whole. (original emphasis)[15]

This is certainly not Williams's meaning. He means that misunderstandings and disputes cannot simply be solved by clarifying the words because underlying the differences are often conflicts of power, class, and group experiences. The extra edge of meaning that *Keywords* might contribute is an increased consciousness of actual conflicts as they are present in the use of words such as 'opportunity' or 'democracy'. This fundamental difference between Empson's air of common sense and Williams's theory of dominant, emergent, and oppositional discourse is the basis of Empson's other disagreements. He is quite angry about Williams on 'education' (that the category is constantly upgraded so that most people are still described as uneducated) and on 'interest' (Williams ends by saying that our main word for attraction or involvement is also a term in finance and property and this in a society based on money relationships).

Williams acknowledges in his introduction to *Keywords* the usefulness for any such project in English of the great *Oxford Dictionary*. The *Dictionary* traces the history of uses of words, giving quotations as examples. Having made this acknowledgement, Williams makes three points. First, because it was compiled effectively from the 1880s to the 1920s it is necessary to look elsewhere for usages after 1920. Especially in dealing with social and political words the *Dictionary* often presupposes orthodox positions: 'The air of massive impersonality which the Oxford *Dictionary* communicates is not so impersonal, so purely scholarly, or so free of active social and political values as might be supposed from its occasional use.'[16] The positions and preferences of the editors must be allowed for in using the *Dictionary*. Here as in his own book, Williams does not believe that value-free scholarship is possible. Second, although the *Dictionary* is deeply interested in meanings it is primarily philological and etymological. Williams is mainly interested in meanings and their context. This involves connections and interactions between words, whereas the *Dictionary* is mainly interested in the range and variations of single words. Third, Williams questions the authority of *written* language because, except for specialized discourses, the source of most meaning in language comes from spoken encounters. The purpose of this last argument is to return creativity in language to those who speak it. Williams is highly critical of the authoritative claims that are often made for dictionaries. Actual difficulties about conflicts in the use of words often cannot be solved by such appeals to authority. The conflicts are often deeply political and social and therefore need to be argued through as such.

Williams's challenge to the authority of the *Dictionary* resulted in a response from R. W. Burchfield, who is in charge of preparing its revised *Supplement*. Burchfield's main argument is that Williams does not have the authority or expertise to compile such a book. He claims that there is little in *Keywords* that is not in either the Oxford *Dictionary* or standard references in political science and sociology. He suggests that Williams lacks necessary linguistic skills. The abbreviations used are not the standard ones, and the choice of words makes *Keywords* of little use to professional economists or sociologists. Williams's book, he concludes, should be shelved in the Dewey system as Education 374 (Adult Education).[17]

Burchfield agrees that the editors of the Oxford *Dictionary* had a Victorian ideology and mentions their drawing-room attitude towards sexuality and their assumptions about 'savages'. The *Supplement* reflects the ideologies of the twentieth century, including new attitudes to race, sexuality, and religion. Burchfield describes his own working-class background in New Zealand and gives statistics about the background and characteristics of the twenty-seven members of his staff. He describes the wide range of sources being used to compile the supplements of the Oxford *Dictionary*.

Thus, while Burchfield seems to acknowledge the theoretical problem that the original and present editors of the Oxford *Dictionary* cannot escape the 'ideology' of their era, he trivializes this hermeneutic problem. The implication is that professional scholarship, using a wide range of sources, can solve the theoretical problems for all practical purposes. In this article for *Encounter* Burchfield presents himself as a reasonable and experienced person but sneers at 'the faintly *Marxisant* basis' of *Keywords*. His fundamental objective is to defend the authoritative status and use of the Oxford *Dictionary*.

The tradition which makes most sense of *Keywords* is the German *Begriffsgeschichte*, which has been associated with the French *Annales* school of history. There is an article in 1930 by Lucien Febvre which describes the history of *civilization*.[18] Study of historical changes of social and political vocabulary is, however, much more developed in Germany. Veit-Brause mentions Williams's *Keywords* as parallel work in an article on the German tradition.[19] The problem of the changing historical meaning of social and political terms grew out of historicist thinking. It cannot be assumed, for example, that the modern concept of 'the state' is adequate for previous historical epochs. In turn, changes in the usage of such words can provide valuable historical evidence.

It was quickly realized that studies of the history of keywords are most useful when a collection or field of words are studied together.[20] This raises questions of the selection of words which constitute such a semantic field. (The German tradition includes ordinary words and formal terminology.) This is in practice based on a knowledge of history and a theory of historical change – for example, the development of the modern world from the end of the eighteenth century. This is a reminder that the selection of the semantic field of *Keywords* was originally founded in the project of *Culture and Society*.[21]

The key to Williams's best known book, *Culture and Society*, is the emergence of the concept of 'culture' in Britain around the time of the Industrial Revolution. Looking back on *Culture and Society* in 1983, Williams reflected that:

The book was organized around the new kinds of problem and question which were articulated not only in the new sense of *culture* but in a whole group of closely associated words. Thus the very language of serious inquiry and argument was in part changed and changing, and my purpose then was to follow this change through in the writing of the very diverse men and women who had contributed to this newly central argument.[22]

This way of reading *Culture and Society*, as a historical study of five keywords, would have been difficult enough because, although there were isolated studies such as William Empson's *The Structure of Complex Words*, there was no tradition of such work in England. The keywords theme was all but blocked by the conditions in which the book was produced. It was finished in 1956 and published, with some difficulty, two years later. It had to be shortened for the publisher by leaving out a chapter on Godwin and another on the English Freudians and Herbert Read. As well as this, the appendix on the keywords, 'Changes in English During the Industrial Revolution', had to be left out.[23]

Although *Culture and Society* had its foundation in workers' education of the 1940s and early 1950s, the book became a rallying point for the new generation that emerged in the late 1950s. Along with a small number of other books and the journal *New Left Review*, Williams's book expressed the interest of the new generation in issues well beyond a narrow definition of politics. This was the case even though the book was written before the emergence of this new generation.

We read *Culture and Society* not only as a book but as a position within a text of readings and re-readings. If the response to a book is part of its reading, Williams's own response deserves to be taken into account as much as any other. Written in isolation in the 1950s, the book looked rather different in the late 1960s. In a lecture given in Manchester in April 1969, Williams comments on two central figures of *Culture and Society*, John Stuart Mill and Matthew Arnold, and therefore on the book itself. The crisis of the 1960s seems to repeat the patterns of the crisis of the 1860s. Arnold's *Culture and Anarchy* was written in the context of public demonstrations for an extension of the franchise and the official response which called for public order. Williams describes Mill as a 'traditional intellectual' who, with all of the limitations this implies, is doing his best to respond to the crisis.[24] Arnold responded rather differently, with anger and calls for repression. The culture he defended then, says Williams, is not excellence but familiarity: 'not the knowable but only the known values'.[25] We read *Culture and Society*, that careful and mediating book, differently if we know that ten years after its publication its author was protesting in the streets of London against the war in Vietnam.

Contrasts

Culture and Society starts with contrasts: between Burke and Cobbett, and Southey and Owen. It is a method that can usefully be continued.

The contrast that will be useful is that of Jean-Paul Sartre's *What is Literature* (1947) and Roland Barthes's *Writing Degree Zero* (1953). A version of Sartre' argument was published in England in *Politics & Letters*.[26] Williams's post-war work shares with that of Barthes an insistence on form, *écriture*, and the history of writing. It is helpful to think of *Culture and Society* in this way, as a European book.[27]

It is, of course, not a matter of choosing either Barthes or Sartre. They share an emphasis on the emergent experience of living as a body in the world and also a critical stance towards bourgeois culture. The singular form of written prose, argues Sartre, is a relationship between writer and reader which implies *freedom*. If Barthes argues against this, that there are many historical forms of writing, that does not mean he is against freedom and in favour of inauthentic writing. It is also commonplace in Williams, Sartre, and Barthes that writing is associated with power and historically was intended for a minority. Yet all three are writers.

It is a simplification – but nonetheless a useful one – that Sartre describes a history of writers, Barthes traces the history of forms of writing, but Williams writes in *Culture and Society* about individual writers in relation to the history of collective forms. There is a very weak notion of literary tradition in *What is Literature*. Sartre describes the backward-looking habits of literary criticism: 'It must be borne in mind that most critics are men who have not had much luck and who, just about the time they were growing desperate, found a quiet little job as cemetery watchmen.'[28] We may take as a response to this the following passage from *Writing Degree Zero*:

Now it is when History is denied that it is most unmistakably at work; it is therefore possible to trace a history of literary experience which is neither that of a particular language, nor that of the various styles, but simply the Signs of Literature, and we can expect that this purely formal history may manifest, in its far from obscure way, a link with the deeper levels of History.[29]

For Sartre freedom is the grammar of all prose writing; but Barthes argues that 'a mode of writing is an act of historical solidarity.'[30] For Barthes, the choice of a form of writing is the moment of the writer's commitment.

In *Culture and Society* there is such a method of attention to the Signs of Literature. Williams brought to the texts, which have become known as the culture and society tradition, his training in close analysis as a student of literature. At the same time, however, it is impossible not to notice the presence of the writers and their commitments: most often used by Williams, as it happens, to excuse or understand a writer with whom one might have thought him to be in strong disagreement. Neither Sartre's method nor that of Barthes would, however, have worked for Williams: for the characteristic of *Culture and Society* is to show that a residual but also oppositional tradition of writing was being used in post-war England in a wholly ideological way.

Notes towards the definition

Although there were debates in England during the 1930s about 'culture' and 'civilization' they did not crystallize out until the post-war years. The anthropology of Malinowski was almost wholly preoccupied with a theory of culture.[31] There was a complex relation with the term 'civilization', which was used by Clive Bell in 1928 as the title of his short book on cultural themes.[32] Two years later 'civilization' came to stand for the deterioration of a vital society in the title of F. R. Leavis's, *Mass Civilization and Minority Culture.*[33] Although there was a debate in the early 1930s about Leavis's use of the word, it was T. S. Eliot's *Notes Towards the Definition of Culture* (1948) which gave the word a new importance. Eliot wrote that: 'I have observed with growing anxiety the career of this word *culture* during the past six or seven years. We may find it natural, and significant, that during a period of unparalleled destructiveness, this word should come to have an important role in the journalistic vocabulary.'[34] Eliot mentions two examples which gave cause for anxiety. The first was the intense wartime debate about the democratization of education in Britain, a process which Eliot opposed. The second was the title proposed in 1945 for the United Nations Educational and Cultural Organization. From Eliot's argument culture is not something that can be organized, especially at an international level.

It is not difficult to deconstruct the absolute terms used by Eliot. Williams would point, for example, to the use of 'natural' in the passage just quoted from Eliot. Frank Gloversmith points out that 'natural' is a key term in arguments about culture in the 1930s which favoured social inequality. The natural differences correspond to the residual notion of innate psychological needs in Malinowski's social anthropology.[35]

Nonetheless, the advance proposed by Malinowski and Eliot's notion of culture is that it challenges the fixed categories of much nineteenth-century social thought. There was a dominance within British anthropology in the first half of the twentieth century of pluralistic and relativistic notions of culture. This involved a rejection of the three axioms of nineteenth-century anthropology: the psychic unity of humankind, the unity of human history, and the unity of culture.[36] Malinowski's interest was in describing actual patterns of culture, and Eliot also insisted on a social perspective. Culture is the pattern of a society as a whole.

This argument was of great theoretical importance to Williams. Eliot had argued that religion and culture were a whole way of life, including potential and not only known culture. This also provides a very strong critique of the alternative notions of culture held by Bloomsbury, Leavis, and Fabian socialists. The argument that culture is a whole way of life rules out the idea of an individual search for culture as a social goal, as in the Bloomsbury fraction. It also rules out the idea, which is the foundation of the *Scrutiny* formation, of a 'minority culture' in isolation from the general society. Eliot also argued against Fabian notions of the extension of an *already existing* culture because culture cannot be democratized without thereby being radically changed. Eliot was, of course, deeply opposed to such change, but the general point against the Fabian notion of the simple extension of a dominant culture still stands.

Although Eliot provided a strong critique of Bloomsbury, Leavis, and social democracy, his own position is described by Williams as a 'new conservatism' because, unlike Edmund Burke and Coleridge, he does not reject the economic system upon which the society he criticizes is based. All of Eliot's points end up as arguments for the existing social and economic system.

The theoretical argument against Eliot is extremely interesting. The problem is that Eliot's theory cannot accept the notion of a contradictory totality. At its simplest, Williams makes the point in this way: 'Eliot seems always to have in mind, as the normal scheme of his thinking, a society which is at once more stable and more simple than any to which his discussion is likely to be relevant.'[37] This is the case for Eliot's theory of class which he derives from the specialization of functional groups within simpler societies. However, after several generations of inheritance and accumulation the function of property may become mainly one of maintaining the privileges of property. The actions and effects of merchants, industrial capitalists, and financiers are far more complex than any specialized social function within an observable community. There is a similar problem, argued Williams, with Eliot's notion of culture as a whole way of life. There is an initial problem that in any real society it would be impossible for one individual to have a working knowledge of all of its culture, defined as ways of life. A more serious objection is that Eliot himself argued that much of culture is not fully knowable: it is unconscious or emergent. Yet Eliot would not allow a potential contradication between an emergent culture and the dominative culture in so far as it only protected a propertied class. Williams accepted the argument about culture and totality, but he insisted that it may be a contradictory totality.[38]

The organization of argument as a book

Unlike *What is Literature* and *Writing Degree Zero*, and other post-war writing including much of the work of Adorno, George Steiner, and Leavis, *Culture and Society* is not written as an essay, or a collection of essays. In Adorno, there is a commitment to the form of written fragments in order not to impose order on a modernity that is itself fragmentary, disordered, and bewildering.[39] Although Williams found the years after the war bewildered and disordering he did not write *Culture and Society* as a series of essays. How, then, is it organized as a book?

Williams rejected the tactic used by Leavis, which was to project the person of the writer as a principle of unity of the work. Williams describes in quite moving terms the personal consequences for Leavis of assuming this role. Every disagreement became something like an attack on Leavis as a person.[40] It is true that some of the figures of *Culture and Society* share the isolation and withdrawal in which Williams wrote the book.[41] Remarks on education, including workers' education, are also relevant to Williams's situation.[42] These personal themes are not, however, the organizational structure of the book.

If *Culture and Society* is not organized by the person of the author perhaps it is organized by the pragmatics of a discipline. Stanley Fish argues in 'What makes an interpretation acceptable?' that the professional institution of literature constructs the facts of a literary text. At least some interpretations of a literary text will not be allowed. An acceptable interpretation must be organized in such a way as to be acceptable to the discipline.[43] There are several problems with this argument. First, the majority of readers of English are not part of Fish's 'class' of readers. He assumes that all meaningful interpretation happens within the university. Second, he denies the possibility of real opposition to instituted English. All alternatives are simply 'subcultures' within the institution. Third, he does not pay attention to the *writing* of interpretations. It is not enough to offer an interpretation of Blake's *The Tyger*: it must be composed and organized as writing which has a quality of Blakean studies. It is not possible to explain the organization of *Culture and Society* in terms of the pragmatics of a discipline. Williams's book was written outside of any university discipline and was intended as a genuine opposition to the dominant discourse about culture in the post-war years. This debate had direct political consequences and its effect went well beyond the institution of the university. It directly involved such matters as the post-war reform of secondary education and intervention by the state to support the arts and the culture industries. The scope of *Culture and Society* extends well beyond the institution and discipline of English studies.

Culture: a paradigm in motion

What makes *Culture and Society* a book rather than a series of essays on English writers is the written practice of keywords. This is the single most innovative feature of the book. Years later, even when Williams had moved some distance from the book, he still described this as the innovation of *Culture and Society* and only regretted that he did not carry it through more strongly.[44] The organizational strategy of the keywords motif results in a book that is both historical and open-ended. In Williams's words, 'It is only by a return to the modulations of the term through history that you can understand the term itself.'[45] This was, of course, the fascination of language as the structuring form of culture and writing in the theoretical discourses of the 1970s: language is an ambiguous and open-ended structure.

Any analysis of the argument of *Culture and Society* must be prefaced by some remarks on Williams's attention to writing. There is a danger that in underlining the innovative method of the book a group of keywords may become abstracted from the complex written argument in which they are found. The method of the book is an extension of the technique of close reading to political, philosophical, critical, and also to some imaginative prose writing. The method can be described as immersion in a text. Indeed, Williams in later years speaks critically of a kind of ventriloquism which came from an undue immersion in a particular writer. The resulting readings have a sympathetic bias since the purpose is to understand the writer's situation and intention. In practice Williams frequently is critical, often quite sharply so. The close reading in which Williams had been trained was not a science of texts but always involved moral and political evaluation.

The large number of quotations in *Culture and Society* are offered as something close to experimental evidence. It is not only that the text is demonstrated. There is also a check on Williams's prose: on his tone and nuance in relation to the text that he is examining. What is being judged is the whole quality of the prose: the writing as a kind of life. As well as this moral pedagogy there is the practice of teaching. *Culture and*

Society was written while Williams was working in adult education. There is a teaching practice of giving sufficient examples to allow students to form their own impressions and argument.

Close attention to writing is even more justified in the texts in which the keyword 'culture' is emergent or is being used in a consciously metaphorical way. This is the case in the opening chapter. For Edmund Burke, there is an argument from actual experience and in opposition to 'industrialization', against which he invokes an 'organic' society, or Spirit of the Nation. Although there is a considerable difference between Burke and the shifting politics of William Cobbett, what they share is something like a theoretical argument: that what will be called 'culture' cannot be understood as a matter of ideas or mechanical invention, but is a kind of foundation or structure of living. The emphasis that matters is that culture is a process.

With the paradigm in motion, subsequent chapters add to its history. The separation of 'art' is associated with the conditions of literary production of the Romantics, in particular a new relationship between writers and the rising middle-class readership. German philosophical thinking about *Kultur* encounters English thinking about industrialization in the person of John Stuart Mill. This is extended in Thomas Carlyle, who also gives 'industrialism' its name. In what Williams then calls 'the industrial novels' the critique of the effects of manufacture is continued, but alongside a new mood. The novelists of the mid-nineteenth century are written by a fear of the action of the organized working class. This continues in J. H. Newman and Matthew Arnold, along with a special emphasis on education. Towards the end of the nineteenth century the cultural critique of industrialization becomes radicalized in writing on architecture and industrial design. In William Morris there is especially a critique based on what in the Marxist tradition is termed the use-value of work and commodities. This is clearly not only a 'cultural' criticism of society; it is criticism aimed at the centre of the capitalist organization of work and production. This way of thinking about art and culture as activities which express human values provokes questions about whether a particular work is worth doing, whether a particular object is worth making. The nearest figure to Morris, concluded Williams, was Cobbett at the start of the century. 'The nearest figure to him in his own century, is Cobbett: with the practice of visual instead of rural arts as the controlling sanity from which the political insights sprang.'[46]

We can begin to put back some of the detail of Williams's written argument by starting from the title. It has often been assumed that the title *Culture and Society* is an unconscious translation of Tonnies's opposition between *Gemeinschaft* and *Gesellschaft* – 'community' and 'society'. This is not the case because as Williams uses them each of these two terms has a different function. The two words are very different. 'Society' is not one of the five keywords. 'Culture' is a process and therefore involves the usual difficulties of studying a process, but 'society' is deeply unknowable and virtually absent from the book. 'Culture' can be traced as an argument in relationship to other keywords through a selected tradition of writing. 'Society' is however quite different. This does not mean that Williams rejects statistical and other systematic techniques of social investigation: on the contrary he consistently supports such research against all romantic and elitist arguments.[47] The point is that Williams's criticism of particular writers is usually for their impoverished vision of what society *might be*. If society is a potential organization of culture, Williams's repeated criticism is the poverty of the offered and imagined institution.

Thus, Edmund Burke, the first figure in the nineteenth-century tradition described *Culture and Society*, is also the last figure in the book whose criticism of industrialization is based on *actual experience* of a residual but existing alternative. Beyond that, what is there? In the Romantics there is an actual exclusion and isolation from effective social institutions, along with high-flown rhetoric about being unacknowledged legislators of the world. In Coleridge there is a proposal for a new class: the Clerisy or National Church. This is to be funded by the state in order to create a third class in addition to the existing classes of landowners and manufacturers. John Stuart Mill put his faith in an extended system of national education. Carlyle combined these notions: a national Literary Class and expanded popular education. He also wrote, as did many other figures in this tradition, in an idealized way about the Middle Ages. The industrial novels are marked by a failure to imagine a solution to the problems of industrialization within the existing society. They typically end in death or in emigration to the colonies. Kingsley recommended Working Men's Colleges. Newman and Arnold wrote about the possibilities of education. It is only with William Morris at the end of the nineteenth century that there is the courage to seek a solution in a different *future*: in a new kind of organization of working and living.

Culture and democracy: the paradigm blocked

In the nineteenth-century tradition the main emphasis is culture as an argument against industrialism. By the 1920s there was a shift in the argument and the debate became mainly one of culture in relation to democracy. The period from 1880 to 1914 is treated in *Culture and*

Society mainly as an interval or pause between the historial tradition and the modern argument. The most important moment of this section of the book is Williams's rejection, in the course of a discussion of T. E. Hulme, of all notions of an isolated pre-social human being. Williams insists that there is no ultimate essential human condition underlying or preceding the manifestations of persons in particular circumstances.[48]

The central twentieth-century debate inherited arguments for the value of art as a criticism of actually existing social relations. A twentieth-century writer such as R. H. Tawney, who essentially continues the nineteenth-century critique of industrialism on the grounds of the need for a shared culture, fails to answer the objection that such democratization would result in a decline in cultural standards. The rejection of individual aestheticism in the 1920s implied a subsequent search for a social foundation on which culture could be sustained against the effects of the twentieth-century cultural industries. The debate between Marxists and the *Scrutiny* formation in the 1930s ended with Leavis in a position of strength mainly because of his attention to language as the material production of literature. The generalized Marxist argument about 'bourgeois' and 'working-class' culture was wholly inadequate when confronted with particular texts.

In spite of his opposition to *fin-de-siècle* aestheticism, I. A. Richards's own theory of literature unconsciously reproduces the central assumption: an isolated observer in relation to a hostile world. Leavis's attention to language was accompanied by his arguments for a cultivated minority in the university in opposition to the cultural industries of publishing, radio, television, and the cinema. The strength of Eliot, as we have seen, is to block both of these arguments. Culture must be a whole way of life and not a matter of individual or minority response. With this, as we have seen, came Eliot's strong argument against democracy on the grounds that most people should remain within the culture in which they were born. It is at this point that *Culture and Society* takes up the paradigm.

Two other twentieth-century figures have a special position in *Culture and Society*. In writing of D. H. Lawrence and George Orwell the prose takes on some of the qualities of the novel *Border Country* which Williams was writing in these years. Lawrence's own working-class background and career as a writer had a direct personal interest. Orwell's background is rather different, although both he and Williams had personal experience of a twentieth-century war.[49] The book that Williams most admires is *Homage to Catalonia*, Orwell's account of the Spanish Civil War.[50] It should be added that although Lawrence and Orwell have a special position in *Culture and Society* they are also the writers whom Williams most rejected in later years.

Lawrence continues the critique of industrialism in a remarkable resemblance to Carlyle eighty years earlier. In his formative period, Lawrence was personally caught up in the ugliness of industry. The ambiguity and uncertainty, which Williams describes in very moving prose, is his formation in a working home by 'the full presence of others', whereas later he became an exile and effectively isolated. 'Lawrence was so involved in the business of getting free of the industrial system that he never came seriously to the problem of changing it, although he knew that since the problem was common an individual solution was only a cry in the wind.'[51]

The case of Orwell is more paradoxical: humanity and inhumane terror, equality and inescapable class difference, socialism and a popularized criticism of it – these exist beside each other in his writing. Williams asks how this may be understood:

He is genuinely baffling until one finds the key to the paradox, which I will call the paradox of the exile. For Orwell was one of a significant number of men who, deprived of a settled way of living, or a faith, or having rejected those which were inherited, find a virtue in a kind of improvised living, and in an assertion of independence.[52]

Lacking the kind of foundation that Lawrence has in the full presence of others from his childhood, Orwell attempts to create a common culture in his writing but often falls into a mood of despair.

The attention to writing which is very much a part of Williams's argument about Lawrence and Orwell derives from the theoretical understanding that Williams himself is writing within a culture. He does not himself want to take the stance of an outsider. The conclusion of *Culture and Society* is a continuation of several articles which Williams published in adult-education journals which commented on terms such as educational 'ladder', 'standards', and 'class'.[53] His main critical attention here is to uses of 'mass' as in mass society and mass-communications. The arguments he uses still stand. Arguments about mass culture ignore the intentions of the author (this does not imply an isolated author but a relationship), issues of reception and response, and usually involve a restricted and biased selection of examples.[54]

Williams's own argument is that working-class culture has the structure of a collective idea. This makes sense in the context of the twentieth-century tradition he has been describing, and can be taken in a fairly crude way to be a sociological hypothesis that working-class life is characterized by solidarity and that of the middle class by individual career patterns. Williams's earlier remarks on the working class in *Culture and Society* are far more complex.[55] His argument here needs to be read carefully. 'The working class, because of its position, has not, since the Industrial Revolution, produced a culture in the narrower sense. The culture which it has produced, and which is important to recognize, is the collective democratic institution, whether in the trade unions, the co-operative movement, or a political party.'[56] We read this against the dominant twentieth-century tradition which saw in such democratic culture a threat to its own rather different sense of 'culture'. Williams's own criticism of his argument in later years is that he was generalizing from the Welsh community in which he grew up.[57] It was in any case a temporary conclusion. A decade later, in his lectures on the English novel, Williams was developing a more elaborated idea of a 'knowable community'. In the Conclusion of *Culture and Society* he writes: 'No community, no culture, can ever be fully conscious of itself, ever fully know itself.'[58]

Notes

1 Williams, *Keywords*, 2nd edn., (Fontana, 1983), p. 11.
2 Williams, *Culture and Society*, (New Left Books, 1979), p. 179.
3 All references to *Keywords* in this chapter are to the revised edition.
4 Terry Eagleton, *Criticism and Ideology*, (London, New Left Books, 1976), p. 22.
5 Patrick Parrinder, 'The Accents of Raymond Williams', *Critical Quarterly*, 26 (Spring and Summer 1984), pp. 47–57; Janet Morgan, 'Unquestioned questions', *Times Literary Supplement*, 4 November 1983, p. 1223. See also 'The end of literary criticism', *Guardian*, 26 January 1984, p. 12; Patrick Parrinder, 'Culture and Society in the 1980s', in his *The Failure of Theory* (Brighton, Harvester Press, 1987), pp. 58–71.
6 Williams, 'The Politics of Nuclear Disarmament', *New Left Review*, 124 (1980), pp. 25–42.
7 Ibid., p. 27.
8 Ibid., p. 32.
9 William Empson, *The Structure of Complex Words*, 3rd edn. (London, Chatto and Windus, 1979), p. 312.
10 Ibid., p. 83.
11 Williams, 'David Hume: Reasoning and Experience', in his *Writing in Society* (London, New Left Books, 1984), p. 140.
12 Empson, *Complex Words*, p. 222.
13 Christopher Norris, *William Empson and the Philosophy of Literary Criticism* (London, Athlone Press, 1979), p. 86.
14 Empson, *Complex Words*, p. 124.
15 William Empson, 'Compacted Doctrines', *New York Review of Books*, 27 October 1977, p. 21.
16 Williams, *Keywords*, p. 18.

17   R. W. Burchfield, 'A Case of Mistaken Identity', *Encounter*, 46 (June 1976), pp. 57–64.

18   Lucien Febvre, 'Civilization: Evolution d'un mot et d'un groupe d'idées', *Première semaine international de synthèse*, f. II (Paris, 1930). Williams also cites Lucien Febvre, 'Capitalisme et Capitaliste', *Annales d'Histoire Sociale* (1939).

19   Irmline Veit-Brause, 'A Note on Begriffsgeschichte', *History and Theory*, 20 (1981), p. 63.

20   Suzanne Ohman, 'Theories of the Linguistic Field', *Word*, 9 (1953), pp. 123–34.

21   Another example of this is Kenneth Burke's 'Dictionary of Pivotal Terms', towards the end of his *Attitudes Toward History*, 3rd edn. (Berkeley, University of California, 1984).

22   Williams, *Culture and Society* (1983 Morningside edition), p. ix.

23   Williams, *Politics and Letters*, p. 99; Williams, *Keywords*, p. 14.

24   Williams, 'A Hundred Years of Culture and Anarchy', *The Spokesman*, no. 8 (1970), pp. 3–5. Reprinted in Williams, *Problems in Materialism and Culture* (Verso, 1980).

25   Ibid.

26   Jean-Paul Sartre, ' "Commitment" in Literature', *Politics & Letters*, vol. 1, nos 2/3 (Winter/Spring 1947–8), pp. 24–33.

27   Lukács, Gramsci, Sartre, Camus, Barthes, Goldmann, and Benjamin are included in the reading list attached to Williams, 'An Introduction to Reading in Culture and Society', in *Literature and Environment*, ed. Fred Inglis (London, Chatto and Windus, 1971), pp. 137–8.

28   J.-P. Sartre, *What is Literature*, tr. Bernard Frechtman, introd. Wallace Fowlie (New York, Harper and Row, 1965), p. 22.

29   Roland Barthes, *Writing Degree Zero*, tr. Annette Lavers and Colin Smith, preface by Susan Sontag (New York, Hill and Wang, 1968), p. 2.

30   Ibid., p. 14.

31   Rhonda Metraux, 'Bronislaw Malinowski', *International Encyclopedia of the Social Sciences* (New York, Macmillan and The Free Press; London, Collier–Macmillan, 1968).

32   Clive Bell, *Civilization: An Essay* (London, Chatto and Windus, 1928), issued as a Penguin paperback in 1938. On culture and civilization see Norbert Elias, *The History of Manners*, tr. Edmund Jephcott (New York, Pantheon, 1978), first published in 1939. For the US cultural debate see Lewis Perry, *Intellectual Life in America: A History* (New York, Franklin Watts, 1984), esp. ch. 6.

33   F. R. Leavis, *Mass Civilization and Minority Culture* (Cambridge, 1930).

34   T. S. Eliot, *Notes Towards the Definition of Culture* (London, Faber and Faber, 1962), p. 13.

35   Frank Gloversmith, 'Defining Culture: J. C. Powys, Clive Bell, R. H. Tawney and T. S. Eliot', in *Class, Culture and Social Change*, ed. Frank Gloversmith (Sussex, Harvester, 1980), pp. 15–44.

36   M. Singer 'The Concept of Culture', *International Encyclopedia of the Social Sciences* (1968), p. 527.

37 Williams, *Culture and Society* (Penguin, 1961), p. 232. All further references are to this edition.
38 Ibid., p. 238.
39 Robert Lane Kauffman, 'The Theory of the Essay: Lukács, Adorno, and Benjamin', Ph. D. dissertation, University of California, San Diego, 1981; T. W. Adorno, 'The Essay as Form', *New German Critique*, 32 (Spring-Summer 1984), pp. 151-71.
40 Williams, 'Seeing a man running', in *The Leavises*, ed. D. Thompson (Cambridge University Press 1984), pp. 113–22.
41 Figures described in *Culture and Society* as isolated include Burke (pp. 24, 27); the Romantics (p. 63), Carlyle (p. 89–90), Wilde (p. 175), Lawrence (p. 203), Richards (p. 245), Orwell (p. 282).
42 For the theme of education in *Culture and Society* see pp. 25, 34, 43–6, 93, 121–3, 128, 206, 249, 295–8, 317.
43 Stanley Fish, 'What Makes an Interpretation Acceptable?', in his *Is There A Text in This Class?* (Cambridge, Harvard University Press, 1980), pp. 338–55.
44 Williams, *Politics and Letters*, p. 109.
45 Ibid.
46 Williams, *Culture and Society*, p. 160.
47 Ibid., pp. 70–71, 91, 105.
48 Ibid., p. 197.
49 This is more noticeable in Williams, 'George Orwell', *Essays in Criticism*, 5 (1955), pp. 44–52.
50 Williams, *Orwell*, 2nd edn. (Flamingo, 1984), p. 59.
51 Williams, *Culture and Society*, p. 203.
52 Ibid., p. 279.
53 Williams, 'Standards', *The Highway*, December 1954, pp. 43–6; Williams, 'Class and Classes', *The Highway*, January 1956, pp. 84–6; Williams, 'A Kind of Gresham's Law', *The Highway*, February 1958, pp. 107–10.
54 For a recent example of an argument in terms of 'masses', see Jean Baudrillard, *In the Shadow of the Silent Majorities* (New York, Semiotext(e), 1983). Williams writes in *Culture and Society* that: 'Inertia and apathy have always been employed by the governed as a comparatively safe weapon against their governors. Some governing bodies will accept this, as at least being quiet' (p. 304).
55 Williams, *Culture and Society*, p. 110. Also the discussion between Hoggart and Williams. 'The Uses of Literacy: Working Class Culture', *Universities and Left Review*, 1, no. 2 (1957), pp. 29–32. These issues resurface in the debate collected in *The Forward March of Labour Halted?*, ed. Martin Jacques and Francis Mulhern (London, Verso, 1981).
56 Williams, *Culture and Society*, p. 315.
57 Williams, *Politics and Letters*, pp. 118–19.
58 Williams, *Culture and Society*, p. 319.

5

The knowable community in the English novel

Williams belongs to that generation of writers and intellectuals, whose work Edward Said dates from about 1936 onwards, who were almost always concerned with concrete situations rather than with abstractions, with methods rather than with universal principles.[1] In another sense, however, Williams belongs with the post-structuralist rediscovery of situations of writing and discourse communities. Williams's discovery in his work on the history of the English novel is an alternative tradition or counter-memory which he calls 'the knowable community'. This complex term describes a strategy in discourse rather than immediate experience or an 'organic' community. Williams reverses the accepted wisdom that traditional communities exist and then historically are disrupted by the mass media. He argues that the experience of 'face to face' community is discontinuous and fragmentary.[2] A community is knowable through a system of extended communication.

From 1840 to 1920 the novel was such a system of extended communication. After the first decades of this century, film, radio, and especially television took over this place of importance. The knowable community belongs to the tradition of the novel. 'Most novels are in some sense knowable communities. It is part of a traditional method – an underlying stance and approach – that the novelist offers to show people and their relationships in essentially knowable and communicable ways.'[3] This literary context is an historical phenomenon through and through. The English novel in the 1840s is important as a form of communicating what can be known of work, desire, speech, and intellectual life: a form of needed communication. The novel may be shaped by the development of industry and the cities, and the continued transformation of the country. The novel may be shaped by the project of the novelist. However, the main argument is that the novel itself actively shapes experience: understanding of connections between individuals and the political, social, and economic structures of history. It is a matter of literature *in* society alongside sermons, newspapers, told stories, political speeches. The novelist is 'defining the society rather than merely reflecting it; defining it in novels'.[4]

Forms of writing are complex historical resources. They allow a writer to make certain connections but make others almost unthinkable. Williams shows this in *The Pelican Book of English Prose*, which traces the history of different forms of writing – including scientific writing – from 1780 to the present day. The central aim of Williams's collection of English prose is to show the development of the novel around the middle of the last century. Such a development was made possible by the tradition of eighteenth-century philosophical and criticial essays. The strengths of this tradition, argues Williams, are the strengths of literacy itself.

The composed page; the sense of time gained, time given; the mind working but also the mind prepared, in an exposition that assumes patience, reference, inspection, re-reading. Such prose, indeed, is a kind of climax of print, and especially of the printed book: a uniformity of tone and address; an impersonality, assuming no immediate relation between writer and reader but only possession, in a social way, of this language; a durability, as in the object itself, beyond any temporary impulse or occasion.[5]

This is a tradition of writing from which we may learn but it is also in history. This composed impersonal page has its advantage of seriousness and uniformity of address. Yet this will be challenged from the 1840s by a new and rather more unstable written form: the counter-tradition of the knowable community. This seems to have four main aspects.

1 There is an instability that is introduced into the form of the English novel by the need to include people and voices that had previously been excluded. The alternative knowable community of George Eliot includes rural workers and their way of speaking. There is then a contrast between these voices and the educated tone of the implied narrator.

2 The actual historical pressure of these voices is part of the emergence of a complex society. It is no longer possible to look and see the workings of the society. There is an evident need in such a developing and complex society to have an overall sense of it.

3 The possibility of an overview of the whole society is, however, subject to radical doubt. The phrase 'knowable community' has a kind of irony because what is being shown is how much of the society is deeply unknowable.

4 Part of what is unknowable is the emergence of the future. The idea of a knowable community implies a contrast with one that is already

known. The counter-tradition of the knowable community includes a subjunctive moment. It asks 'what if' this or that imagined future came to pass.[6]

The emergence of a majority form

Williams's argument in *The Pelican Book of English Prose* and *The English Novel* is that the dominant tradition of the novel in England developed in an epoch on minority literacy. The English country of Jane Austen is a fictional polite society of large houses. It is not yet a knowable community.

It is outstandingly face to face; its crises, physically and spiritually, are in just these terms: a look, a gesture, a stare, a confrontation; and behind these, all the time, the novelist is watching, observing, physically recording and reflecting. That is the whole stance; the grammar of her morality. Yet while the community is wholly known, within the essential terms of the novel, it is as an actual community very precisely selective.[7]

This face-to-face world is selected by social class. The selected community is composed of people in large houses who may be socially recognized and visited. It does not include people who live in the neighbourhood and work on the land. Williams's point is not only that most people have been excluded. As well as this, the important social and economic patterns of the society are present only through this restricted pattern of knowing. The achievement of a settled and confident way of seeing and judging is possible because of this. Jane Austen is candid and precise, but in particular ways.

She is for example more exact about income, which is disposable, than about acres, which have to be worked. Yet at the same time she sees land in a way that she does not see 'other sources' of income. Her eye for a house, for timber, for the details of improvement, is quick, accurate, monetary. Yet money of other kinds, from the trading houses, from the colonial plantations has no equivalent; it has to be converted to these signs of order to be recognized at all.[8]

The underlying social and economic patterns, the consolidation and expansion of an existing social class, can be shown in the novels of Jane Austen only in so far as this process is converted into the symbols of the big house and an estate that is being visibly improved.

The contrast with this apparently settled and poised community is the fictional world of Charles Dickens. For beyond the pages of Jane

Austen, the working class in the country and the city had its own popular culture of speech, song, ballad, story. Austen's tone of equanimity is achieved by excluding this as well as the lives and work of most people. Dickens's project takes up this popular culture and incorporates it into a then radically changed and disturbed form of writing. In part this is because of actual historical changes. In the rapidly expanding nineteenth-century city there was no longer a separation of folk culture and high culture. The contrast is now rather different: between a popular urban culture and an educated class. This is more evidently a *relation*, as between a popular writer like Dickens and his readership, than the kind of *exclusion* which Jane Austen at least seemed to make plausible.

The point is then to understand what Dickens is borrowing from the urban popular culture which he shares. Both this urban culture and the novels of Dickens exist to make knowable the transformations of an urban capitalist formation whose workings are now quite hidden from view but whose effects are felt by every life in this metropolitan centre. Dickens is responding to this felt crisis but also acting on it, showing ways in which it may be experienced, given a kind of reality, and perhaps even changed. Dickens's originality, says Williams, is that:

He is able to dramatize those social institutions and consequences which are not accessible to ordinary physical observation. He takes them and presents them as if they were persons or natural phenomena. Sometimes as the black cloud or as the fog through which people are groping and looking for each other. Sometimes as the Circumlocution Office, or Bleeding Heart Yard, where a way of life takes on physical shape. Sometimes as if they were human characters, like Shares in *Our Mutual Friend* and of course the Great Expectations. This connects with his moral naming of characters: Gradgrind, McChoakumchild, Merdle. It connects also but in a less obvious way with a kind of observation which again belongs to the city: a perception one might say, that the most evident inhabitants of cities are buildings, and that there is at once a connection and a confusion between the shapes and appearances of buildings and the real shapes and appearances of people who live in them.[9]

This is a form of writing a rapidly changing society and city. It is a way of showing the economic transformations which Marx identifies in a necessarily more abstract way. It is an understanding that the structures of political economy, objectified and shown in buildings, business houses, the Stock Exchange, are shaping the reality and appearance of people who live within this rapidly changing whole. People seem to have the same shape as these buildings. The buildings themselves have a kind of hidden yet knowable dynamic.

An argument about power–knowledge

In some recent arguments the way of knowing a community in Dickens has been presented as an effect of power rather than as useful knowledge. For Michel Foucault the social sciences are a prison-house of knowledge. 'The carceral network constituted one of the armatures of this power–knowledge that has made the human sciences historically possible. Knowable man (soul, individuality, consciousness, conduct, whatever it is called) is the object-effect of this analytical investment, of this domination-observation.'[10] There is actually little disagreement here. Williams is equally critical of observation from a distance whether it is Mass Observation from the 1930s or fiction which simply observes without involving the writer's intentions. Nor does Williams have any time for writing which isolates individual persons whether as 'personal' experience or psychological interpretation. Williams's interest is not in 'knowable man' but knowable communities in which the connections between persons, collectivities, and underlying patterns of history are shown.

Foucault's argument has been taken up, although in a qualified way, in Jonathan Arac's *Commissioned Spirits*. His discussion of Dickens selects many of the same themes as Williams but uses them to make quite a different argument.[11] Arac and Williams have a shared understanding of the motifs of the railway and the house in Dickens: the railway as disruptive social motion, the home as somewhere hidden. For Arac, however, the railway is also a force for surveillance: 'The railways also acted as forces of compression within each city. This compression increased the "knowability" of the city, both by condensing certain districts along the railroad into epitomes of social problems and by clearing a space from which an observer could survey the scene. . .'[12] Arac recognizes that Dickens's project is to show the web of connections in the city, against the individualistic emphasis of Benthamism. However, he finds in Dickens another aspect of utilitarianism: the need for government action, inspection, and centralization. According to Arac, 'The increasingly spatializing overview that Dickens assumes as the narrative perspective from which to reveal the coherence of his London depends upon, and embodies fully as much as any of the midcentury Utilitarian pioneers of the welfare state, the power of observation.'[13] In his conclusion, Arac qualifies this criticism of Dickens's overview by arguing that there may be a good side to administration and organization. The fundamental historical issue is who is surveying whom and for what purposes.[14]

Williams's claim for the counter-tradition of the knowable community is that it is an experience of needed and useful knowledge. Which intuition do we accept, that of Williams or Arac? It is useful to point out that Williams's whole argument in the knowable community tradition is made close to the language of the novels. Arac's interpretation employs metaphors of perception and architecture: the gaze of the novelist, the physical look-out point. Williams describes a complex and by no means unified form of writing. Confronted with a relatively unknowable city, Dickens may wish for an omniscient stance from which to see into the hidden sum of so many lives but in his writing he employs and changes the techniques of the novel as well as the grammar of an urban popular culture.

Gender and desire

There is a rather different dynamic in the fiction of Charlotte and Emily Brontë. What is present here, in ways that are genuinely new, is the experience of passion and desire. Williams's point is that the response to poverty and oppression is felt in the texture of personal relationships as much as in work, housing, and other conditions. 'We need not look only, in a transforming history, for direct or public historical event and response. When there is real dislocation it does not have to appear in a strike or in a machine-breaking. It can appear as radically and as authentically in what is apparently, what is actually, personal or family experience.'[15] It is then part of the counter-tradition of the knowable community to make the connections between what is never simply 'personal' experience and the experience of actual historical transformations. Where Dickens's fiction draws on an urban popular culture of which he was part, the Brontës are involved in a history of gender. Through the mid-nineteenth century there is the development of a new masculine mode, a new rigidity, a soberness of dress, a learning not to show emotion in public. The ruling class is masculine, but more specifically educated in the new public schools to suppress all outer show of emotion. The experience of intensely living in and through another person is evidently relegated to childhood and to the realm of women. It is then the specific role of a novel such as *Wuthering Heights* to refuse such specialization and to be a counter-memory, against the dominant culture, of desire *in* another, of relations of intense sharing.

Knowable communities

Williams first used the term 'a knowable community' in an article on George Eliot.[16] The argument is that the novels of George Eliot expanded the community of the novel to include people who actually work in the country. There is then a kind of disruption in the texture of the novel. The new families that are included are shown mainly in direct speech. There are then severe problems of form.

> In the very texture of her writing, in the basic construction of her novels, she has to resolve a conflict of grammars: a conflict of 'I' and 'we' and 'they, and then of the impersonal constructions that in a way inevitably come to substitute for each. . . .There is then a new kind of break in the texture of the novel: between the narrative idiom of the novelist and the recorded language of her characters. . .[17]

The problem of form is the problem of these new voices. It is the problem of the relationship between an analytic and observing narrator and an emotional identity with the newly described lives in the novel. If Williams has specific criticisms to make of each of Eliot's novels, he is admiring enough to say that she has not so much continued the tradition of the novel as invented a new form.

The central concern of this new form is the relation between knowing and community. This is not only a matter of the relation between analysis and description; it is a relation between *educated* and *customary* ways of life and thought.[18] This is central in the novels of Thomas Hardy about a rural society that is in a continual process of historical change. In *Tess* the mother speaks the dialect, but her daughter who has been educated by a London teacher speaks the dialect at home and ordinary English outside.

In Williams's argument the novels of Thomas Hardy are the most important case in the counter-tradition of the knowable community. They show ordinary speech, work, and desire. They show not a timeless rural countryside but the underlying and varied patterns of change, economic forces, mechanization of farming, the anonymous connections by which food is delivered from farms to people in the city. Hardy is both a participant and an observer of this world. This is the reason for the range and variability of his writing and also his eventual bitterness and withdrawal: for he was writing of the country for educated people who saw it as empty nature or a place of their inferiors.

This problem of observation and participation, of customary and educated language, is also central in D. H. Lawrence. If Lawrence's later work moved away from a knowable community to intense personal relations, his early work is rather different. Williams makes his main point about observation and participation in Lawrence as a point about language. He quotes from the short story 'Odour of Chrysanthemums':

> . . . She heard the engine move slowly, and the brakes
> made no sound. The old woman did not notice.
> Elizabeth waited in suspense. The mother-in-law
> talked with lapses into silence.
>   'But he wasn't your son, Lizzie, an' it makes a
> difference. Whatever he was, I remember him when he
> was little, an' I learned to understand him and to
> make allowances. You've got to make allowances for
> them–'
>   It was half past ten, and the old woman was saying:
> 'But it's trouble from beginning to end; you're never
> too old for trouble, never too old for that–' when
> the gate banged back, and there were heavy feet on the steps.
>   'I'll go, Lizzie let me go,' cried the old woman
> rising. But Elizabeth was at the door. It was a man in
> pit clothes.
>   'They're bringing 'im, Missis,' he said.[19]

Williams comments on this passage in which a dead miner is brought home that the language of the narrator is at one with the direct speech of the two women. It is the same world, the same language. 'What is new here, really new, is that the language of the narrator is at one with the language of his characters, in a way that hadn't happened, though George Eliot and Hardy tried, since the earlier smaller community of the novel had been extended and changed.'[20]

This relation between observation and participation, between the narrator and direct speech in the novel, is not something established. It is fragile and vulnerable: not a completed project. It has been continued since the 1920s to some extent in other media: radio, television, film.

Writing voices

What Williams found and admires in Lawrence's 'Odour of Chrysanthemums' is a unity of language between narrator and direct speech. Is there a difference between this and the affirmation of multi-voiced discourse by M. M. Bakhtin? Consider Bakhtin's study of heteroglossia in *Little Dorrit*. The novel is a development of what Bakhtin calls the English comic tradition. The founders of this tradition are Fielding,

Smollett and Sterne. In these novels there are parodic stylizations of various levels of language and literary genres. This is continued in Dickens but the difference between levels and genres is reduced.[21]

Bakhtin's examples from *Little Dorrit* involve the juxtaposition of official, ceremonial, and high-epic style within the frame of Dickens's authorial speech. These 'quoted' speech styles are, however, not marked off from the authorial discourse.

This varied *play with the boundaries of speech types*, languages and belief systems is one of the most fundamental aspects of comic style. Comic style (of the English sort) is based, therefore, on the stratification of common language. . . . *It is precisely the diversity of speech, and not the unity of a normative shared language, that is the ground of style.* (original emphases)[22]

This diversity of language is marked in the early history of the English comic tradition. In Dickens, the many varied voices co-exist in ways that are not so obvious but which yield to Bakhtin's close reading and demonstrations. The novels of Dickens are multi-voiced and dialogical. There is no unified language of the narrator, much less of the narrator and direct speech.

In some ways there is no difference between this argument and that of Williams. The disruptive mode of the knowable community replaces the unity of a normative shared language in the restricted social world of Jane Austen. What is present in Dickens is something rather different. When we read Dickens we can see, writes Williams:

. . .that the popular tradition, which has been so much neglected, gives its life not only to continuations of itself – a crowded many-voiced, anonymous world of jokes, stories, rumours, songs, shouts, banners, greetings, idioms, address. It gives its life also through its highly original use by this remarkable writer, to a very novel form of sustained imaginative creation – to a unique and necessary way of seeing and responding to what was then an unprecedented world; to the crowded, noisy miscellaneous world of the nineteenth-century city, and of the industrial-capitalist civilization of which the city and above all the metropolis, was the principal embodiment.[23]

So there is a recognition in Williams of what Bakhtin calls the dialogism of a multi-voiced miscellaneous world. However, Williams insists that Dickens is more than a comic writer: he is part of the history of the counter-tradition of the knowable community. This intention of finding ways of knowing what was experienced as confused and emergent living – what in retrospect we call the development of the nineteenth-century city and industrial capitalism – exists alongside the dialogic comic tradition identified by Bakhtin. There is surely always a need for this moment of observation. Dialogism by itself need not be liberating. Here it is significant that Williams is as interested in work, sexuality, and death in the novel as he is in direct and indirect speech. The real point, however, is that dialogism is hardly progressive if the voices which interpenetrate are selected, with many other actual voices, even a majority, completely silenced and left out.

The moment that Williams admires in Lawrence's short story – it is only a moment and not sustained – has little to do with the comic deflation of official and high speech. It involves the recognition in equal terms of voices which the dominant tradition left out or treated *only* in comic ways. The knowable community for Williams is a genuinely oppositional form. It may indeed be usefully continued.

So much more of life, it can seem to many, is now incorporated, processed, perpetually informed and communicated. It can seem a reasonable strategy to continue the novel by a kind of negative definition: what the other media are not, or more generally what the public world doesn't bother, doesn't know enough, to report. Very few of us live as now most of us read. I mean as having parts, consciousness, in that official and daily history.[24]

The tradition of the knowable community was until about the 1920s an alternative to the dominant form of the English novel. It is still potentially an alternative, no longer mainly to the novel but to a general informed, processed, and communicated hegemony.

What emerges is a diverse tradition of discursive prose. The journal, memoir, and letter overlap with the novel. It is sometimes difficult to tell, says Williams, in a single paragraph by Orwell what is report and what is fiction.[25] Some of Williams's own historical writing about literature overlaps with his own fiction.[26] Some of his essays are close to the qualities of his fiction: remembering F. R. Leavis running, always running, with little time to talk but with a bundle of letters to post.[27] Some of Williams's television columns for *The Listener* have the same feeling as his novels. Apart from these mixed and varied forms, Williams continues to write full-scale novels in which he continues and expands the counter-tradition of Eliot, Hardy, Lawrence.

It is then significant and perhaps not surprising that Williams's argument about knowable communities has been best understood outside the departments of literature. The argument has always been that it is through cultural forms such as the novel that the historical patterns of economy and society show and show through varied and necessarily incomplete communities. There is a kind of necessary crossing-over, as in Williams's conclusion about Dickens: 'It does not matter which way we put it: the experience of the city is the fictional method; or the fictional method is the experience of the city. What matters is that the vision – no single vision either, but a continual dramatization – is the form of the writing.'[28] This emphasis on written form has been taken up most seriously by anthropologists who have come to see the problem of setting experience in patterns of the world political economy as a problem of writing culture. One such anthropologist, George Marcus, writes: 'Williams has precisely defined text construction as the crucible for integrating the macro into the micro, combining accounts of impersonal systems into representations of local life as cultural forms both autonomous and constituted by the larger order.'[29] Marcus agrees with Williams that the problems of this kind of text construction are great. There are few examples of written knowable communities in which the necessary connections with historical patterns of economy and culture are convincingly made. Yet to have understood the problem of the novel, ethnography, and many other kinds of writing in this way is both a theoretical and a practical advance in understanding.

Notes

1 Edward W. Said, 'Labyrinth of Incarnations: The Essays of Maurice Merleau-Ponty', *Kenyon Review*, 29 (1967), p. 54.
2 Williams, *May Day Manifesto* (Penguin, 1968), pp. 39–40. This theme is developed in *The Country and the City* in the following way: It is very striking that in response to the city and to a more deeply interrelated society and world we have developed habitual responses to information, in an altered sense. The morning newspaper, the early radio programme, the evening television, are in this sense forms of orientation in which our central social sense is both sought and in specific and limited ways confirmed (Paladin, 1975, p. 355).
3 Williams, *The English Novel*, (Paladin, 1974), p. 13. For a rather different counter-tradition see Ken Worpole, 'Expressionism and Working Class Fiction', in his *Dockers and Detectives* (London, Verso, 1983), pp. 77–93; reviewed by Williams in *New Society*, 5 January 1984, pp. 17–18.
4 Williams, *The English Novel*, p. 11.
5 Williams, *The Pelican Book of English Prose* (1969), p. 31. Also in Williams, *Writing in Society* (Verso, 1984), p. 80.
6 Examples of the subjunctive in the tradition Williams is describing would include ch. 80 of *Middlemarch*; ch. 16 of *The Rainbow*; and the conclusions of Hardy's novels such as *Tess of the D'Urbervilles*, *Jude the Obscure*, and *The Woodlanders*. An interest in the subjunctive moment is the foundation of Williams's interest in science fiction as examples of imagined communities that connect with our existing experience. See Williams, 'Utopia and Science Fiction', in his *Problems in Materialism and Culture* (Verso, 1980), pp. 196–212.
7 Williams, *The English Novel*, p. 21.

8 Ibid., p. 19.

9 Ibid., p. 30.

10 Michel Foucault, *Discipline and Punish: The Birth of the Prison*, tr. Alan Sheridan (New York, Vintage, 1979), p. 305.

11 Jonathan Arac, *Commissioned Spirits: The Shaping of Social Motion in Dickens, Carlyle, Melville, and Hawthorne* (New Brunswick, Rutgers University Press, 1979).

12 Ibid., p. 20.

13 Ibid., p. 69.

14 Ibid., pp. 189–90.

15 Williams, *The English Novel*, p. 54. John Hutcheson describes the 'subdued feminism' of the knowable community tradition in 'Subdued Feminism: Jane Austen, Charlotte Brontë and George Eliot', *International Journal of Women's Studies*, vol. 6, no. 3 (1983), pp. 230–57.

16 Williams, 'The Knowable Community in George Eliot's Novels', *Novel*, 2 (1969), pp. 255–68.

17 Williams, *The English Novel*, p. 65.

18 Ibid., p. 80.

19 This story is part of the collection of Lawrence's stories, *The Prussion Officer*, first published in 1914.

20 Williams, *The English Novel*, p. 140.

21 M. M. Bakhtin, 'Discourse in the Novel', in his *The Dialogic Imagination: Four Essays*, tr. Caryl Emerson and Michael Holquist (Austin and London, University of Texas Press, 1981), pp. 302–8.

22 Ibid., p. 308. Katrina Clark and Michael Holquist argue in their biography, *Mikhail Bakhtin* (Cambridge and London, Harvard University Press, 1984), pp. 268–72, that Bakhtin is arguing with the 'centralization' of 'official genres' of socialist realism in the Soviet Union through the 1930s.

23 Williams, 'Introduction', to *Dombey and Son*, by Charles Dickens (Penguin, 1970), p. 15.

24 Williams, *The English Novel*, p. 154.

25 Williams, *Pelican Book of English Prose*, p. 52.

26 See the discussion of writing his novel *Border Country* in Williams, *The Country and the City*, pp. 359–60. Also, an interview with Williams, 'Making It Active', *The English Magazine*, no. 1 (Spring 1979), pp. 4–7.

27 Williams, 'Seeing a man running', in *The Leavises*, ed. Denys Thompson (Cambridge University Press, 1984), pp. 113–22.

28 Williams, *The Country and the City*, p. 191.

29 George E. Marcus, 'Contemporary Problems of Ethnography in the Modern World System', in *Writing Culture: The Poetics and Politics of Ethnography*, ed. James Clifford and George E. Marcus (Berkeley, University of California, 1986), p. 170. See also George E. Marcus and Michael M. J. Fisher, *Anthropology as Cultural Critique: An Experimental Moment in the Human Sciences* (Chicago and London, University of Chicago Press, 1986), ch. 4, 'Taking Account of World Historical Political Economy: Knowable Communities in Larger Systems'.

6

Complex seeing in drama and television

Williams wrote on drama for all of his professional life. Starting from his interest in Ibsen he described a selective tradition of European drama in *Drama from Ibsen to Eliot*, revised his argument in the course of lectures at Cambridge in the 1960s (published in *Modern Tragedy*) and then presented this revised argument in *Drama from Ibsen to Brecht*.[1] The existentialist themes of his early work on Ibsen are revised and replaced by the idea of 'complex seeing' from Brecht. The central issue throughout is the discovery of forms of drama which allow expression for what is ordinarily silenced in everyday life.

Although Williams's early work on drama was influenced by Leavis and the *Scrutiny* formation, Leavis himself paid little attention to drama.[2] Williams's choice of drama as a topic of research in the 1940s and 1950s is therefore a challenge to what may be loosely called Leavis's 'structure of feeling'. There are two aspects to this. First, drama includes design in space: gesture, staging, moving pictures. Leavis was above all a dramatized *consciousness*. Second, whereas Leavis was interested in qualities of experience in literature, Williams's attention from the start was on drama as a *cultural form* and the ways in which forms of drama change in history.

Since all drama employs dialogue of some sort there is an important issue of the emergence of 'ordinary' speech, replacing aristocratic and middle-class speech. A related theme is the emergence of 'ordinary' actions, especially the dramatic showing of the rhythms of work.

The issue of a development of *majority* cultural forms is also important. Most significant drama for a century after 1870 came from a critical minority of middle-class dramatists. Any simple analysis of 'bourgeois' drama is therefore inadequate. What Williams describes in his books on drama is a minority alternative tradition to commercial theatre. Within this tradition there are important examples of drama written for working-class audiences. There are also important connections after the 1920s between drama and majority cultural forms such as radio, film, and newspapers. This is the case in expressionistic drama, which sometimes uses film on stage, the forms of newspaper headlines, or radio announcements. There is an important development of these techniques in the plays of Brecht.

Among Williams's most individual essays are the pages on tragedy and revolution in *Modern Tragedy*. In an ordinary life through the middle years of the twentieth century, Williams has known tragedy in several different ways. Thus, he writes:

I have known tragedy in the life of a man driven back to silence, in an unregarded working life. In his ordinary and private death, I saw a terrifying loss of connection between men, and even between father and son: a loss of connection which was, however, a particular social and historical fact: a measurable distance between his desire and his endurance, and between both and the purposes and meanings which the general life offered him.[3]

This is both a personal and a more general experience. Williams finds this loss of connections built into a factory and a city;[4] and an attempt to educate people that this loss of hope and desire is normal. There is a more general experience of tragedy in this century in the experience of war and social revolution. These are not separate from ordinary living but constantly break into it with new rhythms and demands. How is this to be understood? At the start of any attempt to understand war and an ordinary death as tragedy there is set a practical and institutional block. To start a discussion by mentioning the use of the word 'tragedy' in ordinary speech and the newspapers can provoke astonishment in the university. It took Williams many years to gather the courage to argue that there is no single tradition or meaning of the word.

An important part of the argument of *Modern Tragedy* is to bring together the history of two keywords: 'revolution' and 'tragedy'. Williams starts his history of tragedy by insisting that the only continuity that can be assumed at the outset is the use of the word 'tragedy' through a complex history of drama.

Modern tragedy

Williams's argument starts by refusing to accept the conventional argument that a mining disaster, a burned-out family, a broken career, or a smash on the roads, however painful, are not tragic. They are accidents. Williams argues against this that:

The events which are not seen as tragic are deep in the pattern of our own culture: war, famine, work, traffic, politics. To see no ethical content or human agency in such events, or to say that we cannot connect them with general meanings, and especially with permanent and universal meanings, is to admit a strange and particular bankruptcy, which no rhetoric of tragedy can finally hide.[5]

The purpose of Williams's argument is to retrieve the history of tragic drama and fiction for everyday understandings. His reflections on tragedy are part of a social phenomenology which refuses to allow event and response, order and accident to be separated. The conventional argument is that an observed death is not tragic but it becomes so through a shaped response. Williams argues against this that it is impossible to separate event and response in this absolute way. The separation of agency and response from human action may be described as an ideology. Order in tragic drama is the result of the action; it is not imposed from above. Order is created in a particular action and there is a direct relation between order and disorder.

What is common in the works we call tragedies is that they dramatize a particular and grievous disorder and its resolution. Tragic meaning is not fixed but is itself an actor in the play. Significant tragic drama is associated not with fixed faiths or stable 'organic communities' but with cultures moving toward violent internal conflict and major transformations. Its usual historical setting is the period preceding substantial breakdown and transformation of an important culture.[6]

Tragedy is the cultural form of revolutionary action. The next generation after the revolution may describe what happened as a narrative; but for those involved in it the action is not epic but tragedy. The subtext of *Modern Tragedy* is the history of the October Revolution of 1917. Since then it is impossible to exclude social revolution from our map of the world. This does not mean an easy position either for or against the Soviet Union. Williams welcomes the October Revolution as an act of human liberation and continues: 'I know also that the revolutionary societies have been tragic societies, at a depth and on a scale that go beyond any pity and fear.'[7] Yet this cannot be a pretext for reducing tragedy to any of its ideological formulations. Human nature is not absolutely evil, nor is it good in any absolute way: humanity is historically shaping and shaped.

Writing in the mid-1960s, in an era of optimism about the management of conflict, the economy, even 'managed' violence in a balance of world power, Williams insists that all of these are literally tragic illusion. Our situation is already tragic. The illusion of stability is again and again challenged: in Korea, Suez, the Congo, Cuba, and Vietnam. The world system of power and nuclear armaments means that each of these conflicts threaten the world and our neighbourhood. The managed consensus of the industrialized nations in the 1960s is only possible because of violence or the threat of violence to the most poverty-stricken areas of the world. The consensus rests on the export of poverty and violence, which consistently threaten to return home. To remain silent in such a world system is implicitly to agree with it. Any serious attempt to deal with the Third World will certainly affect the daily fabric of life in the industrialized parts of the world. Yet the real tragedy is not that this would involve a massive redistribution of resources, experience, and expectations, but that this kind of fundamental change would be widely and strongly resisted.

Our situation is tragic because the revolution has already started. The choice is between the pity of the poor of the world, and the fear of overwhelming social change.

Williams's detailed writings on drama are particularly complex and it will only be possible to select a number of themes which are relevant for an overall understanding of his work. These themes are:

1 The ambiguity of his notion of a dramatic 'structure of feeling'.
2 His insistence that terms such as 'realism' and 'naturalism' must be considered historically rather than as formal categories.
3 The identification of a dramatic tradition of Social Expressionism which corresponds to the 'knowable community' in Williams's treatment of the English novel. Of particular interest is the possibility of dramatizing a subjunctive or possible world.
4 An argument that certain dramatic forms, with a new technology, cross over from the theatre to film and especially to television in a rapidly changing ratio of experience and cultural form.

Structures of feeling

The idea of a 'structure of feeling' is often considered to be the major invention of Williams's sociology of culture. As a concept it refers to something more general than the ideas of a period, yet something more organized than its culture. Williams used the phrase in his general sociology of culture, for example in an attempt to describe the 'structure of feeling' of Britain in the 1960s in the third part of *The Long Revolution*. Attempts to clarify the meaning of the term have not been very successful.[8] Williams himself makes a connection with Lucien Goldmann's notion of a 'genetic structure'. This has led to the understanding that what he has in mind is something like an emergent pattern of general experience. Each 'structure of feeling' is loosely associated with a generation of writers or artists: the Romantics, the Victorian novel, Expressionism, and so forth. This notion has been criticized because it seems to lack any sense of conflict within a single generation. As well as this there are often practical problems in identifying such generations. In practice in his work on drama Williams can describe the 'structure of feeling' of a single dramatist (such as Sean O'Casey) and at the same time use the notion to cover patterns of drama that extend well beyond one, two or even three generations.

Williams no longer uses the term in the general sense of the structure of experience of a whole generation. In *Marxism and Literature* the term is given the specialized meaning of a pre-emergent cultural phenomena: a trend that is developing but is not yet clearly emergent. We may have a sense of something new developing but as yet not fully formed: it is very difficult to describe it at this stage. This is a particularly interesting phenomenon and it is useful to have a term which refers to it.[9]

Nonetheless, the problems which caused Williams to introduce the term in *Preface to Film* (1954) are themselves of considerable interest. The term was introduced to make a link between dramatic *conventions* and written *notations*. Drama, including film and television, involves relationships between written notations and dramatic conventions. In this way, Williams considers drama as a material practice which involves issues of writing as notation or script.

The conventions of drama are more obviously deeply social than those of poetry and of the novel. Whereas Leavis could consider a poem to be a matter of the 'full personal experience' of living, it is much more difficult to avoid the matter of conventions in performed drama. All drama proceeds through conventions which are acceptable to audience and playwright. This tacit agreement is absolutely necessary for the play. Williams describes some general conventions:

With the slightest of indications, we will accept that the events we are watching are occurring four thousand years before Christ, or in the Middle Ages, or in a flat in Paris on the same night as we are in a theatre in Manchester. The men whom we see as inspector and criminal we recognize as having seen last week as criminal and inspector, or as butler and peer, but we do not challenge them. We accept, we agree; these are the conventions.[10]

Yet even though these basic conventions are accepted there may be difficulties. We accept that a man puts on a grey cloak and is therefore invisible even though we continue to see him; but if another actor turns to the audience and addresses us directly, we feel uneasy: it seems 'unreal'. The explanation for this is that there is a relationship between the conventions of a period and what Williams calls its 'structure of feeling'. All the products of a community are essentially related, though in ways that may be difficult to describe. The structure of feeling is the total or common experience of a period.

We examine each element as a precipitate, but in the living experience of the time every element was in solution, an inseparable part of a complex whole. And it seems to be true, from the nature of art, that it is from such a totality that the artist draws; it is in art primarily, that the effect of the totality, the dominant structure of feeling, is expressed and embodied.[11]

Dramatic conventions, for example, are a part of this overall structure of feeling. In a period of change, such as the 1890s, a new structure of feeling demands the creation of new conventions.

In this 1954 book, the notion of a 'structure of feeling' is used in the sense of a general or shared culture. It may better be considered as a kind of hermeneutic. Williams describes the idea as developing out of attempts to deal with scripts and literary texts.[12] This hermeneutic starts with notations on a page. It is a productive reading, because as we have noted, dramatic scripts have a deep dependence on conventions shared with the audience. To read drama is to read parts, to read for a cultural history – including the material conditions of the performance of the drama. Williams's hermeneutic is to read a general history into particular scripts.

A debate about realism

Williams's historical studies of drama as notation, convention, and performance were subject to criticism in the 1970s. At its best this criticism may usefully extend Williams's cultural materialism. Much of it, however, mistook his work for a much simpler and less interesting theory of realism

In his 1974 article, 'Realism and the cinema: notes on some Brechtian theses', Colin MacCabe describes what he calls 'the classic realist text' in the nineteenth-century novel and in film: 'A classic realist text may be described as one in which there is a hierarchy amongst the discourses which compose the text and the hierarchy is defined in terms of an empirical notion of truth'.[13] In the novel there is a hierarchy in which the various voices are organized by the narrative. In film the viewer is invited to take this position: an ironic position which surveys and unifies the various discourses. This subject position is identified by MacCabe as an historical feature of bourgeois culture.

Furthermore, the classic realist text cannot deal with fundamental conflict since its function is more or less to create a unity of discourses. It is also argued that the classic realist text cannot deal with the fact of its own material production since this would disrupt its apparent unity. The implied criticism of Williams is that a non-contradictory notion of 'structure of feeling' acts in a similar way as a kind of guarantee of the ideological unity of the realist text. Against this, MacCabe holds the example of Brecht's drama which disrupts the relation between levels of discourse and does not allow the viewer to take an ironic position outside and above the voices of the play. Brecht's drama also draws attention to its own material production.

Williams rejects this formal description of 'the classic realist text' and insists on an historically based argument. In a lecture given at a SEFT/*Screen* weekend school on Realism in 1977 he makes the following arguments. He denies that realism as a method is a property of bourgeois culture: he gives examples starting with a medieval nativity play and implies that realism as a method would also exist well beyond bourgeois culture. Furthermore, he argues that realism is not something that can be understood in itself but only makes sense in relation to other methods in a play and to the *intention* of the work. In the realism of the bourgeois drama of the eighteenth century Williams identifies the following characteristics. First, the drama is extended so that the action includes social groups which had usually been excluded. Second, the action tends to be removed from the past and sited in the present. Third, the action is secular; it is no longer set in a religious or metaphysical frame. With these three general emphases bourgeois drama developed as a major form, with many variations in the method.

It is important to treat definitions as historically variable and to avoid abstracting the intention of the drama from its method. Williams's purpose here is to:

take the discussion of realism beyond what I think it has been in some danger of becoming – a description in terms of a negation of realism as single method, of realism as an evasion of the nature of drama, and the tendency towards a purely formalist analysis – to show how the methods and intentions are highly variable and have always to be taken to specific historical and social analysis, and then with that point established, to begin to approach what are at once the significant realist works and the quite unresolved problems of this kind of work.[14]

Realism is not one form but many different kinds of method and intention. From Williams's position realism is not a unifying ideology but an unfinished practice with often quite unresolved problems of its own. In specific ways that are described in the next section, Williams is interested in an extended kind of realism. This has not prevented him writing a book *Drama in Performance* – on the material production of drama. Furthermore, the relation between drama as notation and dramatic conventions is itself part of this material production. Williams's interest in film is in part because the processes of photography and sound recording are a radically different type of dramatic *notation* which both change the material conditions of production and greatly extend the possibilities of dramatic forms.

The emergence of social expressionism

The argument of Williams's *Drama from Ibsen to Brecht* is centrally a hermeneutic reading of two 'structures of feeling' within a minority and oppositional dramatic tradition. The main alternative tradition that Williams describes is a feeling of personal isolation and despair. This emerges in the late drama of Ibsen and Strindberg and repeats itself in the drama of the next three or four generations through to the drama of unknowable worlds in Pirandello and Beckett. An alternative dramatic tradition corresponds to the tradition of the knowable community in the English novel, but is much weaker, more difficult to sustain, and more vulnerable.

The problem of this alternative tradition is to search for ways of showing a subjunctive moment using dramatic conventions that an audience can accept as 'real'. The pattern that emerges is of a wholly unstable combination of social naturalism and social expressionism. Social naturalism goes beyond showing individual experience to finding ways of dramatizing patterns of collective or social action. Social expressionism is an attempt to find ways of dramatically showing a future or potential society. This is what Brecht calls 'complex seeing'. It is a way of showing through actual action the ways in which that action could be different.

Although the movement of German Expressionism ended in the early twenties, Sean O'Casey's *The Silver Tassie* (1928) is at least in part an experiment in expressionist drama. The expressionist moment is mainly in the second act of the play, which Williams describes as 'still one of the most remarkable written in English in this century'.[15] The action shows anonymous soldiers standing for humanity, protesting the horrors of war. Williams then fits this into a description of O'Casey's 'structure of feeling'. It is a mixture of a richness of a kind of crowded language, with at least a partial lack of real connection. Williams reacts to the colourful language in much the same negative way he reacts to Welsh rhetoric.[16] The lack of reasoned connections, the overall feeling of entrapment, he connects with O'Casey's partial exile: needing the vitality of the city but actually living, first on a border country looking for an educated response, then in actual exile.

In his discussion of Ernst Toller's *Hoppla! Such is Life* (1927) Williams distinguishes *individual* expressionism, which starts with the late plays of Strindberg, from *social* expressionism: 'the characterization, often critical and even revolutionary, of a social system'.[17] Williams is sympathetic to this kind of social typification as a method. 'In any complicated society, in which major social forces are bound to appear as in many respects impersonal, the schematic, typifying method of expressionism may in fact reveal more than immediate, "unexaggerated" description or reproduction'.[18] His criticism of Toller is actually that he did not go far enough in making a society knowable. Toller's frantic typification in *Hoppla!* seems to be full of doubt about presenting these patterns of experience, against a more usual pattern of *individual* tragedy. Nonetheless, the dramatic method is a gain in expressing emotion and presenting social structures. It is a way of getting beyond external observation of a known world. As such it would be taken up – in an innovative way – in the dramatic world of Bertolt Brecht.

Williams restricts his discussion in *Drama from Ibsen to Brecht* to two themes: Brecht's rejection of naturalist theatre, and the late plays, especially *Mother Courage and Her Children* and *The Life of Galileo*. The techniques of Brecht's 'open' theatre are important. They are part of a materialism in which people produce their own lives. An earlier and simpler materialism described people as determined by their environment. In this earlier naturalism, the presentation of the determining environment is then a means to human truth. The rejection of this early form of materialism is more than a technical matter. Williams refuses to separate the techniques of Brecht's 'open' theatre from its intention: its conventions and structure of feeling.

Brecht's originality, argues Williams, is not in developing new theatrical techniques, but in a kind of 'complex seeing' which is found in the best of his plays. This is found in the written play. It is not only a matter of the play's reception. What Brecht does at his best is to create a 'complex action' on stage. This is an extremely valuable extension of the method of expressionist theatre. Williams gives as one of the simplest and most brilliant examples of this the creation of *two* alternative but co-existing characters in *The Good Woman of Sezuan*:

The methods of expressionist drama, which had normally been used to show an intolerable tension within a single consciousness, are extended to show the tension of a common experience: a method of critical examination rather than sensational exposure. The play does not show the world through the actions and tensions of a single mind, but through an objective action in which Shen

Te and Shui Ta are at once created characters and yet, by this fact of creation, reveal the processes by which they have produced themselves.[19]

Williams most values the use of this complex seeing in Brecht's historical plays: the 'structure of feeling' of *Mother Courage* and *Galileo*. The complexity of action in *Mother Courage* is this woman who moves through a war with an enormous physical determination which at the same time also destroys her family. In *Galileo* the complexity is of consciousness. Galileo is able to continue his scientific work, but in isolation from those he might have taught. The one play creates a complex action; the other dramatizes a complex consciousness. Williams argues, however, that Brecht retains the structure of feeling of expressionist drama: an isolated individual in the face of a total world. What Brecht does is to change the values: the isolated individual is only a symptom and not the centre: the total world is now the source of values and explanation. The intermediate connections of any knowable community are simply absent. In this extension of an expressionist structure of feeling, there is a separation between a complexly seen action, and a complexly seen consciousness. This separation between action and consciousness is the actual history that Brecht lives out.[20]

A dramatized world

Williams's writing on television is a continuation of his writing on drama, radio, film, and even the English novel. Most dramatic performances now actually take place in film and television studios. This makes a qualitative change in the audience: 'We have never as a society acted so much or watched so many others acting.'[21] Representative democracy itself has been transformed into a kind of public drama. On television alone, the majority of viewers see up to three hours of drama each day. It is not a matter of drama on special occasions:

For the first time a majority of the population has regular and constant access to drama, beyond occasion or season. But what is really new – so new that I think it is really difficult to see its significance – is that it is not just a matter of audiences for particular plays. It is that drama, in quite new ways, is built into the rhythms of everyday life.[22]

It is of course necessary to ask what people are watching, though the answer will depend on who is asking and how the question is put. But the fundamental fact, Williams argues, is this new kind of audience.

Till the eyes tire, millions of us watch the shadows of shadows and find them substance; watch scenes, situations, actions, exchanges, crises. The slice of life, once a project of naturalist drama, is now a voluntary, habitual, internal rhythm; the flow of action and acting, of representation and performance, raised to a new convention, that of a basic need.[23]

Why is this? It is because our society is more mobile, more complex, and therefore more unknowable than ever before. Yet it is also more pressing, more penetrating and determining. We look for information in abstract statistical forms, but we also look for experimental, investigative dramatizations of social order.

Dramatizations of social order have, however, not been available for several generations. The naturalist play, from Ibsen onwards, left the palaces, the streets, the public forums, and created a drama of the enclosed room. There is then a cross-over from the work of the great naturalist dramatists to what is now a majority experience.

They created, above all, rooms; enclosed rooms on enclosed stages; rooms in which life was centred but inside which people waited for the knock on the door, the letter or the message, the shout from the street, to know what would happen to them; what could come to intersect and to decide their own still intense and immediate lives. There is a direct cultural continuity, it seems to me, from those enclosed rooms, enclosed and lighted framed rooms, to the rooms in which we watch the framed images of television: at home in our lives, but needing to watch what is happening, as we say 'out there': not out there in a particular street or a specific community but in a complex and otherwise unfocused and unfocusable national and international life. . .[24]

This is what Williams means by a dramatized society. What was emergent in Ibsen and Strindberg, as a naturalist slice of life, a flow of experience that needed interpretative signs to be made intelligible, is now a majority experience. For most people it is now actual: a daily habit and need. It is a necessary flow of experience that is also a technology.

Then the subtext of power enters fully into the argument. Drama and ritual have been part of the presentation of the political power of kings, or as a way of making gods present. There is a residual use of drama in this way in a society such as Britain. What is far more important is the continuation of a different kind of dramatization of consciousness. On the public stage, improbable but plausible figures continue to claim to represent us. Representation is a political issue as well as an issue in the theory of cultural forms. These figures on the public stage make the claim to speak for Britain. It is this form, this dramatization of consciouness that Williams challenges. Even if we reject particular figures such as Prime Minister Wilson or Heath, it is much more difficult to reject the whole form of dramatized consciousness of a country or nation.

To this extent, experience is not self-organizing but has been colonized by the *form* of television. This is far more serious than if we have allowed ourselves to be persuaded about certain issues. Studies of the effects of television have missed what is most important. There is a kind of autonomy against this colonization in what Williams calls thisness, hereness; but this is in practice the experience of privacy. We are offered roles for this, not least by what Williams calls the 'domestic romance' of television advertising. Beyond this there is the irreducible experience of a personal life, already a dramatic convention of dissent in Beckett (for example), but in effect powerless against the other public representation of the voice that claims to speak for the nation.

Distance

These are difficult ideas and it will be useful to work through two of Williams's detailed examples in which television made possible a particular kind of dramatized consciousness. The first example is his commentary on the tragic events at the 1972 Olympic Games in Munich. The second is a long article written ten years later on the television coverage of the Falklands/Malvinas crisis.

At Munich, television was itself part of what happened. The presence of television cameras and the estimated audience of one-third of the world's population made the Munich Olympics such an attractive target for the raid that took place. What happened, as Williams describes it, is that the arranged coverage of events was torn aside, that there was a break in the colonization of experience. The experience, centrally, is that of the athletes who are organized by both national officials and the television coverage of the Games into the conventional politics of nation states: the medals tables by country, the flags, the semi-military ceremonies. There are occasions when the athletes' experience breaks through this structure, though at Munich two athletes were suspended for (among other actions) talking during a national anthem. The raid cannot be understood as the invasion of sport by politics: this was not its shock. What was shocking, says Williams, was that the prepared versions of politics and sports were momentarily torn aside. It went from the highly visible arranged coverage of the Games to film of a different quality, the obscurity of darkness, flashes of a repeating rifle. 'What was shocking at Munich was that the arranged version of what the world is like was invaded by an element of what several parts of the world are actually like. It happened, with a certain inevitability, because the act of arranged presentation had created a point of political pressure.'[25] Many of the states represented at the Games came into being through a similar kind of violence. Other acts of war can be watched on television on almost any evening. Who has not wished that the world was like the Olympic Games: enjoyable exciting television coverage. Then, concludes Williams, the cover is ripped aside.

Television was even more a part of the war in the Falkland/Malvinas Islands. Williams's essay of June 1982 deals mainly with the form of television programming of the crisis: a general form that he calls the culture of distance. The features of this were the great distances involved in the naval campaign which at once posed problems for the producers of television programmes and guaranteed that, except for the sailors and soldiers involved, the war was being conducted at a very safe distance from those watching it on television in Britain. It was different from the television coverage of the Vietnam War because for many weeks there was no close fighting to be shown: only the slow movement of the fleet towards the islands.

This kind of distance is the essence of tele-vision (seeing from afar) but this should not be understood as some kind of technological inevitability. There are in practice many different ways of seeing. Williams describes a correspondence between the television professionals and the Army's own public relations and advertising campaigns. It seemed at times a matter of professionals understanding professionals: the need for good clear television. The distances involved and the absence of anything like military action directed this in a particular way: the use of maps, models, and film clips from military exercises. This resulted in one particular kind of distance: of a push-button war rather like a video game of 'invaders'.

It was a military operation seen through the conventions of television. This includes the time of television in which six or seven weeks of waiting seems a very long time. Actual negotiations in international relations take many months, even years without building up the impatience that resulted. 'The long, slow approach to the islands was a material reality. But then: to go all that way and do nothing? To hear those discussions night after night, as in an unusually extended pre-match analysis? To want at least something to happen, as in the ordinary rhythms of television?'[26] The conventions and the rhythms of time are those of television coverage of sports events. A television clip of an Argentine crowd looked like the rougher kind of football crowd. It may be difficult to put these conventions into motion and after all that to have no contest.

Although Williams describes very vividly the shaping effect of television (in no way simply recording events that are happening elsewhere), this is nothing like a world in which all contradictions have collapsed. Oppositional views were allowed on television, even though they were placed at once as dissident. *Panorama* showed alternative views although this programming independence had again to be defended (continuing a long history of controversy about showing alternative viewpoints in Northern Ireland). It was never a matter of a wholly dominant television coverage. Williams happened to be in Ireland at the start of the crisis and the political contradictions came through quite clearly in Irish television: both Labour and Conservative Governments had supplied advanced weaponry to the regime in the Argentine; the rhetoric was of a war with a military fascist government, but Britain was meanwhile in active co-operation with Chile. The hegemonic television coverage, what Williams describes here as a culture of distance, cannot contain all of experience. It must be unconvincing to those of Williams's generation, and others, who have experience of an actual war and are watching this televised version.

After several days of it, feeling the rhythms soaking in, I happened to pass a bonfire of rags and oil in the village, and suddenly, in an overwhelming moment, I was in a field in Normandy and the next tank, with my friends in it, was burning and about to explode. I think I then understood the professional culture of distance. Its antiseptic presentation of the images of war was skilled but childish.[27]

A hegemonic culture simply cannot account for the diversity of experience through which it will be received. For any description of war there will be at least some persons who have actually been in a war. For any description of 'Britain' at war there will be those who will insist that they are not British but Welsh or Scottish.

The point is extended by Williams to a strong criticism of parliamentary democracy: to all forms of political representation. The Falkland/Malvinas crisis showed the Cabinet acting with absolute sovereign powers and (at very least in the early stages) with no pretence of representing people. The use of these kinds of sovereign powers, in conjunction with particular uses of television and opinion polls, is what Williams calls constitutional authoritarianism. The point of this name is that different forms of democracy are possible. Yet a majority of people in Britain were organized in support of a war which had many features of a nuclear war. A majority of people in Britain were organized in support of a war, in a culture of distance, 'within which men and women are reduced to models, figures and the quick cry in the throat.'

Television

Whereas Williams's arguments about 'drama in a dramatized society' are generalizing and speculative, his *Television: Technology and Cultural Form* is written in quite a different mode. The book makes its arguments through a skilful accumulation of detail. This is so much the case that it is at times difficult to see that a quite specific and theoretical argument is being made, often against other unnamed arguments.

The opening argument against all forms of technological determinism is perhaps the most straightforward. Williams lists nine versions of an argument which he quite rightly says dominates professional and ordinary discussions of television. Then, by a detailed account of the scientific and technological history, he reinserts the *intention* that had been left out. The detailed historical argument is characteristic of the book as a whole. The matter of intention is more difficult. Williams does mean to restore individual intentions, but he mainly means the directions in which the form of the society pushed scientific research and the selection for technological development of some scientific research and in particular ways. Television is the applied technology of a late form of capitalist society that is increasingly complex and increasingly mobile. It is the chosen communications of a particular kind of household. It is the dominant form of communication in a society where information and communication are centralized in their origin.

Part of Williams's historical approach is the contrast between British and American television. This contrast is important in the argument and is there on almost every page. His visit to Stanford in 1973 (he had refused many invitations previously as a protest against the war in Vietnam) had the effect of defamiliarizing British television, about which he had been writing for a number of years.

This contrast between Britain and the United States is much more specific than generalizations about 'television' as a form of commodity or as a spectacle. Williams does not make his argument in these general terms. The contrast with US television is particularly apt since, as Williams points out, a major characteristic of television since the 1950s is its domination by US programming.

Williams's discussion of the *forms* of television has a definite theoretical underpinning. Most forms of television are extensions of existing forms of communications (gossip, news) to a much wider audience than ever before possible. As a generalization, Williams views this transformation from a minority public to a majority as a positive achievement. There have been so many arguments against television that his general position comes as a genuine surprise. He is able to show (to take one example) that television news is very similar to the news coverage of the serious minority papers and in his opinion the extension of this to a much wider audience is a positive thing. Having said that, he makes strong and specific arguments in criticism of this news: the way it sets limits to discussion, or simply assumes a consensus which it then strongly enforces, without prior public discussion.

Williams makes a similar argument about drama. In Britain especially in the 1960s, ten or twelve million people watched BBC's *Wednesday Play* presentations of a new generation of dramatists who wrote directly for television (Dennis Potter, David Mercer). This is a remarkable extension of a minority form to a much increased audience.[28]

Much of television is an extension of ordinary conversation. It depends wholly on the foundation of people's interest in talk, exchange of experience, interest in seeing other people's lives, and the ordinary enjoyment of music and dance. Television is often simply an extension of a body of talk and movement and of the human interest in it. Williams is then critical, especially of the centralized sources of *broadcasting*. However, the main argument is wholly different from those who say that television inaugurates a new and different kind of society, or who dismiss television in a general argument about a society of the spectacle. Television often *does* colonize experience: but the more generalizing arguments throw the baby out with the bath water. Argument that experience is deeply colonized come easily if that experience is given very little value to start with. Williams's argument makes more sense: he says that people would not be much interested in television except that it is founded in some real human interest in talk, seeing, information, and entertainment.

One of the best examples of what Williams has in mind is the weekly serial 'The Riordans' in Irish television. It is a dramatization of the majority experience of farming in the Irish countryside. It has a very wide audience. The programme is often talked about in ordinary conversation on the following day, in the same way as local gossip. Williams also gives the example of anti-authoritarian elements in variety theatre which gain a much wider and delighted audience through television. His point is that each of these forms has to be examined, historically, in its own right. The traditions, which were often very mixed in content and quality, come to have an equally complex existence for television viewers.

Williams is able to show, using quite conventional categories, that the programming on three British stations and two American stations has many important differences. In Britain, BBC 2 devoted 29 per cent of its broadcasting time for education in one week in 1973, whereas an

American commercial station gave only 2 per cent. Using similar conventional categories it is posible to show other differences of this kind. Williams then makes an interesting but very tentative attempt to sketch a 'cultural set' based on this kind of observation. It is possible to make some observations on the value put on personal relations between members of a family, which in a kind of quiz show are treated very lightly, as against the treatment of the aviation industry, which in a documentary is treated very seriously indeed.[29] However, Williams does not put a great deal of emphasis on this kind of analysis.

His main emphasis is on the effects of a *flow* of television programming. Unlike a book or a film, but with some affinity to magazines, television is not a matter of discrete units but a flow of programming. This became evident in a kind of culture shock when Williams first watched American television, with its much greater frequency of advertisements and trailers for several films to be shown later that evening. 'I still cannot be sure what I took from that whole flow. I believe I registered some incidents as happening in the wrong film, and some characters in the commercials as involved in the film episodes, in what came to seem – for all the occasional bizarre disparities – a single irresponsible flow of images and feelings.'[30] The flow of programming can be described in terms of an evening's schedule, still keeping the idea of programmes but with the emphasis on their connections and overall effect. The flow can be examined on paper more closely, as descriptions of units of two or three minutes or less: the items in a newscast and the advertisements. At the closest examination the flow of television can be studied in terms of words, camera distance and position, and images. Williams offers examples of these three kinds of analysis. His commentary on the effects of the flow is of particular interest: for example, an item of news can be affected by an advertisement which has preceded it.

Williams is drawing on his previous work in three ways. First, his medium-range and close description of the flow of television is a development of the problem of devising notations for dramatic performances. This is one of the main themes of *Drama in Performance*. There his main emphasis is on problems of production; here the same problems arise in describing the experience of reception. Second, his particular descriptions of the flow of images and sounds is in part derived from his descriptions of the modernist novel, especially Joyce's *Ulysses*. The argument is that what was emergent as a new experience in Joyce is now a widespread majority experience. Third, Williams's description of television as a form of communications is a development of his work in *The Long Revolution*. The connection between the two books is quite explicit.

Williams refuses the trivialized version of studies of the 'effects' of television. They inevitably operate within assumed models of the nature of the society. Studies of violence and television, for example, assume that the societies are themselves not violent. At the time of writing Britain was engaged in military action in Northern Ireland, and the United States was still in Vietnam. As in the argument of *The Long Revolution*, Williams insists on a critical sociology of society as a totality. Television has its effects within this totality and not as a matter of isolated causes and effects. This totality is a matter of interconnections and not a simple determined whole. Williams rejects notions such as 'mass society' or 'global village' as essential descriptions of whole societies.

Television ends with a discussion of the possibility of democratic communities of communication as against most existing models of 'broadcasting'. The problems that had already seemed difficult for literacy and printed forms are now much more difficult. There is nothing inevitable in this, especially with the development of inexpensive video recording equipment. The centralized 'penetration' of households belongs to a particular history of nationally organized broadcasting and commercial provision. Alternatives such as a town meeting through video have been tried on an experimental basis. Newly developed technology could make interactive communication possible on a scale never before imagined. Much of the development and design of this technology is, however, being done with quite other priorities in mind. Williams makes an argument against these authoritarian intentions and profit motives on the ground that what they are dealing in is not any commodity but something as central as human communication and its future.

Visible fictions

The one serious encounter with Williams's ideas about television is John Ellis's book on cinema, television, and video. His argument is based on a theoretical distinction between film and television. Ellis draws on an extensive theoretical literature about film: semiotics, a psychoanalysis of looking, the theoretical formation of *Screen* magazine. There is much less theoretical work on television and Ellis draws heavily on Williams's book on television. Ellis's argument is that the cinema viewer is a voyeur, but we only glance at television. Film is high on visual information, television is low. Cinema is fascination, television is gesture. Cinema is primarily visual whereas television sound is of prime importance.

However, Ellis finds a residual notion of discrete event underlying Williams's notion of the flow of television. Ellis insists that the unit of television is not something like a programme but units of about 30 seconds to three minutes. He argues that television has the form of a segmented commodity.[31] The basic unit is that of an advertisement spot. Ellis generalizes Williams's description of the 'domestic romance' of commercial television: a magic stream of voices and images that sells almost everything as a commodity.

The difference between Ellis and Williams seems at first to be not very great: a technical difference within a shared framework. Yet in the end the differences are enormous. On almost every point, Williams shows that the features which Ellis describes as integral to 'television' are a historical feature of the particular uses that have been made of television in our kind of society. Take, for example, the issue of television sound. For Ellis, sound is of prime importance: to get attention in a busy room for the small flickering screen. The image is an illustration for sound. The characteristic forms of television all rely heavily on voice: the news broadcast, the documentary with its broadcast voice-over, the bulk of TV comedy shows.[32] For Ellis, this is a defining feature of 'television', although he makes exceptions: for example, films that are shown on TV and television drama.

Williams's analysis is quite different. Very early in his columns on television for *The Listener* he complained about the intrusion of voices into material where they were not necessary. In the very first column, irritated by the sports commentators, he suggests turning off the sound and just watching the athletics competitions. A few weeks later, discussing the right to speak on television, he extends the point:

Many relationships are possible, in the presentation of talk, but what is most stultifying is the all-purpose presenter, through whom all men and issues flow, and who in the end is a substitute for men and issues. There are too many of these presenters to list, in current affairs and sports programmes, but it would also be unkind to list them as individuals; it is the *function* that needs to be criticised. (original emphasis)[33]

This is a point to which Williams returns many times. He suggests that the unnecessary intrusion of voices is due to a deep insecurity that listeners must be *directed how to look*. This carries over a general insecurity to cases where it is a distracton from what could otherwise be good television. Describing programmes that are mainly conceived for visual reasons (for example, helicopter views of the country), Williams comments that 'so much that is exciting and delightful is now filmed that the persisitence of commentary must be ideological.'[34]

The difficulties are even greater in the case of presenters of documentaries and chairpersons of discussions. One of the greatest problems of politics on television, argues Williams, is that too few people say far too much. He means elected politicians and offical spokespersons of all kinds; but he also means the familiar voices and figures of television reporters and commentators. At this point his overall argument emerges clearly. These nationally recognized voices are *hegemonic* in relation to the voices of most other people. 'All I have to say', he continues, 'is that nobody would believe that there are 56 million people in Britain: we see and hear so few of them.'[35]

If we were to generalize (though it does not really hold in every case) we might say that television is not predominantly a sound medium but that hegemonizing voices attempt to have us look at the television images in certain patterned ways. Williams's theoretical argument is that television is itself contradictory because the visual material is always much richer, capable of many more interpretations, than the spoken commentary. Williams describes a *24 Hours* programme about the second anniversary of the Russian invasion of Czechoslovakia: 'I find the political argument about the Prague Spring very difficult to resolve, but it happened that one of the slogans – "socialism with a human face" coincided with the face of Dubcek in an unguarded moment: the mobile intelligent face so saddened that "human", as a description, took on a quite different sense from the political definition. . .'[36] Or another programme, the *World in Action* special on the 1972 Democratic Party Convention. The contradiction here was described in the programme's title '*How to steal a party*'. The commentators described the McGovern people trying to move in and establish a new kind of politics. The contradiction was expressed in the programme itself: this tough beating the bosses at their own game (stealing a political party) along with the desire for a new open style of politics. What Williams remembers is another face. 'But there was one woman delegate who clearly believed in open politics, as something more than a slogan, and her face, intermittently seen, silent and puzzled among the contending groups, had its own testimony.'[37] These kinds of programmes cannot but show us images like these. A human face can express much more subtle meaning than any phrase of commentary, or political slogan. Television has to show us images and these images keep threatening to disrupt any simple meaning: hence the perceived need for the insistent voices.

Notes

1 Williams and M. Y. Orrom, *Preface to Film* (Film Drama, 1954); Williams, *Drama from Ibsen to Eliot* (Peregrine, 1964); Williams, *Drama in Performance* (Basic Books, 1968); Williams, *Drama from Ibsen to Brecht* (Pelican, 1973); Williams, *Television* (Fontana, 1974). All references are to these editions.

2 For Leavis's neglect of drama see Jonas Barish, *The Anti-Theatrical Prejudice*, (Berkeley, University of California Press, 1981), pp. 419–20; Ian Wright, 'F. R. Leavis, the Scrutiny Movement and the Crisis', in *Culture and Crisis in Britain in the Thirties*, ed. Jon Clarke (London, Lawrence and Wishart, 1979), p. 47.

3 Williams, *Modern Tragedy* (London, Verso, 1979), p. 13. All references are to this edition.

4 See Williams's novel, *Second Generation* (Chatto and Windus, 1964).

5 Williams, *Modern Tragedy*, p. 49.

6 Ibid., p. 54.

7 Ibid. p. 74.

8 See the discussion in Williams, *Politics and Letters* (New Left Books, 1979), pp. 156–65.

9 Williams, *Marxism and Literature* (Oxford University Press, 1977), pp. 128–35. 'I now feel very strongly the need to define the limits of the term', says Williams in *Politics and Letters*, p. 164.

10 Williams, *Preface to Film*, p. 18.

11 Ibid., p. 21.

12 Thus Williams says in *Politics and Letters*, p. 158, that the notion of a structure of feeling 'was initially developed from the accessible evidence of actual articulations in texts and works that I could read'.

13 Colin MacCabe, 'Realism and the cinema: notes on some Brechtian theses', in his *Theoretical Essays: Film, Linguistics, Literature* (Manchester, Manchester University Press, 1985), p. 34. The argument of this essay was amended by MacCabe in 1976, 'Theory and film: principles of realism and pleasure', also in *Theoretical Essays*, pp. 58–81. I have taken the earlier essay to stand for the theoretical arguments of a specific intellectual formation of the early 1970s rather than a statement of MacCabe's present position.

14 Williams, 'A Lecture on Realism', *Screen*, 18 (Spring 1977), p. 73.

15 Williams, *Drama from Ibsen to Brecht*, p. 167. Breon Mitchell, 'Expressionism in English Drama and Prose Literature', in *Expressionism as an International Literary Phenomenon*, ed. Ulrich Weisstein (Paris, Librarie Marcel Didlier; Budapest, Akademiai Kiado, 1973) says that the extent and origin of the expressionist influence in O'Casey's drama is not yet resolved, though much has been written on the subject. His own conclusion is that there is little evidence of the influence of Toller and German expressionism (p. 188).

16 See the earlier discussion of O'Casey which is almost entirely in terms of his colourful language, in Williams, *Drama from Ibsen to Eliot*, pp. 187–92.

17 Williams, *Drama from Ibsen to Brecht*, p. 297.

18 Ibid., p. 301.

19 Ibid., p. 323.

20 See also Williams, 'English Brecht', *London Review of Books*, 16 July – 5 August 1981, pp. 19–20; Williams, 'Discussion on St. Joan of the Stockyards, 1973', in *A Production Notebook to St. Joan of the Stockyards*, ed. M. D. Bristol and D. Suvin (Montreal, McGill University, 1973), pp. 184–98. Williams has not attempted anything like a full account of Brecht. For developments in this direction see Darko Suvin, *To Brecht and Beyond: Soundings in Modern Dramaturgy* (Sussex, the Harvester Press; New Jersey, Barnes and Noble, 1984)

21 Williams, *Drama in a Dramatised Society*, (Cambridge University Press, 1975), p. 4. All references are to this edition. This inaugural lecture is reprinted in Williams, *Writing in Society* (Verso, 1984), pp. 11–21; and in *Raymond Williams on Television: Selected Writings*, ed. Alan O'Connor (Toronto, Between the Lines, 1988; London and New York, Routledge, 1989).

22 Ibid., p. 5.

23 Ibid., p. 7.

24 Ibid., pp. 8–9.

25 Williams, 'What happened at Munich', *The Listener*, 14 September 1972, p. 322. Reprinted in *Raymond Williams on Television*.

26 Williams, 'Distance', *London Review of Books*, 17–30 June 1982, p. 19. Reprinted in *Raymond Williams on Television*.

27 Ibid., p. 19.

28 Williams makes this argument against John McGrath, *A Good Night Out: Popular Theatre; Audience, Class and Form* (London, Eyre Methuen, 1981). McGrath's argument is for a theatre based on working-class forms of entertainment. Apart from the difficulty of getting oppositional work past the controllers, television would seem to be attractive for this project. However, McGrath argues that the main difficulty is the ordinariness of television viewing (with carpet slippers, cocoa, and biscuits to nibble), which he says blunts the effects of any challenge. In his Foreword to McGrath's book, Williams says that this is still an open question. For Williams's influence, see McGrath, 'The Theory and Practice of Political Theatre', *TQ: Theatre Quarterly*, vol. 9, no. 35 (1979), pp. 43–54. McGrath recognizes the sexism of working-men's clubs. This is also described by Barbara Rogers, 'Men only, please', *New Statesman*, 3 February 1984, pp. 9–10.

29 Williams, *Television*, p. 86.

30 Ibid., p. 92.

31 John Ellis, *Visible Fictions: Cinema, Television, Video* (London, Routledge and Kegan Paul, 1982), p. 119. Chris Motterhead's review of *Television* in *Screen Education*, no. 14 (Spring 1975), pp. 35–8, provides a good summary of the book and criticizes Williams for lacking a *method* for

studying television as a flow of programming. The relative absence of serious discussion of his writing on television is remedied by Stephen Heath and Gillian Skirrow, 'An Interview with Raymond Williams', in *Studies in Entertainment*, ed. T. Modleski (Indiana University Press, 1986), pp. 3–17.

32   Ibid., p. 129.
33   Williams, 'The Miner and the City', *The Listener*, 7 November 1968, p. 623. This and the next four items are reprinted in *Raymond Williams on Television*.
34   Williams, 'A Noble Past', *The Listener*, 17 April 1969, p. 543.
35   Williams, 'Shoot the Prime Minister', *The Listener*, 10 October 1968, p. 483.
36   Williams, 'Breaking Out', *The Listener*, 27 August 1970, pp. 286–7.
37   Williams, 'Hassle', *The Listener*, 27 July 1972, p. 124.

7

Marxism and theory

It has become usual to describe a break in Williams's work about the mid-1970s and the publication of *Marxism and Literature*. The usual point is his willingness to start his arguments in Marxist texts, which is taken as a new political declaration by him. An assessment of Williams's politics must start from the history of his political activities described in Chapter 2. However, an 'epistemological break' in his theoretical texts does not make good sense. The argument made here is for a *fundamental* theoretical continuity although there were shifts and changes. The significant change is a consolidation of Williams's fundamentally decentred approach to the world. Whatever ambiguity there was in the early work about a fundamental plentitude is firmly struck out in the later theoretical essays and in *Marxism and Literature*.

The Long Revolution

The first part of *The Long Revolution* consists of a fairly extended theoretical discussion of culture and politics. The fundamental argument is an emphasis on *process* and *relationship*. This is a radicalization of conservative arguments about organic connections which must not be allowed to be broken by rapid social change or by 'ideology'. Williams accepts the general emphasis on a totality of everyday practices. It is indeed the case that ideological concepts ignore human activity and material processes. Williams takes the fundamental insight of conservative philosophy about the organic connections of everyday life and uses this insight in an oppositional argument.

Williams's theoretical argument in *The Long Revolution* is a deconstruction of concepts that have been given an ideological centrality. These concepts are the headings of his chapters: the creative mind, culture, individual and society. His challenge to these terms is mainly historical: to say that they are changing ideas and they have their own history. Instead of these false absolutes we need to investigate actual relations.

The first chapter is a deconstruction of the notion of 'the creative mind'. Williams traces the long history of the word 'creative'. The general movement is away from Aristotle's universal concepts. An important part of this in the nineteenth century is a move away from a belief in God. Since creativity can no longer be moulded by universals or a transcendental which has simply to be uncovered, it is increasingly held to exist within the individual artist: the creative mind. Creativity is a special kind of seeing. Williams argues against this that many other lines of thought have been cut off. The idea of the creative mind serves a complex ideological function. Williams uses scientific studies of human perception to deconstruct this notion of individual seeing. Studies of perception show that we learn to see a thing by learning to describe it.[1] There is therefore no ordinary or natural seeing with which creative seeing can be contrasted. In a frequently quoted passage, Williams insists that: 'The emphasis that matters is that there are, essentially, no "ordinary" activities, if by "ordinary" we mean the absence of creative interpretation and effort.'[2] Creativity cannot be specialized to the individual artist and all other activity described as ordinary. The activities which have been described in these ways are deeply social in their foundation and human in their activity.

We learn to see by learning to describe. The historical studies of Part II of *The Long Revolution* are about this historical process of learning to describe. Education, literacy, the popular Press, standard English, the history of writers, and of forms of drama and fiction: these are changing aspects of how we learn to see things and relationships. To see things anew is the work of art, but also of science and everyday communication. Williams describes this seeing as an embodied process, especially a matter of rhythm: body, voice, sound, colour, form, pattern. There is skill in this certainly, but that is the real point and not a dichotomy between art and non-art. 'We must see art, rather, as an extension of our capacity for organization.'

Williams deconstructs a notion of culture as the product of 'the creative mind'. Again there are two arguments here. First, what we know as culture is a *selective* tradition. It has been shaped and selected in an active process, within certain institutions and under certain pressures. The second argument is to look for structures of relationships, structures of feeling within 'culture'. This is made somewhat easier because historians and critics have often found such notions as the Romantics, or the Victorian novel, not only useful but necessary in their work. Williams wishes to argue that these are not only ideal types (idealized but useful constructs) but have a complex historical foundation. This is a matter of the writer's experience and of the written form.

The individual, including the individual writer, is not a creative mind but an ensemble of social relationships. Williams's argument therefore deconstructs the categories of individual and society. There are various possible *relationships*, such as member, subject, rebel, exile, vagrant. These relations are a matter for actual historical investigation. Thus, for example, we may pay attention to the changing relationship between writer and patron or publisher, or between writer and readers. There are also many images of 'society'. These include kingdom, nation, military structures, and various images of democracy. To defend 'culture' as a symbol of individual freedom is a false argument since what is really at stake is how culture changes with changing structures of human relationships.

Williams's argument aroused an enormous amount of hostility. He challenged orthodox thinking in three ways. First, he denied the whole foundation of debates about art versus reality by showing that both depend on a deep social structure and on creative interpretation and effort. Second, his discussion challenges the naturalized assumption that it is simply the *best* art and writing that survives. The third challenge is more directly political. It provides some evidence of the ideological function of notions of individual creativity in the 1950s and early 1960s. The argument that an individual is an ensemble of social relations within the foundation of a 'structure of feeling' means that there is a false grammar in sentences such as: 'Western society is good because it allows freedom of the individual'; and 'Literature is a sign of a cultivated individual'. Williams will not allow individual and society to be used in these absolute ways. He insists on historical study of language, literacy, education, communication, and so forth.

While *The Long Revolution* was being attacked from the right it was also criticized from the left. Edward Thompson wrote a two-part response in *New Left Review* in which he recognized that Williams was arguing strongly against the conservatism of T. S. Eliot. In this he finds Williams's tone to be overly academic. The terms 'pattern of culture' and 'way of life' are from the conservative tradition. Power and conflict seem not to exist. Williams describes seemingly impersonal forces rather than actual people and struggles.[3]

There is a substantive argument here but many of Thompson's argument and asides are *ad hominem* assumptions about working-class writers crossing the socialist 'river of fire' in the wrong direction – into the academy. (By the time *The Long Revolution* was published Williams was teaching at Cambridge.) The temperment of the two men is also entirely different. Whereas Williams is interested in patient descriptions of social structures and cultural forms, Thompson's histories are of people and action.

Williams describes three 'social characters' within the structure of feeling of the 1840s. These are of the dominant middle class (itself in a process of change), the residual aristocracy, and the subordinated working class. Since the structure of feeling of the decade of the 1840s corresponds mainly to the middle class 'social character' the concept is clearly a critical rather than simply a descriptive one. Williams also has no hesitation in naming capitalism, imperialism and Empire. His explanation of the substantive argument with Thompson, many years later, was that whereas Thompson was attracted to historical periods of working-class militancy, Williams himself, writing in the late 1950s, sought to explain ways in which during other periods class conflict is mediated and blocked.[4]

Materialism and culture:
New Left Review essays

The Long Revolution created an oppositional argument using elements of science, social psychology, and historical research. It belonged to no discipline, though it helped to create the new discourse of cultural studies in the 1960s. When it appeared in 1961 it was in many respects a lone book.[5] This is the noticeable change in a series of theoretical essays by Williams, which often originated as talks for particular occasions, but were published from 1973 onwards mainly in *New Left Review*. These essays, starting with 'Base and superstructure in Marxist cultural theory', can be seen to belong with the elaborated Marxist theoretical discourse of the 1970s.[6]

Having said this, it is then necessary to point to the underlying continuity in argument. The fundamental strategy of 'Base and superstructure' is to deconstruct a category which had been treated as an absolute: the Marxist category of 'the base'. In a strategy that is familiar from Williams's earlier writing, he insists that the 'base' must be understood as productive activities (as processes), and as structural relations. How is this structure to be understood? Williams criticizes Lukács's concept of 'totality' here on the grounds that simply to show connectedness is not enough: it is also necessary to have some account of determination. This argument may also be taken as a criticism of a similar emphasis in *The Long Revolution*. The notion of 'structure of feeling', which has that sense of totality, is to be replaced by the rather different notion of 'hegemony'.

Williams is critical of those who use the notion of hegemony to mean ideology, in a superficial sense. Hegemony operates at the same fundamental depth as what Williams had indicated by the 'structure of feeling' of a generation. It is a body of practices and activities that are deeply part of the everyday. If the effective dominant culture were only a matter of an ideology, if we were held by it that lightly, it would be much easier to challenge and change. The hegemonic culture is a process within educational institutions, training in the family and at work, and a selective tradition of culture from the past. The dominant culture can even tolerate some alternative cultural practices. The theoretical problem for Williams's deeply sociological imagination is to explain the possibility of emergent oppositional cultural practice. Whence does it come?

Williams rejects all metaphysical explanations and all accounts in terms of individual creativity. Emergent and alternative cultural practices are possible because the effective dominant culture must select from a very large observable range of action and practices those over which it will exercise a hegemonic control. It necessarily excludes large amounts of social and cultural practice. As in *The Long Revolution*, Williams rejects the notion that emergent culture derives from 'the creative mind'. In the earlier argument, 'individual' and 'society' were rejected as false absolutes. The real interest is in actual and possible relationships: member, rebel, and so forth. In 'Base and superstructure' the emphasis that matters in cultural creation is the *relation* between an individual project and a collective mode.

A 1978 essay by Williams takes this argument further. In 'Means of communication as means of production' there is further argument against a restricted use of the category of 'the base'. In advanced capitalist society it is absolutely necessary to include here the processes of cultural production. Existing communications theory invariably operates with an abstract notion of 'the individual' who transmits or receives a message. Williams's own theoretical account absolutely denies this separation.

For Williams, communications starts with the body of gesture, rhythm, and talk. Most theories of communications mention and then set aside this 'ordinary' communication. For Williams it is the basis of communication through time and over space. As well as this, he insists that: 'In all modern and foreseeable societies, physical speech and physical non-verbal speech ("body language") remain as the central and decisive communicative means.'[7] This is an important emphasis: it connects the production of culture to lived practices, and in an increasingly divided world it connects the cultural technology of the North to the spoken word of the South. Williams sets out a project for the study of means of production of communication. He describes the development of means of transmitting embodied communication over space (live radio broadcasting) and over time (various systems for storing communication). A very important development, which has a very long history, is means of communication which may be described as alternatives to the body of gesture and rhythm. This is a difficult theoretical distinction. We may include architecture, though some forms of housing have the mark of a human hand and life. Interestingly, Williams includes film and edited television because the process of editing creates something that is alternative to the recorded speech and gesture.[8]

A third *New Left Review* essay (1978) is devoted to Sebastiano Timpanaro, author of a study of Italian poet and philosopher Giacomo Leopardi (1798–1837), a philological examination of Freud's interpretations of verbal errors under the title *The Freudian Slip*, and a collection of essays titled *On Materialism*. The central matter here is Williams's rather complex response to Timpanaro's materialism. Williams prefaces his discussion by pointing out that knowledge of the material world is subject to a continuing process of radical revision. Such knowledge can be falsified or the initial and all subsequent categories rejected for new categories. Two significant problems arise from this. There is a contradiction in any claim for material*ism* because properly understood, it cannot be a doctrine but must be subject to change. A second problem arises when materialism is assumed to be fixed and becomes affiliated with a particular political position. Marxism was founded in opposition to exactly such frozen forms and their political consequences.

Williams dissents from the start with Timpanaro's linking of the struggle for communism with 'the struggle against nature'. Nature is intrinsic to human beings and Williams cannot allow the suggestion of externality and control in Timpanaro's phrase. What Williams does accept is the acknowledgement of the priority:

Of the physical level over the biological level, and of the biological level over the socio-economic and cultural level; both in the sense of chronological priority (the very long time which supervened before life appeared on earth, and between the origin of life and the origin of man), and in the sense of the conditioning which nature *still* exercises on man and will continue to exercise for the foreseeable future (original emphasis).[9]

The physical world existed before life, and other forms of life before humankind. However if we wish to think about the *continued* effects of this we must reject the false universals of 'nature' and 'man'. Nature is intrinsic to humans, for example in evolved physical organs. There is an 'external situation' of nature which is beyond human control: the middle and far reaches of our physical environment. These reaches are *conditions* for our existence, but Williams insists they are not material for conquest. Williams distances himself from Timpanaro's formulations about the 'passive' world upon which we act. Timpanaro was reacting to a tendency which reduced all science to epistemology and by implication the physical world to human activity. However Williams insists that it is not a matter of passive versus active regions. 'There are dimensions quite beyond us, or there are basic forces – the obvious examples are gravity and light – which have entered so deeply into our constituted existence that they are conditions of everything we do, over the whole range from the active to the passive modes.'[10] What is 'passive' (in the sense of given or relatively unwilled) is the character of many basic physical processes which are conditions of life. There is also the much more difficult matter of our participation in our genetic inheritance. However, 'passive' strikes the wrong relational and emotional note. Physical conditions and processes can better be understood as constitutive rather than passive.

From this point – a point about Timpanaro's prose and his philosophical inheritance from Leopardi's 'pessimism' – Williams's arguments are somewhat different from those of Timpanaro. He agrees that Marxism would benefit from more attention to science, though he also stresses that the physical and social sciences are themselves social practices. Williams accepts the renewed emphasis on physical conditions and processes. However, whereas Timpanaro stresses such physical realities as illness, the process of ageing and death, Williams enters a reminder about sexual love, the love of children, and the pleasures of the physical world. Any Marxism that ignores the reality of illness and ageing can seem to be a petty bullying or bureaucracy. Equally, however, to ignore the realities of physical fulfillment, especially in the advanced capitalist countries, is a kind of political dogmatism. There is a sadness in Timpanaro that is expressed in terms of physical limits. 'Yet the true sources of this depth of sadness', argues Williams, 'are surely predominently historical.'[11] His emphasis is on elements of a material practice within a continuing social process. Materialism must itself be understood as such a practice. A renewed emphasis on physical conditions and limits, as in the politics of ecology, is welcome. However, our understanding of 'physical' and 'material' are open to a process of change.

Marxism and literature

In 1977 Williams published a systematic discussion of theoretical positions which had been emergent in his writing for some time.

Marxism and Literature is the basis of the position which he calls 'cultural materialism'. The book is recognizably Williams's: not only are the chapters organized by keywords; the discussion itself starts with the changing history of 'economy', 'society', 'culture', and 'civilization'. There is one possible misunderstanding which needs to be dealt with at once. Williams is *not* recommending the use of all of the keywords in the chapter headings. He is very critical of some of them: even his own notion of 'structure of feeling' is substantially revised.

The initial arguments of *Marxism and Literature* are quite recognizable. There is, first, the principle that we create our civil society, our culture. There is no *inherent* historical direction in this. There is no absolute division between nature and society, and a *constitutive* relationship between society and economy. Finally – and this is more particularly Williams's own argument – there is a demonstration that Marxism tended to make cultural history secondary (to economic or political processes) when what is needed is to make cultural history *material*. The crucial place to start is with language which is not in any way secondary, but is itself material.

For Williams the materiality of language implies two principles: first, that language is historical; and second, that language is practical constitutive activity, or practical consciousness. The argument is made in his own terms, but also in a dialogue, mainly with Volosinov's *Marxism and the Philosophy of Language*. There is also mention of the Italian linguist Rossi-Landi.

Volosinov and Rossi-Landi are both Marxist thinkers but they are very different style. What they share is a sense of *connectedness* in language, practical consciousness, and action. The general emphasis in Rossi-Landi is that speech is a practical activity and not separate from work. His aim is to demonstrate the practical homology between linguistic production and material production. There are many levels of this homology: for example, he argues that a sentence corresponds to a tool in economic production. It is not possible to separate work and speech because spoken communication is an integral part of work activity and training for work. This is a foundation which Williams and Rossi-Landi share.

Nonetheless, Williams's style of argument is different in at least two ways. Rossi-Landi explicitly sets out to develop a semiotic homology for the discourses of linguistics and Marxist economics. Williams deliberately decides not to write *Marxism and Literature* as a homology of two discourses: a settled body of theory or doctrine in relation to known general properties of another settled body of work, or kinds of works.[12] A second difference is that Williams does not in any way limit practical activity to *work*. Rossi-Landi is certainly aware of a wide range of symbolic actions[13] but his central emphasis is on language as work and not merely as use.[14]

The criticism of language as use is part of Rossi-Landi's critical work on Wittgenstein. Rossi-Landi criticizes Wittgenstein for assuming the existence of an individual *prior* to language instruction; for not considering how a word is originally produced, considering communicative instruments as a sort of wealth that is freely available; for not considering *why* language 'goes on holiday' or produces 'mental cramps' – for having no theory of linguistic *alienation*; and finally for an uncritical substitution of Wittgenstein's social formation ('we') at Oxford and Cambridge for all of the social world.[15] This kind of argument is very close to Williams.

The main source for Williams's argument on language in *Marxism and Literature* is Volosinov's *Marxism and the Philosophy of Language*.[16] Linguistic theory has been based on either the documents of dead languages, or on an objectivist relationship to various colonized languages. It is necessary to restore the many dimensions of a language that is actually in use. Volosinov rejects theories of subjective expressionism and also systematic abstractions of language. His aim is in part to demonstrate that the connection between base and superstructure is to be found not in social psychology but in language. Language in use, as opposed to language that is a residue, has its value because of its position in a system of linguistic signs, but also in the local situation of its use. Language in use carries the intention of the speaker, but with (or against) the instituted intentions of other speakers, both past and present. Language is a social institution but of a very special kind: it pervades all other social institutions and the social self. There is a complex relationship between *inner speech* (and silent reading) and the spoken word. Volosinov does not comment on this to any great extent except to say that their *grammars or structures are very different*. Williams notes this and comments that this is a problem which urgently needs further research.[17]

Indeed, the purpose of Williams's lengthy chapter is to establish a theoretical foundation for the chapter to follow in which he rejects the category of 'literature' and replaces it with a notion of written linguistic practice. What Williams looks for in Volosinov is a notion of language as social practice and as historical institution. This seemingly ecumenical account of language will have substantial polemical bite against the dominant Western notions of literature. Since Volosinov rejects the notion of an individual person outside of language, the figure of the writer must now be understood as a *relationship* rather than as a person. Williams welcomes the emphasis in Volosinov on creative practice, but this must be understood in the 'short waves' of history rather than in the 'long waves' of evolution or the discursive structure of an epoch.

The discussion of language is then taken forward into Williams's deconstruction of the concept of 'literature'. He argues against the dominant definition of literature in English-speaking parts of the world as a set of valued written works which deal with 'full, central, immediate human experience'. This is meant to contrast with such abstractions as society, politics, or ideology. His argument about language will not allow that human experience is full, central, or immediate in that way, or separate from society and politics. All are founded in linguistic practice that is both constitutive and has its own history.

Williams also makes a *historical* argument showing the conditions for the emergence of this ideological specialization of 'literature' from a whole existing range of written practices. Yet simply to show that literature has a historical and social construction does not *in itself* diminish its value. It may show its appropriation by certain social classes and institutions. His main point is that in our own century these social relations and means of production are rapidly changing and a different set of practices are emergent. It is not surprising, he continues, 'that the specialized concept of literature developed in precise forms of correspondence with a particular social class, a particular organization of learning, and the appropriate particular technology of print, should now be so often invoked in retrospective, nostalgic, or reactionary moods, as a form of opposition to what is correctly seen as a new phase of civilization.'[18] The challenge to literature in theory is an expression of new social relations and technologies. Much writing, for example, is now done for speech in recorded and electronic transmission rather than for print. There is also the development of new selective traditions of writing (for example, women's writing), mainly outside the old class relations of literature and outside the teaching institutions.

The arguments that Williams uses against the notion of literature are equally effective against the category 'ideology'. It is useful to have a general name for signification as a central social process. Nonetheless, most uses of the term, including much of the Marxist tradition, is deeply faulted. Williams's emphasis is that consciousness and its products are part of the material process itself.[19] It is much easier to show bourgeois ideas to be 'ideological' than to explain their actual conditions of practice.

The second part of *Marxism and Literature* is an expansion of the argument of 'Base and superstructure in Marxist cultural theory'. Williams clearly intends to contribute a cultural materialism from *within* the traditions and developments of a Marxist discourse. He spends an amount of space going through these arguments, frequently ending in substantial disagreement with them. As in the essay 'Base and superstructure in Marxist cultural theory' the starting-point is the notion of a determining base and a determined superstructure, even though from a strictly theoretical viewpoint 'this is not, in fact, where we might choose to begin'. Indeed, what Williams is proposing is a set of arguments considerably revising what we might have thought Marxist cultural theory to be. These arguments reject a fixed or centred *concept* of the 'base' (concepts must be historically open) and also the idea of an actual relatively *enclosed* socio-economic arena. In Williams's words:

The force of Marx's original criticism had been mainly directed against the *separation* of 'areas' of thought and activity (as in the separation of consciousness from material production) and against the related evacuation of specific content – real human activities – by the imposition of abstract categories. The common abstraction of 'the base' and 'the superstructure' is thus the radical persistence of the mode of thought which he attacked. (Original emphasis)[20]

This emphasis on process and connectedness is familiar from Williams's early work. Most attempts to restore the sense of activity to the base–superstructure model focus on the superstructure. A properly Marxist approach, argues Williams, is to deny the reduction of the base to a category or specialized area.

What, then, distinguishes Marxism from a sociology of social action or process? Williams agrees that Marxism without some notion of determination is worthless; but an economism of 'natural laws' is equally worthless. After some discussion Williams opts for the formulation that Marxist determination is the *setting of limits* and the *exertion of pressures*. Much of the discussion in subsequent chapters is an elaboration and more specific description of what this means.

Williams retains a notion of productive force which is not equivalent to 'human relations' of production, as in the sociology of work. However, neither can the idea of productive force be specialized to 'material production' under capitalist conditions. Williams insists that, in a human historical process, we produce ourselves and our society and variable forms of material production within these forms of social knowledge and organization. The specialization of 'productive force' may be explained historically. Marx was describing and protesting capitalist institutions and material production which seemed to dominate the society in an external way. Yet the ruling classes must also pay attention to the material production of the social and political order: palaces, courts, military, schools. In the twentieth century it is impossible to draw a distinguishing line between the older sense of material production (heavy industry, transport) and this broader sense of the production of 'defence', 'law and order', and 'entertainment'.

Notions of reflection, mediation, typification, and homology need to be approached critically. They are generally concepts to bridge a 'gap' between base and superstructure. However, Williams's whole argument questions this formulation of the problem. In addition, he argues that it is always necessary to avoid the assumption of a *known* world to which a phenomenon is then, with a complex concept, simply related. That assumption of a fully known social reality must be challenged. 'There is a persistent presupposition of a knowable (often wholly knowable) reality in terms of which the typification will be recognized and indeed (in a normal process in "Marxist criticism") verified. This presupposition repeats, if in a more complex and at times very sophisticated form, the basic dualism of all theories centred on the concept of "reflection". . .'[21] Some of these formulations, notably in the hands of Benjamin or Goldmann, avoid the implication of cultural activity as secondary to forces of production. They do not always avoid assumptions of known qualities of an epoch, rather than a complex and many-dimensional historical process.

Although Williams admires the work of Goldmann and Benjamin, it is clear that his own preference is not for the notions of homology or correspondence. The weight of Williams's position is on the rather different notion of hegemony. This notion should be understood as replacing that of structure of feeling from his early work. The older concept is now used in a rather different and specialized sense. The switch to the concept of hegemony includes a notion of determination as the placing of limits and the exertion of pressures. In other words, there is a constitutive notion of power which was lacking in the earlier notion of structure of feeling. Still retained, however, is the emphasis on everyday practice. Williams is hostile to notions of hegemony which in effect transform it into the older notion of ideology. Hegemony is primarily a matter of social process rather than a formal system of belief, meanings, or values.

It is a whole body of practices and expectations, over the whole of living: our senses and assignments of energy, our shaping perceptions of ourselves and the world. It is a lived system of meanings and values – constitutive and constituting – which as they are experienced as practices appear reciprocally confirming. It thus constitutes a sense of reality for most people in the society. . .[22]

However, this everyday culture includes relations of domination and subordination. This form of power in culture is mainly found in the advanced capitalist countries. Historically and in other countries simple direct control is often of more importance and indeed is of increasing importance in the systems of authoritarian democracy in Britain, West Germany, the USA, Canada, and Japan in the 1980s.

The new emphasis on hegemony is related to the argument of *The Long Revolution* in two ways. First, it is a continuation of Williams's theorizing about new forms of capitalist society. (The *May Day Manifesto* was also important here.) In advanced capitalism 'culture' includes relationships of domination. Second, Williams's argument has an emphasis on a *depth* of analysis. As in the earlier book, the emphasis is on the depth and thoroughness at which the cultural hegemony is lived. It is nothing like a superstructure, entertainment, or art; it is the material of everyday living.

Hegemony can never be expressed as a total system or ideology. It involves relations of domination and subordination produced with and as part of multiple and concrete relationships and processes. As Williams argued in 'Base and superstructures in Marxist cultural theory', the dominant reality includes *alternatives*, but also *excludes* very many possible practices. The significant and exciting areas for study are often unstable aspects, or the emergence of new areas of practice or production. The openness or multi-voiced character of forms of art are often fertile places to observe this historical dynamic.

The new concept of 'structure of feeling' mainly refers to this moment of pre-emergence of a new or changed cultural form, *Traditions* are shaped within the contemporary dynamic of domination and subordination. A tradition is always selective within this kind of dynamic. Cultural *institutions*, including the so-called mass media, have a shaping effect on the cultural forms themselves. A more subtle relationship is the kind of informal social network that Williams calls a 'formation'.[23] A historical analysis must recognize the effective presence of *residual* cultures (for example, the Church) as well as signs of the *emergent*. Each may be dominant, oppositional, or only alternative. These are terms for a concrete sociology of culture rather than a fully worked-out cultural theory.[24]

However Williams does not mean a sociology of 'knowledge' or mass communications. What he intends is a study of the whole material of culture. The sign system, or cultural semiotic, has a whole series of social relations internal to it. This set of working concepts is sufficiently different from a sociology of culture, or cultural studies, to deserve the new name that Williams gives to it: 'cultural materialism'.

Writing

The general approach and working concepts described so far are used in the third part of *Marxism and Literature* as part of a literary theory, even though the general approach could be used for music, visual art, radio, television, film. Williams's discussion assumes a writerly practice which can never be fully described. It is not only that such descriptions are a matter of concrete studies (themselves open to correction and revision) but also that the *emergent* in writing catches us by surprise.

Williams describes two characteristics of writing. The first is its 'distinctive practice of objectified material composition of language'.[25] By this he means writing as *notations* and the reader–writer relationship to these material marks. The second general characteristic is the multiplicity of writing. *The Penguin Book of English Prose*, edited by Williams, includes scientific prose, nature writing, social observation, imaginative prose, philosophical essay, biography, and other forms. The lines between these forms are in part a matter of interpretation and the lines can be drawn and redrawn. This process can be described historically in terms of shifting categories: personal, objective, factual, and so forth.

The most difficult is the distinction of aesthetic from other situations of writing. Here, Williams argues against attempts, as in Lukàcs, to define an aesthetic category, and the formalists' attempt to isolate 'poetic language'. Williams refuses to separate the aesthetic situation or poetic language from social and material processes. Once we recognize 'the variability, the relativity, and the multiplicity of actual cultural practice', any attempt to reserve the category of art or poetry can be seen to have evident ideological functions.[26] Among these is the separation of artistic work from its material processes.

The actual practice is a range of situations of writing. It is clear from the discussion in *Politics and Letters* that Williams includes natural science writing. He insists that psychoanalysis involves interaction and observation but there is then a process of written composition.[27] The point is not to objectify writing but to describe practices of writing as constitutive of their subject. Writing does not have an intermediate status but in one of many other material practices including cutting stone, shaping clay, making sound with instruments, wearing costume, controlling body movement and voice, and so forth. The reason for insisting on the materiality of these processes is that materiality *changes historically*. A materialization of experience, as in visual art, produces an object but may also affect something as deeply social as our experience of objects.[28]

The idea of written notations is important to Williams's cultural materialism. It is a fundamentally decentred notion. On the one hand, notations are a mode of production of communication; on the other, they are 'locally materialized' indications. Writing is at once extraordinarily productive: we can lose ourselves in a printed story or be carried away by a written argument. At the same time, writing is curiously inert: marks on paper, an abandoned film. Writing is a material production of human sociality and it is also marks on a surface. These two come together in ways that are both complex and social. The production of communication joins locally produced indications in an extremely complex process. Williams gives some parameters of this. The most important dimensions of this process are conventions, forms, and creative practice. The last is a reminder that Williams is not offering a systematic theory of 'literary production' but some guidelines for thought and research.

Notations include, for example, the division of a book into Parts I, II, III. A convention is more historical. It may be understood as a social relationship or the ground of a relationship. It can concern rules of speech such as *limits* to intersubjectivity or polyphony which are necessary to distinguish sense from redundancy and noise. There are historically changing conventions about narration and description. There are conventions about the description of work, death, and sexuality. There are conventional orthographic notations for variations in speech.

Williams sets aside the notion of 'genre' in favour of cultural 'form' *as a social relationship*, with an active material basis. The relationship within the form is of individual intentions to collective modes. This kind of relationship must be understood as varying historically, some periods having different kinds of individual–collective relationships. It must also be understood as a material, physical process. Williams intends to indicate by this:

real processes but always physical and material relational processes. This is true of the most 'subjective' generative moments – the poem first 'heard' as a rhythm without words, the dramatic scene first 'visualized' as a specific movement or grouping, the narrative sequence first 'grasped' as a moving shape inside the body – as of the most 'objective moments' – the interaction of possible words with an already shared and established rhythm, the plasticity of an event 'taking shape' in its adaption to a known form, the selection and reworking of sequence to reproduce an expected narrative order.[29]

This kind of process happens in works that we call literary but also, in direct continuity with them, in everyday conversation: shared sounds and rhythms. This is a material process of production and recognition. Form is a relation between individual intention and collective mode. It is less obviously a social relationship than a writer's 'commitment' but yet there is a direct continuity: for as Williams concludes, 'To write in different ways is to live in different ways. It is also to be read in different ways, in different relationships, and often by different people.'[30]

Notes

1   See also Sidney Hook, *Towards an Understanding of Karl Marx: A Revolutionary Interpretation* (London, Victor Gollancz 1933), p. 89; M. Merleau-Ponty, *Phenomenology of Perception*. tr. Colin Smith (London, Routledge and Kegan Paul, 1962).
2   Williams, *The Long Revolution* (Penguin, 1965), p. 54. All references are to this edition.
3   E. P. Thompson, 'The Long Revolution', *New Left Review*, 9 and 10 (May/June and July/August 1961), pp. 24–33 and 34–9
4   Raymond Williams, *Politics and Letters* (New Left Books, 1979), pp. 134–6.
5   However, Williams admired E. E. Hirschmann, *On Human Unity* (London, Victor Gollancz, 1961). See Williams's comments in *Twentieth Century*, 172 (1963), p. 137; and his review of *On Human Unity*, 'Universal Borotherhood', *Guardian*, 30 June 1961, p. 7.
6   Williams. 'Base and Superstructure in Marxist Cultural Theory', in his *Problems in Materialism and Culture* (Verso, 1980), pp. 31–49.
7   Williams, 'Means of Communication as Means of Production', in his *Problems*, p. 55.
8   This general programme of research explains the organization of Williams (ed.), *Contact: Human Communication and its History* (Thames and Hudson, 1981).
9   Williams, 'Problems of Materialism' in his *Problems*, p. 106. From Sebastiano Timpanaro, *On Materialism*, tr. Lawrence Garner (London, Verso, 1980), p. 34.
10 Williams, 'Problems of Materialism', p. 108.
11 Ibid., p. 115.
12 Williams, *Marxism and Literature*, (Oxford University Press, 1977), p. 1.
13 Ferrucio Rossi-Landi, *Language at Work and Trade: A Semiotic Homology for Linguistics and Economics*, tr. Martha Adams and others (Massachusetts, Bergin and Garvey, 1983), p. 52. For an introduction see Augusto Ponzio, 'On the signs of Rossi-Landi's work', *Semiotics*, 62 (1986), pp. 207–21.
14 Rossi-Landi, *Language as Work and Trade*, pp. 78, 128.
15 Ibid., 31–2.
16 V. N. Volosinov, *Marxism and the Philosophy of Language* tr. Ladislav Matejka and I. R. Titunik (New York, Seminar Press, 1973).
17 This is the most serious theoretical problem in Williams's work and is

thoughtfully described in Michael Scrivener's excellent review of *Marxism and Literature* in *Telos*, 38 (Winter 1978–9), pp. 190–98. 'What is the relationship between language and pre-linguistic, non-linguistic experiences, inchoate feelings, memory, silence and dreams? (p. 193). I would myself extend the question in the following way: what is the relationship between Williams's emphasis on language as constitutive of experience and his equally important insistence on the theme of human embodiment in the world?

18 Williams, *Marxism and Literature*, p. 54.
19 Ibid., p. 61.
20 Ibid., p. 78.
21 Ibid., pp. 101–2.
22 Ibid., p. 110.
23 For Williams's own studies of formations see, 'The Bloomsbury Fraction' in *Problems*, pp. 148–69; Williams, 'The Uses of Cultural Theory', *New Left Review*, 158 (July/August 1986), pp. 19–31; Williams, *Culture* (Fontana, 1981), ch. 3.
24 Anthony Barnett, 'Towards a theory', *New Society*, 21 July 1977, pp. 145–6, makes this point in a wholly negative way when he describes *Marxism and Literature* as only a preliminary and conceptual study and looks forward to a general theory of the specific, historical application of the concepts.
25 Williams, *Marxism and Literature*, p. 146.
26 Ibid., p. 153.
27 Williams, *Politics and Letters*, pp. 327–9 on science writing; and pp. 331–4 on Freud's writing. Also, Williams, 'Foreword', in *Languages of Nature*, ed. L. Jordanova (Free Association Books, 1986), pp. 10–14.
28 This is also the case for new technologies such as film, television, and recorded music.
29 Williams, *Marxism and Literature*, pp. 190–1.
30 Ibid., p. 250. See also Nicholas Garnham and Raymond Williams, 'Pierre Bourdieu and the sociology of culture: an introduction', *Media, Culture and Society*, 2 (1980). The interest in Bourdieu at this moment is his resolutely materialist approach to what he calls symbolic power and Williams in *Marxism and Literature* calls cultural hegemony. For an earlier review of Bourdieu see Williams, 'French Connection', *New Society*, 5 May 1977, pp. 239–40.

8

Conclusion: writing and politics

It will be no surprise to discover a politics in the writing of Raymond Williams. Much of his own work has been this kind of discovery. The main argument of Williams's essay on David Hume, for example, is that Hume's discovery of a philosophy was his discovery of a way in which to write.[1] This has its own politics, Williams's argument is that:

The sceptic has arrived at a way of living with his scepticism, and this way, paradoxically, is one of affirmation. For 'a true sceptic will be diffident of his philosophical conviction'. It is in this way that Hume's essential tension is, if not resolved, negotiated. Here decisively, is the discovery of how to write.[2]

Hume's philosophical decision, as Williams demonstrates, a choice of style which depends upon and finds expression in certain conventions. Williams challenges the institutions of knowledge in the university by reading Hume as literature and as philosophy. He writes, as did Hume, to maintain the republic of letters.[3] He stresses the *secular* nature of Hume's thought. He also calls attention to the body writing: Hume's ardour, sickness, fatigue, and the demands of his senses. Williams's main argument, however, turns on the conventional use of the keyword 'society' in Hume's discourse. Williams shows that Hume uses 'society' in a complex way, mainly to restrict its usage to the *company* of members of his own social class.

What, then, of Williams's own project in which politics is also something like the education of desire? It will not do to forget the material conditions of his work in adult education and at the university. It is equally necessary to remember the history of institutions of publishing, broadcasting, cultural creation. Williams's novels and plays stand as something like experimental evidence for his project. Perhaps the other writing which most shows the grain of his intention is his television column in *The Listener* between 1968 and 1972.

This column is often a kind of diary of a writer. It includes Williams's life: building a stone wall; inside because of the bad October weather; watching when he is tired at the end of term; or with his nephews whom he had to fetch ten miles because they were stranded without a set; watching children's programmes with his granddaughter. The columns also include the Czech crisis of 1968; Williams's visit to a student in prison; the general election of 1970; Northern Ireland; and a sense of failure of the left in the early 1970s. Especially in two later columns in January 1974, there is a real sense of tiredness and crisis.

The columns have a kind of development, from the first in which Williams introduces himself, to the last regular column in December 1972, which is a farewell kind of summarizing. There is an initial settling down, and then the strong theme of opposition to television commentators: to voices that attempt to organize and contain the visual images, to limit the response and the kind of questions that may be asked. There are a few columns that deal with a subject matter rather than with the television: work, housing, the Chinese Cultural Revolution. There are a few columns that deal with one programme: about Northern Ireland, about a debate that ended in a row about women's issues. There are two columns that deal with the institutions of broadcasting, one of these on advertising policy.

The main emphasis, however, is on different *forms* of television. Williams's criticism at this point is that so much of life is seen through such forms as police and doctor series rather than through everyday forms of talk. This can be understood as a broadening of his criticism of intrusive presenters and commentators. Thus, for example, Williams criticizes the habit of showing places through selected people. He compares his own experience of Venice with the mood that James Cameron brought to his programme *Venice – the Vanishing Lady*. The selection is so deep that it appears natural. Cameron is a travelled and humane man but now:

He had the mood of this culture which the BBC selects so regularly: the sad vanishing past, the muddled and hateful present. There must be a whole group of Englishmen, in the BBC and elsewhere, who have got so used to seeing the world in this way that they think it's the camera or the sentences doing it: the medium itself having this kind of watercolour soul.[4]

Williams remembers being shown a new steel works in Venice, in a very different mood, by two women who were full of hope for this industry in their city. The nostalgia presented through the person of Cameron is not a property of television as a medium. Although it is not a matter of surface information either, it is an *alterable* aspect of a form of presentation.

The relationship between hegemony and resistance is central to the analysis of Williams's writing on television. The hegemonizing relations come in very subtle forms. The sad version of Venice, the habit of seeing places through a celebrity presenter, is deep within ourselves as viewers. Yet the resistance is also there. We have been to Venice and had it shown by different kinds of people. Or eventually they will show such a programme about somewhere that you know well. So Williams's descriptions of his own experience, tired at the end of term, or with his nephew, is properly part of his writing on television. Any account that leaves that out needs to be carefully thought about.

Williams is critical of what he sees as an irresponsible flow of images and voices: a use of montage on television to say nothing new. He makes his point in particular contexts: for example, the use of clips from a demonstration against the Vietnam War in Grosvenor Square in a trailer for a BBC 2 adaption of Dostoevsky's *The Possessed.*

Where reason, fact and discrimination are now urgently necessary, we are sodden with montage. What was originally a creative technique to express newly perceived relationships has become a manipulative evasion of all substantive connections. Nothing flows, nowadays, so well as an Oxo commercial, a genteel art film, an elderly commentator's reminiscences of history. In this kind of work, where form is everything, we see dissolves of sunlit woods and revolutionary crowds and waves breaking and mouths opening and rockets and streaming hair. At any time in a generation in which so much art or pseudo art is produced, the production habits of a majority of professionals compose a structure of associations, images, tones, which sets limits to actual insights and perceptions, yet ensures, in the programmes that follow each other so closely, a certain confidence of address. The sheer bloody nerve of that trailer for *The Possessed* was not, as the people concerned might like to think, intellectual or creative daring. It was a busy producer's unsurpassable confidence in the currently available clichés.[5]

The cliché is the reduction of popular politics in the street – a demonstration against the war in Vietnam – to disruption and mindless violence. The purpose of Williams's writing is to interrupt the flow of images and voices which he describes. He makes connections between material that was separated by the flow of programming, but in any ordinary analysis would be brought together. It is a difficult theoretical question to describe how Williams's assembled flow of items in his written narrative is different from the flow of television, apart, of course, from the fact that one is written and the other audio-visual.[6]

The answer is that the intention is different. A good example of Williams's own descriptive 'montage' is his column entitled 'Combined operations', in which the contrast is between a transatlantic race, a publicity stunt that seems to have been connected with the sale of British military aircraft, and another plane in which a pilot in West Africa is attempting to save a harvest from destruction by locusts. The rhetorical structure is composed of different kinds of repetition. A narrative about the first plane, another narrative about the second. These narratives are interwoven and there is a deliberate shock effect.

It looked like a dance: the women in white, moving in repeated half-circles, lifting their loose dresses until they swayed like sails. It was a few peasant women in East Africa trying desperately to drive away a huge swarm of locusts which was settling on their crops. . . . Some help was coming from a little control room, from a few light planes. And then within minutes we were in another control room, at the top of the Post Office Tower. With a sense of urgency from this other operations room we were taken to New York where a chimpanzee was 'giving a press conference'. . . . They were so short of resources, fighting the locusts. They were poor people in poor countries. It is, then, not that the Air Race was a conspicuous waste of resources; in television terms it was a waste and a diversion of attention.[7]

But not just a diversion of attention. A manufactured news item as part of a sales campaign for British military aircraft and arms exports. Then, the Eritrean, a former fighter-pilot fighting his way through the locusts. It is not often, says Williams, that 'an evening's television dramatizes, so visibly, the conflicts and contradictions of a politically intolerable world.' There is this political intention in Williams's analysis. He ends the column by briefly mentioning a documentary which studied the amounts spent on military advertising in various countries. Yet Williams rejects in Durrenmatt's *Conversation at Night* (shown on BBC 2) the mood of sad resignation. 'Sad, empty, resigned: this neutral post-war humanism, with the knife on stage: sophistication, dwindling down above empty streets.' As in many of his columns, Williams does not end on that note. He ends by remembering the one line that stuck in his mind from this play broadcast in 1969: 'I'm delighted to hear that education is becoming a danger once again.'

Where, then, do we start? 'Culture is ordinary: that is where we must start', writes Williams in 1958.[8] 'We begin to think where we live', says Williams in 1968.[9] We hear this and we may think of a simple sense of community: the place where we grew up, for example. In fact even when Williams was writing *Culture and Society* he was coming to terms in his first novel with living in at least two communities: home and university. The simpler notions of community are not of much use to think about an actual way of life that is geographically, educationally and politically mobile. What Williams now wants to argue for therefore, is that 'ordinary culture' and 'where we live' is multiple and structured in many complex ways. At a conference held in Yugoslavia in 1985 to discuss socialism on the threshold of the twenty-first century, Williams gave a talk with the title 'Towards Many Socialisms.'[10] The starting place is that since there are many people and cultures there will be many socialisms.

The argument of Williams's *Towards 2000* is to make hope for an alternative future practical. Characteristically, the book is organized by keywords which include industry, democracy and culture. It will not be possible to trace all of Williams' arguments but it will be useful to note how it is a continuation of a kind of subjunctive realism which connects general argument with a future that is imagined in some detail. Williams's method assumes no fixed human nature, no simple nature of things, but a series of discourses through which we know each other and our world. His method is to start within the ways we speak and write the world rather than either a presumed naturalness or abstract theory.[11]

What might be a socialist future for what is called the economy? In the 1970s and 1980s there was much valuable experience of work in collective and co-operative organizations. Most of this experience of collective decision-making has been in small organizations. There is a need therefore to think also about problems of co-ordination on a larger scale. This raises issues of representation which will be discussed in a moment.

To continue thinking about work, the priorities for our economy exclude most kinds of necessary human caring: cooking, housekeeping, care of children and elderly persons. What are the existing priorities which describe such caring as 'unemployment'? It is clearly a social life that is being determined by economic calculation rather than one in which resources are used for social needs. Williams describes a possible immediate goal and a long-term goal. The immediate goal would be an extension of democratic decision-making to existing situations of work. The long-term goal would be a reorganization of resources for social needs rather than economic calculations of profit and return.

There is then the matter of decision-making beyond a single place of work or activity. In thinking about a socialist future there are clear intermediate goals. The most obvious is to change unfair and archaic electoral systems. Williams makes an argument that Britain adopt a system of proportional representation such as exists in West Germany. The long-term goal would be to rethink the whole meaning of 'representative democracy'. Here, Williams is at his most radical: for he points out that the system of representative democracy was historically introduced as a compromise by the middle class to the more radical demand of popular democracy.

The system of representative democracy implies a unity of community in those represented. It must, however, be clear that there is no such unity but a radical conflict of interest. The principle of a delegate who is subject to recall must replace the present illusion of representation and consensus. Clearly this active democracy would be much helped by the possibilities of new interactive electronic communications systems.

Another major area for planning discussed by Williams is the increasingly important areas of culture and communications. The intermediate policy must be to defend social provision against the current policy of increasing the commercial control of newspapers, radio, television, film, and the new electronic systems. The aim must be to reduce the control of the advertising which in the long term pushes the culture in its own direction and priorities. There are a great many other short-term objectives which are worth fighting for: for example, the right of a magazine to be properly distributed and displayed, as present enshrined in law in France.

Williams repeats as a long-term goal his argument in *Communications* that the means of production and distribution of news, music, film, video, information of all kinds, must be controlled collectively by cultural workers themselves.[12] Where this is not possible because of the huge investments involved, the means of production and transmission must be owned in a trust fully protected from political interference and leased to diverse groups of cultural producers.

Clearly there is no consensus about these matters but, rather, real conflict and actual resistance. This comes most obviously from those who benefit from the undemocratic and profit-oriented arrangements that presently exist. However, it is also true that within ourselves there are ways of thinking which block the kinds of proposal that Williams is offering for discussion. Among these blocks is the commercial culture of short-term immediate advantage. There is also a widespread colonization of an ordinary wanting to belong in particular ideological uses of nationalism. This was evident in England and Wales at the time of the Falklands/Malvinas military adventure.

Against this culture what hope is there for an alternative? At this point it is useful to note that the argument of *Towards 2000* was made in many left periodicals: *New Socialist, New Left Review, Socialist Review*, and in talks for the Socialist Society and the Socialist and Environment Resources Association.[13] Williams's resources for hope include the organized working class but also the new social movements: ecology, peace, and women's organization. He writes this but these political intentions and movements write him.

Notes

1   On Hume's writing see Jerome Christensen, 'Hume's Social Composition', *Representations*, 12 (Fall 1985), pp. 44–65; Dagmar Barnouw, 'Skepticism as a Literary Mode: David Hume and Robert Musil', *Modern Language Notes*, 93 (1978), pp. 852–70; David Simpson, 'Hume's Intimate Voices and the Method of Dialogue', *Texas Studies in Literature and Language*, 21 (1979), pp. 68–92; and a series of articles by Michael Morrisroe Jr. including 'Rhetorical Methods in Hume's Works on Religion', *Philosophy and Rhetoric*, 2 (1969), pp. 121–37.

2   Williams, 'David Hume: Reasoning and Experience', in *The English Mind*, ed. H. Sykes and G. Watson (Cambridge University Press, 1964), p. 40. Also in Williams, *Writing in Society* (Verso, 1984), pp. 121–41.

3   See Williams's argument for a Faculty of Humanities in 'Beyond Cambridge English', in his *Writing in Society*, pp. 212–26.

4   Williams, 'Death Wish in Venice', *The Listener*, 4 September 1969, pp. 322–2, and reprinted in *Raymond Williams on Television*, ed. Alan O'Connor (Toronto, Between the Lines, 1988; London and New York, Routledge, 1989).

5   Williams, 'To the Last Word', *The Listener*, 20 February 1969, pp. 248–9, and reprinted in *Raymond Williams on Television*.

6   There is an interesting historical connection. Williams points out that Joyce worked for a time as a cinema manager. See Williams, 'In Praise of Films', *The Listener*, 20 May 1971, p. 634.

7   Williams, 'Combined Operations', *The Listener*, 15 May 1969, p. 697. Also in Williams, *Communications*, 3rd edn. (Penguin, 1968), pp. 96–9, and reprinted in *Raymond Williams on Television*.

8   Williams. 'Culture is Ordinary', in *Conviction*, ed. N. MacKenzie (MacGibbon and Kee, 1958), p. 74.

9   Williams, 'Culture and revolution: a comment', in *From Culture to Revolution*, ed. T. Eagleton and B. Wicker (Sydney, Sheed and Ward, 1968), p. 24.

10 Williams, 'Towards Many Socialisms', *Socialist Review*, 85 (January–February 1986), pp. 45–65.

11 Raymond Williams, *Towards 2000* (London: Chatto and Windus, 1983). For discussion see Francis Mulhern, 'Towards 2000, or News From You-Know-Where,' *New Left Review* 148 (November–December 1984), pp. 5–30; David Slater, 'Social Movements and a Recasting of the Political,' in *New social movements and the state in Latin America* ed. David Slater (Amsterdam, CEDLA, 1985), pp. 1–23. For an interesting recent study of keywords see Raymond Williams, 'Mining the Meaning: Key words in the miners' strike', *New Socialist*, March 1985, pp. 6–9.

12 Williams, *Communications*, 3rd edn, pp. 170–79.
13 Williams, *Socialism and Ecology* (pamphlet, 1982); Williams, *Democracy and Parliament* (pamphlet, 1982); Williams, 'An Alternative Politics', *Socialist Register* (1981), pp. 1–10; 'The Politics of Nuclear Disarmament', *New Left Review*, 124 (1980), pp. 25–42; Williams 'Democracy and Parliament', *Marxism Today*, June 1982, pp. 14–21; Williams, 'Problems of the Coming Period', *New Left Review* 140 (1983), pp. 7–18; Williams, 'Splits, Pacts and Coalitions', *New Socialist*, March/April 1984, pp. 31–5.

A Raymond Williams
Bibliography

References within each section of the bibliography appear in chronological order of publication, with the exception of the first and last sections (Bibliographical essays and Select bibliography), in which references appear in alphabetical order by author. The bibliography is divided into sections as follows.

Bibliographical essays

Works by Raymond Williams

1 Books
2 Short stories, novels, and plays
3 Chapters in books
4 Pamphlets
5 Books in translation
6 Articles: general
7 Book reviews in the *Guardian*
8 Articles in *Tribune*
9 Article on politics in Britain in *The Nation*
10 Television column in *The Listener*
11 Book reviews in *New Society*
12 Published interviews
13 Letters to newspapers
14 Williams as editor

Works about Raymond Williams

Selected bibliography on Williams

Bibliographical essays

Borklund, Elmer, 'Williams, Raymond (Henry)', in *Contemporary Literary Critics*, 2nd edn, Detroit, Gale Research Company, 1982.

Gilpin, George H. and Hermione de Almeida, 'Williams, Raymond (Henry)', in *Thinkers of the Twentieth Century: A Biographical, Bibliographical and Critical Dictionary* ed. by Elizabeth Devine et al., Detroit, Gale Research Company, 1983.

Page, Malcolm, Bibliography and short essay, in *Contemporary Novelists*, 3rd edn, New York, St Martin's Press, 1982.

Temple, Ruth and Martin Tucker, 'Raymond Williams (1921–)', in *A Library of Literary Criticism; Modern British Literature*, vol. III, New York, Frederick Unger, 1966.

Wakeman, John, 'Williams, Raymond (Henry)', in *World Authors 1950–1970*, New York, H. W. Wilson Company, 1975.

Works by Raymond Williams

1 Books

Reading and Criticism, Man and Society series, London, Frederick Muller, 1950. Reprinted 1962.

Drama from Ibsen to Eliot, London, Chatto and Windus, 1952. New York, Oxford University Press, 1953. Revised edn. Harmondsworth, Peregrine, 1964. London, Chatto and Windus, 1968.

Raymond Williams and Michael Orrom, *Preface to Film*, London, Film Drama, 1954.

Drama in Performance, London, Frederick Muller, 1954. Revised edn, The New Thinkers Library, London, C.A. Watts, 1968. New York, Basic Books, 1968. Harmondsworth, Pelican, 1969.

Culture and Society 1780–1950, London, Chatto and Windus, 1958. New York, Columbia University Press, 1959. New York, Doubleday, Anchor Press, 1959. Harmondsworth, Penguin, 1961; reprinted with Postscript, 1963. New York, Harper and Row (paperback edn.), 1966. New edition, New York, Columbia University Press, 1983, with a new Introduction. Translated into Italian, Japanese, Portuguese, German.

The Long Revolution, London, Chatto and Windus, 1961. New York, Columbia University Press, 1961; reissued 1983. Harmondsworth, Pelican, 1965, with additional endnotes; reissued 1984. Westport, Conn., Greenwood Press, 1975.

Britain in the Sixties: Communications, Penguin Special, Harmondsworth, Baltimore, Penguin, 1962. Danish edition. Second edition, London, Chatto and Windus, 1966. New York, Barnes and Noble, 1967. Harmondsworth, Penguin, 1968. Spanish translation. Third edition, Harmondsworth, Penguin, 1976.

Modern Tragedy, London, Chatto and Windus, 1966. Stanford, Stanford

University Press, 1966. Reprinted without play 'Koba', 1977. New edition also without play 'Koba', and with new Afterword, London, Verso, 1979.

Stuart Hall, Raymond Williams, Edward Thompson (eds), *May Day Manifesto*, London, May Day Manifesto Committee, 1967. 2nd edn, Penguin Special, Harmondsworth, Penguin, 1968.

Drama from Ibsen to Brecht, London, Chatto and Windus, 1968. New York, Oxford University Press, 1969. Harmondsworth, Pelican, 1973. London, Hogarth Press, 1987.

The Pelican Book of English Prose, Volume 2: From 1780 to the present day, ed. Raymond Williams, Harmondsworth, Baltimore, Penguin, 1969.

The English Novel from Dicken to Lawrence, London, Chatto and Windus, 1970. New York, Oxford University Press, 1970. Paper edn. Marrimack, 1970. St Albans, Herts., Paladin, 1974. London, Hogarth Press, 1985.

Orwell, Fontana Modern Masters series, Fontana/Collins, 1971. New York, Viking, 1971. New York, Columbia University Press 1981. 2nd edn, Fontana, Flamingo paper editions, 1984.

The Country and the City, London, Chatto and Windus, 1973. New York, Oxford University Press, 1973. Paperback edn 1975. St Albans, Herts. Paladin, 1975. London, Hogarth Press, 1985.

Joy and Raymond Williams (eds), *D. H. Lawrence on education*, Harmondsworth, Penguin Education, 1973.

Raymond Williams (ed.), *George Orwell: A Collection of Critical Essays*, Twentieth Century Views, Englewood Cliffs, N.J., Prentice-Hall, 1974.

Television: Technology and Cultural Form, Technosphere series, Fontana/ Collins, 1974 (paperback). New York, Schocken, 1975. Italian translation.

Keywords: A Vocabulary of Culture and Society, Fontana Communications series, Fontana paperbacks, 1976. London, Croom Helm, 1976. New York, Oxford University Press, 1976. 2nd edn, London, Fontana Paperbacks, 1983. New York, Oxford University Press, 1984.

Marie Axton and Raymond Williams (eds), *English Drama: Forms and Development: Essays in Honour of Muriel Clara Bradbrook*, with an Introduction by Raymond Williams, Cambridge, New York, Cambridge University Press, 1977.

Marxism and Literature, Marxist Introductions series, London, New York, Oxford University Press, 1977. Italian translation.

Politics and Letters: Interviews with New Left Review, London, New Left Books, 1979. New York, Schocken, 1979. Verso paperback edn 1981.

Problems in Materialism and Culture: Selected Essays, London, Verso, 1980. New York, Schocken, 1981.

Culture, Fontana New Sociology Series, Fontana Paperbacks, 1981. U.S. edn, *The Sociology of Culture*, New York, Schocken, 1982.

Raymond Williams (ed.), *Contact: Human Communication and its History*, London and New York, Thames and Hudson, 1981.

Cobbett, Past Masters series, Oxford, New York, Oxford University Press, 1983.

Towards 2000, London, Chatto and Windus, 1983. Harmondsworth, Penguin,

1985. US edn, *The Year 2000*, with a Preface to the American Edition, New York, Pantheon, 1984.

Writing in Society, London, Verso, 1984. US edn, 1984.

Merryn Williams and Raymond Williams (eds), *John Clare: Selected Poetry and Prose*, Methuen English Texts, London and New York, Methuen, 1986.

Raymond Williams on Television: Selected Writings, Preface by Raymond Williams, ed. Alan O'Connor, Toronto, Between the Lines, 1988; New York, London, Routledge, 1989.

2 Short Stories, novels, and plays

Short stories

Short story, in *Cambridge Front*, no. 2 (1941). Perhaps 'Red Earth', listed in *Politics and Letters* chronology. Source: *Outlook: A Selection of Cambridge Writing*, Raymond Williams, Michael Orrom, Maurice James Craig (eds), Cambridge, 1941.

'Sack Labourer', in *English Story 1*, edited by Woodrow Wyatt, London, Collins, 1941.

'Sugar', in *Outlook: A Selection*, pp. 7–14.

'This Time', in *New Writing and Daylight*, no. 2, 1942–3, ed. John Lehmann, London, Collins, 1943, pp. 158–64.

'A Fine Room to Be Ill In', in *English Story 8*, ed. Woodrow Wyatt, London, Collins, 1948.

Novels

Border Country, London, Chatto and Windus, 1960. New York, Horizon Press, 1962. Book club edn, Readers Union/Chatto and Windus, London, 1962. Harmondsworth, Penguin, 1964. Reissued by Chatto and Windus, 1978.

Second Generation, London, Chatto and Windus, 1964. Reissued 1978. New York, Horizon Press, 1965.

The Fight for Manod, London, Chatto and Windus, 1979.

The Volunteers, London, Eyre Methuen, 1978. Paperback edition, London, Hogarth Press, 1985.

Loyalties, London, Chatto and Windus, 1985.

Plays

Koba, in Raymond Williams, *Modern Tragedy*, London, Chatto and Windus, 1966.

A Letter from the Country, BBC Television, April 1966, *Stand*, 12 (1971), pp. 17–34.

Public Inquiry, BBC 1 Television, 15 March 1967, *Stand*, 9 (1967), pp. 15–53.

The Country and the City (television documentary, Where We Live Now series), 1979.

Williams' unpublished plays include a television play, *The Volunteers*. See *The Listener*, 20 February 1969.

3   Chapters in books

'Culture is ordinary', in *Conviction*, ed. Norman Mackenzie, London, MacGibbon and Kee, 1958, pp. 74–92. American edn, New York, Monthly Review Press, 1959.

'The Social Thinking of D. H. Lawrence', in *A D. H. Lawrence Miscellany*, ed. Harry T. Moore, Carbondale, Southern Illinois University Press, 1959, pp. 295–311. From *Culture and Society*.

In *Popular Culture and Personal Responsibility*, London, National Union of Teachers, 1960.

Witness for the defence, in *The Trial of Lady Chatterley: Regina v. Penguin Books Limited*, the transcript of the trial, ed. C. H. Rolph, Penguin Special, Baltimore, Harmondsworth, Penguin, 1961, pp. 133–5.

'Lawrence's Social Writings', in *D. H. Lawrence: A Collection of Critical Essays*, ed. Mark Spilka, Englewood Cliffs, N.J., Prentice-Hall, 1963, pp. 162–74. From *Culture and Society*.

'Recent English Drama', in *The Modern Age*, vol. 7 of the Pelican Guide to English Literature, ed. Boris Ford, 2nd edn, Harmondsworth, Penguin, 1963, pp. 531–45. Revised from *Twentieth Century* (1961).

'David Hume: Reasoning and Experience', in *The English Mind*, ed. Hugh Sykes and George Watson, Cambridge, Cambridge University Press, 1964, pp. 123–45. Reprinted in *Writing in Society*.

'Towards a Socialist Society', in *Towards Socialism*, ed. Perry Anderson and Robin Blackwood, London, Fontana, 1965, pp. 367–97. From *The Long Revolution*.

'Strindberg and Modern Tragedy', in *Essays on Strindberg*, published by the Strindberg Society, Sweden, Stockholm, Beckmans, 1966, pp. 7–18. From *Modern Tragedy*.

'Dylan Thomas's Play for Voices', in *Dylan Thomas: A Collection of Critical Essays*, Twentieth Century Views, ed. C. B. Cox, Englewood Cliffs, N.J., Prentice-Hall, 1966, pp. 89–98. From *Critical Quarterly*, 1959.

'General Profile'; 'Criticism', in *Your Sunday Paper*, ed. Richard Hoggart, London, University of London Press, 1967, pp. 13–29, 150–63. Book commissioned by ABC Television in relation to a series of thirteen adult-education programmes.

'Paradoxically, if the book works it to some extent annihilates itself', in *McLuhan: Hot and Cold*, ed. Gerald E. Stearn, New York, Dial Press, 1967, pp. 186–9. See response by McLuhan, pp. 283–4. Reprinted from *University of Toronto Quarterly* (1964).

'Culture and revolution: a comment', in *From Culture to Revolution: The Slant Symposium 1967*, ed. Terry Eagleton and Brian Wicker, London, Sydney, Sheed and Ward, 1968, pp. 24–34, 296–308.

'Another Pheonix', review of *Pheonix II*, by D. H. Lawrence, in *The Bedside Guardian 17: A Selection from the Guardian 1967–68*, ed. W. L. Webb, London, Collins, 1968, pp. 246–8. From the *Guardian*.

'The Meanings of Work', concluding essay in *Work: Twenty Personal Accounts* vol. 1, ed. Ronald Fraser, Harmondsworth, Penguin in association with New Left Review, 1968, pp. 280–98.

'A social commentary', in *The Press: a case for commitment* ed. Eric Moonman, Fabian Tract 391, London, Fabian Society, 1969, pp. 1–4.

'From The May Day Manifesto', in *The New Left Reader*, ed. by Carl Oglesby, New York, Grove Press, 1969, pp. 111–43. From 1967 *May Day Manifesto*.

'Introduction', in *National Convention of the Left April 1969 Report and Proposals*, London, National Convention of the Left, 1969 (mimeo).

'Introduction', in *Three Plays*, by D. H. Lawrence, Harmondsworth, Penguin, 1969, pp. 7–14.

'The Realism of Arthur Miller', in *Arthur Miller: A Collection of Critical Essays*, Twentieth Century Views, ed. Robert W. Corrigan, Englewood Cliffs, N.J., Prentice-Hall, 1969, pp. 69–79. From *Critical Quarterly* (1959).

'Dickens and Social Ideas', in *Dickens 1970*, ed. by Michael Slater, London, Chapman and Hall, 1970, pp. 77–98. Reprinted in *Sociology of Literature and Drama*, ed. T. and E. Burns, Harmondsworth, Penguin.

'Radical and/or Respectable', in *The Press We Deserve*, ed. Richard Boston, London, Routledge and Kegan Paul, 1970, pp. 14–26.

'The Industrial Novels: Hard Times (1958)', in *Charles Dickens*, Penguin Critical Anthologies, ed. Stephen Wall, Harmondsworth, Penguin Education, 1970, pp. 405–9. From *Culture and Society*.

'Introduction', in *Dombey and Son*, by Charles Dickens, ed. Peter Fairclough, Harmondsworth, Penguin, 1970, pp. 11–34.

'From Modern Tragedy 1966', in *Henrik Ibsen*, Penguin Critical Anthologies, ed. James McFarlane, Harmondsworth, Penguin, 1970 pp. 312–19.

'Crimes and Crimes', in *A Listener Anthology: August 1967-June 1970*, ed. Karl Miller, London, British Broadcasting Corporation, 1970, pp. 210–22. From *The Listener* (21 August 1969).

'On Reading Marcuse', in *The Cambridge Mind: Ninety Years of the Cambridge Review 1879–1969*, ed. Eric Homberger, William Janeway, Simon Schama, Boston, Little, Brown, 1970, pp. 162–6. From *The Cambridge Review* (1969).

'An Introduction to Reading in Culture and Society', in *Literature and Environment: Essays in Reading and Social Studies*, ed. Fred Inglis, London, Chatto and Windus, 1971, pp. 125–40.

'The Realism of Arthur Miller', in *Arthur Miller: The Crucible; Text and Criticism*, ed. Gerald Weales, New York, Viking, 1971, pp. 313–25. From *Critical Quarterly* (1959).

'On Solzhenitsyn', in *Literature in Revolution*, ed. George Abbott White and Charles Newman, New York, Holt, Rinehart and Winston, 1972, pp. 318–34.

'Ideas of Nature', in *Ecology: The Shaping Inquiry*, ed. J. Benthal, London, Longman, 1972. Based on a lecture at the Institute of Contemporary Arts, 1971. Reprinted in *Problems in Materialism and Culture*.

'Introduction', in *Racine*, by Lucien Goldmann, tr. Alister Hamilton, Cambridge, Rivers Press, 1972. London, Writers and Readers, 1981, pp.

vii-xxii. Text of lecture, Cambridge, 26 April 1971. From *New Left Review* (1971).

'Realism and the Contemporary Novel', in *Twentieth Century Literary Criticism: A Reader*, ed. David Lodge, London, Longman, 1972. From *The Long Revolution*.

'Discussion on St. Joan of the Stockyards, 1973', in *A Production Notebook to St. Joan of the Stockyards* ed. Michael D. Bristol and Darko Suvin, Montreal, McGill University, 1973, pp. 184–98. Transcript of discussion in Montreal, March 1973.

'Social Darwinism', in *The Limits of Human Nature*, ed. J. Benthall. London, Allen Lane, 1973. From lecture at the Institute of Contemporary Arts, London, 1972.

'Thomas Hardy', in *Thomas Hardy: The Tragic Novels*, ed. R. P. Draper, pp. 341–51. From *Critical Quarterly* (1964).

'Observation and Imagination in Orwell', in *George Orwell: A Collection of Critical Essays*, ed. Raymond Williams (1974). From *Orwell*.

Untitled, in *Bookmarks*, ed. Frederic Raphael, London, Quartet Books, 1975, pp. 162–5. In connection with the Authors' Lending Rights Society.

'Welsh Culture', in *Culture and Politics: Plaid Cymru's Challenge to Wales*, Plaid Cymru, 51 Cathedral Road, Caerdydd, CF1 9HD, 1975, pp. 6–10. From talk on BBC Radio 3, 27 September 1975.

'You're a Marxist, Aren't You?' in *The Concept of Socialism*, ed. Bhikhu Parekh, London, Croom Helm, 1975, pp. 231–42.

'Sean O'Casey', in *Sean O'Casey: A Collection of Critical Essays*, Twentieth Century Views, ed. Thomas Kilroy, Englewood Cliffs, N.J., Prentice-Hall, 1975, pp. 53–60. From *Drama from Ibsen to Brecht*.

'Raymond Williams Comments (1972)', in *World Authors 1950–1970*, ed. John Wakeman, New York, H. W. Wilson Company, 1975, pp. 696–7.

'Communications as Cultural Science', in *Approaches to Popular Culture*, ed. C. W. E. Bigsby, London, Edward Arnold, 1976, pp. 27–38. From *Journal of Communication* (1974).

'Realism and Non-Naturalism', *Official Programme of the Edinburgh International Television Festival* (1977). May be Claire Johnston, ed., *Edinburgh '77 Magazine*, London, BFI, 1977.

Untitled, in *My Cambridge*, ed. Ronald Hayman, London, Robson Books, 1977, pp. 55–70. US edn *My Oxford, My Cambridge*, ed. Ann Thwaite and Ronald Hayman, New York, 1979.

'Literature in Society', in *Contemporary Approaches to English Studies*, ed. Hilda Schiff, London, Heineman for The English Association, 1977, pp. 24–37.

'The Press We Don't Deserve', in *The British Press: A Manifesto*, Communications and Culture Series, London, Macmillan, 1978, pp. 15–28. From the Action Society Press Group presentations to the McGregor Commission on the Press.

'Foreword', in *The Critical Twilight: Explorations in the Ideology of Anglo-American Literary Theory from Eliot to McLuhan*, by John Fekete, International

Library of Phenomenology and Moral Sciences, London, Routledge and Kegan Paul, 1978, pp. xi-xiv.

'The press and popular culture: an historical perspective', in *Newspaper History: From the Seventeenth Century to the Present Day*, ed. George Boyce, James Curran and Pauline Windgate, London, Constable; Beverly Hills, Sage Publications, 1978, pp. 41–50.

'Forms of English Fiction in 1848', in *1848: The Sociology of Literature*, Proceedings of the Essex Conference on the Sociology of Literature, July 1977, ed. Francis Barker et al., University of Essex, 1978, pp. 277–90. Reprinted in *Literature, Politics and Theory* ed. F. Barker et al, London Methuen, 1986, and *Writing in Society*.

'Social environment and theatrical environment: the case of English naturalism', in *English Drama: Forms and Development*, ed. Marie Axton and Raymond Williams, 1978, pp 203–23. Reprinted in *Problems in Materialism and Culture*.

'Wessex and the Border (1973)', in *The English Novel: Developments in Criticism since Henry James: A Casebook*, ed. Stephen Hazell, London and Basingstoke, Macmillan, 1978, pp. 190–205. From *The Country and the City*.

'The Growth and Role of the Mass Media', in *Media, Politics and Culture: A Socialist View*, ed. Carl Gardner, London, Macmillan, 1979, pp. 14–24. From *Wedge* (1977); *International* (1977).

'The Institutions of Technology', in *Communication and Class Struggle*, 2 vols, ed. Armand Mattelart and Seth Siegelaub, Vol. 1 *Capitalism, Imperialism*, New York, International General; Bagnolet, France, International Mass Media Research Centre, 1979, pp. 265–67. From *Television*.

'Utopia and Science Fiction', in *Science Fiction: A Critical Guide*, ed. Patrick Parrinder, London, Longmans, 1979. From *Science Fiction Studies* (1978).

'Effects of the technology and its uses', in *Communication Studies: An Introductory reader*, ed. John Corner and Jeremy Hawthorn, London, Edward Arnold, 1980, pp. 174–86. From *Television*; not in the 2nd edn.

'Hardy and Social Class', by Raymond Williams and Merryn Williams, in *Thomas Hardy: The Writer and His Background*, ed. Norman Page, London, Bell and Hyman, 1980, pp. 29–40.

'The Bloomsbury Fraction', in *Keynes and The Bloomsbury Group: The Fourth Keynes Seminar held at the University of Kent at Canterbury, 1978*, ed. Derek Crabtree and A. P. Thirlwall, London, Macmillan, 1980. Reprinted in *Problems in Materialism and Culture*.

'Tragedy and Contemporary Ideas (1966)', in *Tragedy: Developments in Criticism: A Casebook*, ed. R. P. Draper, London and Basingstoke, Macmillan, 1980, pp. 182–9. From *Modern Tragedy*.

'Foreword', in *A Good Night Out: Popular Theatre: Audience, Class and Form*, by John McGrath, London, Eyre Methuen, 1981, pp. vii-xi.

'Foreword', in *The Language of Television: Uses and Abuses*, New Accents Series, by Albert Hunt, London, Eyre Methuen, 1981, pp. vii-x.

'Editor's Introduction', in *Medieval Readers and Writers 1350–1400*, English Literature in History Series, London, Hutchinson; New York, Columbia University Press, 1981, pp. 9–12. General Editor's Introduction reprinted in other volumes in this series.

'Raymond Williams', in *The Forward March of Labour Halted?*, ed. Martin Jacques and Francis Mulhern, London, Verso in Association with *Marxism Today*, 1981, pp. 142–52.

'The Analysis of Culture', in *Culture, Ideology and Social Process*, ed. Tony Bennett et al., An Open University Reader, London, Batsford, 1981, pp. 43–52. From *The Long Revolution*.

'Lecture', in *The Arts Council: Politics and Policies*, London, The Arts Council of Great Britain, c.1981, pp. 9–16.

'The New Metropolis', in *Introduction to the Sociology of 'Developing Societies'*, ed. Hamza Alvai and Teodor Shanin, New York and London, Monthly Review Press, 1982. From *The Country and the City*.

'The Politics of Nuclear Disarmament', in *Exterminism and Cold War*, ed. New Left Review, London, New Left Books, 1982, pp. 65–85. Reprinted from *New Left Review* (1980).

'Region and Class in the Novel', in *The Uses of Fiction: Essays on the Modern Novel in Honour of Arnold Kettle*, ed. Douglas Jefferson and Graham Martin, Milton Keynes, The Open University Press, 1982, pp. 59–68. Reprinted in *Writing in Society*.

'Working-Class, Proletarian, Socialist: Problems in Some Welsh Novels', in *The Socialist Novel in Britain: Towards the Recovery of a Tradition*, ed. H. Gustav Klaus, Brighton, Sussex, The Harvester Press, 1982, pp. 110–21.

'Exiles', in *James Joyce: New Perspectives*, ed. Colin MacCabe, Sussex, The Harvester Press; Bloomington, Indiana University Press, 1982, pp. 105–10. Reconstruction of part of a lecture (1947).

'British Film History: New Perspectives', in *British Cinema History*, ed. James Curran and Vincent Porter, London, Weidenfeld and Nicolson, 1983, pp. 9–23.

'Cultural Revolution', in *British Socialism: Socialist Thought from the 1880's to 1960's*, ed. Anthony Wright, London and New York, Longman, 1983, pp. 170–81. From Part III of *The Long Revolution*.

'Culture', in *Marx: The First Hundred Years*, ed. David McLellan, Fontana paperbacks, 1983, pp. 15–55.

'Lecture', in *The Arts Council: Politics and Policies*, The 1981 W. E. Williams Memorial Lecture, London, Arts Council, 1983, pp. 9–16.

'Monologue in Macbeth', in *Teaching The Text*, ed. Susanne Kappeler and Norman Bryson, London, Routledge and Kegan Paul, 1983, pp. 180–202.

'Seeing a man running', in *The Leavises: Recollections and Impressions*, ed. Denys Thompson, Cambridge, Cambridge University Press, 1984, pp. 113–22.

Untitled, in *Writings on the Wall: A Radical and Socialist Anthology 1215–1984*, ed. Tony Benn, London, Faber and Faber, 1984, pp. 115, 116–17. From 'Culture is Ordinary' (1958) and *May Day Manifesto*, 1968.

'Socialists and Coalitionists', in *The Future of the Left*, ed. James Curran,

Cambridge, Polity Press and New Socialist, 1984, pp. 182–94. From *New Socialist*.

'State Culture and Beyond', in *Culture and the State*, ed. Lisa Appignanesi, London, Institute of Contemporary Arts, 1984, pp. 3–5.

'Forms of English fiction in 1848', in *Literature, Politics and Theory: Papers from the Essex Conference 1976–84*, ed. Francis Barker et al., London, Methuen, 1986, pp. 1–16. Reprinted from *1848: The Sociology of Literature*, ed. F. Barker et al., University of Essex, 1978.

'Foreword', in *Languages of Nature: Critical Essays on Science and Literature*, ed. Ludmilla Jordanova, London, Free Association Books, 1986, pp. 10–14.

'Pierre Bourdieu and the sociology of culture: an introduction', by Raymond Williams and Nicholas Garnham, in *Media, Culture and Society*, ed. Richard Collins et al., London, SAGE, 1986, pp. 116–30. Reprinted from *Media, Culture and Society*, 1980.

'Towards Many Socialisms', in *Socialism on the Threshold of the Twenty-First Century*, London, Verso, 1986. First published in *Socialist Review* (1986).

'Alignment and Commitment', in *Contemporary Literary Criticism: Modernism Through Postmodernism*, ed. Robert Con Davis, New York and London, Longman, 1986, pp. 124–9. From *Marxism and Literature*.

'Base and Superstructure in Marxist Cultural Theory', and 'The Multiplicity of Writing', in *Debating Texts*, ed. Rick Rylance,Toronto: University of Toronto Press, 1987, pp. 204–16, 217–20. From *Problems in Materialism and Culture* and *Marxism and Literature*.

'Conventions', in *Twentieth-Century Literary Criticism*, ed. Vassilis Lambropoulos and David Neal Miller, Albany, State University of New York Press, 1987, pp. 185–90. From *Marxism and Literature*.

'Language and the avant-garde', in *The Linguistics of Writing: Arguments between language and literature*, ed. Nigel Fabb, Derek Attridge, Alan Durant, Colin MacCabe, New York, Methuen, 1987, pp. 33–47. From a conference on 'The Linguistics of Writing' at Strathclyde University in 1986.

'Fact and Fiction', in *International Encyclopedia of Communications*, Oxford University Press, 1988.

'Beckett, Samuel', in *Modern Irish Literature*, ed. Denis Lane and Carol McCrory Lane, New York, Ungar, 1988, p. 10. From *Modern Tragedy*.

'Dominant, Residual, and Emergent', in *Twentieth-Century Literary Theory: A Reader*, ed. K. M. Newton, New York, St Martin's Press, 1988, pp. 121–6. From *Marxism and Literature*.

'The politics of the avant-garde', and 'Theatre as a political forum', in *Visions and Blueprints*, ed. Edward Timms and Peter Collier, Manchester, Manchester University Press, 1988, pp. 1–5, 307–20.

4 Pamphlets

Unsigned [Raymond Williams and Eric Hobsbown]. Pamphlet on the Russo-Finnish War. Communist Party of Great Britain, 1940. This may be a pamphlet by the Russia Today Society, *Finland–the Facts*, London [Communist Party], 1939.

Communication and Community, William F. Harvey Memorial Lecture, Bedford College, University of London, 1961.

The existing alternative in communications, Fabian Tract no. 337, Socialism in the Sixties series, London, Fabian Society, 1962.

Drama in a dramatised society: An Inaugural Lecture, Cambridge, Cambridge University Press, 1975. Reprinted in *Writing in Society* and *Raymond Williams on Television*.

The Welsh Industrial Novel, Cardiff, University College Press, 1979.

Socialism and Ecology, London, Socialist Environment and Resources Association [1982].

Democracy and Parliament, with an Introduction by Peter Tatchell, London, Socialist society Pamphlet, 1982.

5   *Books in translation*

Catalan

Cultura i Societat, Barcelona, Laia, 1974. Translation of *Culture and Society*.

Danish

Massemedierne, Copenhagen, 1963. Translation of the first edition of *Communications* with material on the Danish press. See 1968 Penguin edition, p. 12.

German

Gesellschaftstheorie als Begriffsgeschichte: Studien z. histor. Semantik von Kultur, tr. Dt. von Heinz Blumensath, Muchen, Rogner and Bernhard, 1972. Translation of *Culture and Society*.

Innovation: uber den Prozesscharakter von Literatur und Kultur, selected and tr. H. Gustav Klaus, Frankfurt am Main, Syndikat, 1979. Selections from *The Long Revolution, From Culture to Revolution, Modern Tragedy, The Country and the City*, also 'Literature and Sociology: in Memory of Lucien Goldmann,' and 'Base and Superstructure in Marxist Cultural Theory.'

Italian

Cultura e rivoluzione industriale Inghilterra, 1780–1950, Piccola bibliotech Einaudi, tr. M. T. Grendi, Torino, G. Einaudi, 1968. Translation of *Culture and Society*.

Marxismo e letteratura, tr. by Mario Stetrema, Roma, Bari Laterza, 1979. Translation of *Marxism and Literature*.

Televisione. Technologia e forma culturale, tr. with an Introduction by Celestino E. Spada, Bari, De Donate, 1981. Translation of *Television*.

Japanese

Translation of *Culture and Society*. See 1983 Columbia University Press edition
p. xi.

Portuguese

Marxismo e Literatura, Rio, Zahar, 1979. Translation of *Marxism and Literature*.

Spanish

Los Medios de comunicacion social, Barcelona, Peninsula, 1971.
Marxismo y Literatura, Barcelona, Peninsula, 1980. Translation of *Marxism and
Literature*.
Cultura, sociologia de la communicacion y arte, Buenos Aires, Barcelona, Mexico,
Paidos, 1982. Translation of *Culture*.
Hacia el Año 2000, Barcelona, Critica, 1984. Translation of *Towards 2000*.

6 *Articles: general*

The Cambridge University Journal (vol. 1, no. 1, 21 October 1939), Williams
editor, April-June 1940.
'Profundities for poets. The Muse in Utopia', 3 February 1940, p. 7.
[Michael Pope] 'The Spoon in the Yellow Liver: First Act of a Great New
Drama', 9 March 1940, p. 2.
[Michael Pope.] Review of *Must the War Spread*, Penguin Special, by D.
N. Pritt.
'Commentary', 27 April 1940, p. 5.
[Unsigned] 'Commentary', 4 May 1940, p. 5.
'Commentary', 11 May 1940, p. 5.
'Commentary', 18 May 1940, p. 5.
'Commentary', 25 May 1940, p. 5.
'Not with a Scream but with a Twitter: Trinity's "Magpie" Released', 25
May 1940.
'Commentary', 1 June 1940, p. 5.
'Commentary: Union Turns Left–But How', 9 November 1940, p. 2.
[Michael Pope] 'Ralph Lynn at Arts', 9 November 1940, p. 2.

Cambridge University Socialist Club Bulletin, 1939.
'Defence Against Air Raids'.   'Literature and the Cult of Sensibility'.

Twentyone, weekly newspaper of the 21st Anti-Tank Regiment, Royal Artillery,
printed at Pinneberg, Germany. Williams editor April-October 1945. See
Politics and Letters, p. 59. The British Library has a single copy, 1
December 1945, which includes a photograph of Williams back at
Cambridge.

1947

'Dali, Corruption and His Critics', review of *Hidden Faces* by Salvador Dali, *Politics & Letters* 1, nos 2/3 (1947), pp. 112–13.

'The Delicacy of P. H. Newby', review of *Agents and Witnesses*, by P. H. Newby, *The Critic* 2, no. 2 (1947), pp. 79–81.

'A Dialogue on Actors', *The Critic* 1, no. 1 (1947), pp. 17–24.

Clifford Collins, Wolf Mankowitz, Raymond Williams, 'Editorial', *The Critic* 1, no. 2 (1947).

—— 'For Continuity in Change', editorial, *Politics & Letters* 1, no. 1 (1947), pp. 3–5.

—— 'Culture and Crisis', editorial, *Politics & Letters* 1, nos 2/3 (1947), pp. 5–8.

'Ibsenites and Ibsenite-Antis,' review of *Ibsen: the Intellectual Background*, by Brian W. Downs; *Ibsen the Norwegian*, by M. C. Bradbrook, *The Critic* 1, no. 2 (1947), pp. 65–8.

'Lower Fourth at St. Harry's', *Politics & Letters* 1, nos 2/3 (1947), pp. 105–6.

'Radio Drama', *Politics & Letters* 1, nos 2/3 (1947), pp. 106–9.

'Saints, Revolutionaries, Carpetbaggers', review of *The New Spirit*, by E. W. Martin; *Writers of Today*, ed. Denys Val Baker, *The Critic* 1, no. 1 (1947), pp. 52–4.

'The Soviet Literary Controversy in retrospect', *Politics & Letters* 1, no. 1 (1947), pp. 21–31.

1948

'A note on Mr. Hoggart's appendices', *Adult Education* 21 (1948), pp. 96–98.

[Michael Pope] 'The American Radio', review of *The American Radio*, by Llewellyn White, *Politics & Letters* 1, no 4 (1948).

'And Traitors Sneer', *Politics & Letters* 1, no. 4 (1948), pp. 66–8.

'The Exiles of James Joyce', *Politics & Letters* 1, no. 4 (1948), pp. 13–21. In *Drama from Ibsen to Brecht*, part 2, ch. 3.

[Michael Pope] Short Review of *A Skeleton Key to Finnegan's Wake*, by Campbell and Robinson, *Politics & Letters* 1, no. 4 (1948).

'Some Experiments in Literature Teaching', *Rewley House Papers* vol. 2, no. 10 (1948–9), pp. 9–15.

[Michael Pope] 'The State and Popular Culture', *Politics & Letters* 1, no. 4 (1948), pp. 71–2.

1949

'Literature in relation to History: 1850–75', *Rewley House Papers* 3, no. 1 (1949–50), pp. 36–44.

'Ibsen's Non-Theatrical Plays', *The Listener* 42, 22 December 1949, pp. 1098–9. From the Third Programme.

1951

'Christopher Fry', *The Highway*, May/September 1951, pp. 42–8. A chapter in *Drama from Ibsen to Eliot*.

'Criticism into Drama', *Essays in Criticism* 1 (1951), pp. 120–138. A chapter in *Drama from Ibsen to Eliot*.

1953

'Film as a Tutorial Subject', *Rewley House Papers* 3, no. 2 (Summer 1953), pp. 27–37.

'The Idea of Culture', *Essays in Criticism* 1 (1953), pp. 239–66.

'Myth and Mr. O'Neill', *The Highway*, May/September 1953, pp. 42–8.

'The Teaching of Public Expression', *The Highway*, April 1953, pp. 247–50.

1954

'Editorial Commentary', *Essays in Criticism* 4 (1954), pp. 341–4. On small magazines.

'Figures and Shadows', *The Highway*, February 1954, pp. 169–72.

'Standards', *The Highway*, December 1954, pp. 43–6.

1955

'George Orwell', review of *George Orwell*, by Laurence Brander, *Essays in Criticism* 5 (1955), pp. 44–52. Early version of a *Culture and Society* chapter.

1956

'Class and Classes', *The Highway*, January 1956, pp. 84–6.

'T. S. Eliot on Culture', *Essays in Criticism* 6 (1956), pp. 302–18.

'Science Fiction', *The Highway*, December 1956, pp. 41–5.

1957

'Fiction and the Writing Public', review of *The Uses of Literacy*, by Richard Hoggart, *Essays in Criticism* 7 (1957), pp. 422–8.

'The New Party Line?', review of *The Outsider*, by Colin Wilson, *Essays in Criticism* 7 (1957), pp. 68–76.

Review of *Edward Thomas*, by H. Coombes, *The Highway*, January 1957, pp. 94–5.

'The Uses of Literacy: Working Class Culture', *Universities and Left Review* 1, no. 2 (1957), 29–32.

1958

'3B at Cement Street', review of four books for children, *New Statesman* 56, 15 November 1958, pp. 682–3.

'A Kind of Gresham's Law', *The Highway*, February 1958, pp. 107–10.

'New Verse Plays', review of *Two Plays*, by George Banker; *Helen in Egypt and Other Plays* by John Heath-Stubbs, *New Statesman*, vol. 56, 27 December 1958, p. 916.

'Poetry Today', review of six books of poetry, *New Stateman*, vol. 56, 6 December 1958, pp. 811–12.

'The Present Position in Dramatic Criticism', review of *The Art of Drama*, by Ronald Peacock, *Essays in Criticism* 8 (1958), pp. 290–8.

'The Press the People Want', *Universities and Left Review* 5 (1958), pp. 42–7. Shortened advance chapter of *The Long Revolution*.

'Realism and the Contemporary Novel', *Universities and Left Review* 4 (1958), pp. 22–5.

Review of *The Poet's Craft*, by A. F. Scott; *English Historians: Selected Passages*, by B. Newman, *The Highway*, April 1958, pp. 188–9.

'Revolution in Cambridge', review of *The Muse Unchained*, by E. M. Tillyard, *New Statesman*, vol. 56, 1 November 1958, p. 604.

'The Social Thinking of D. H. Lawrence', *Universities and Left Review* 4 (1958), pp. 66–71. Advance chapter of *Culture and Society*.

1959

'Arguing About Television', review of *Television and the Child*, by Hilde T. Himmelweir, *Encounter* 12 (June 1959), pp. 56–9.

'The Bearing of Literature', review of *The Uses of the Imagination*, by William Walsh; *Poetry and Morality*, by Vincent Buckley, *New Statesman*, vol. 57, 21 March 1959, p. 410.

'The Critic as Biographer', review of *Katherine Mansfield and Other Literary Studies*, by J. Middleton Murray, *New Statesman*, vol. 57, 9 May 1959, pp. 662–3.

'Critical Forum', *Essays in Criticism* 9 (1959), pp. 171–9. Reply to Ian Gregor and Malcolm Pittock on *Culture and Society*, reviewed by Richard Hoggart.

'Definitions of Culture', review of *Culture in Private and Public Life*, by F. R. Cowell, *New Stateman*, vol. 58, 25 July 1959, p. 114.

'Dylan Thomas's Play for Voices', *Critical Quarterly* 1 (1959), pp. 18–26.

'Going on Learning', *New Statesman*, vol. 57, 30 May 1959, pp. 750–1.

'Grammar of Dissent', review of *Voices of Dissent: A selection of articles from Dissent Magazine*, *The Nation* 188 (1959), pp. 174–5.

'Literature and Morality', review of *Three Traditions of Moral Thought*, by Dorothea Krook; *The Ethical Idealism of Matthew Arnold*, by William Robbins, *New Statesman*, vol. 58, 31 October 1959, pp. 588–90.

'Our debt to Dr. Leavis' [Symposium], *Critical Quarterly* 1 (1959), pp. 245–7.

'The Press and Popular Education', *The Highway*, April 1959, pp. 183–8.

'Priestly Against Topside', review of *Topside, or the Future of England*, by J. B. Priestly. *New Statesman*, vol. 57, 10 January 1959, pp. 47–8.

'Realism and the Contemporary Novel', *Partisan Review* 26 (1959), pp. 200–13.

'The Realism of Arthur Miller', *Critical Quarterly* 1 (1959), pp. 140–9. Reprinted in *Universities and Left Review* 7 (1959), pp. 34–7. Reprinted in *Arthur Miller* ed. G. Weales, New York, Viking, 1971.

'Science and Culture', review of *T. H. Huxley: Scientist, Humanist and Educator*, by Cyril Bibby, *New Statesman*, vol. 57, 25 April 1959, p. 584.

'Tribune's Majority', review of *Tribune 21*, ed. Elizabeth Thomas, *New Statesman*, vol. 57, 24 January 1959, p. 124.

'Verse and Drama', review of *The Third Voice*, by Dennis Donoghue, *New Statesman*, vol. 58, 26 December 1959, p. 916.

1960

'Class and Voting in Britain', *Monthly Review* 11, no. 9 (January 1960), pp. 327–34.
'Freedom and Ownership in the Arts', *New Left Review* no. 5 (September–October 1960), pp. 53–7. Advance chapter of *The Long Revolution*.
'Ibsen restored', *New Statesman*, vol. 60, 2 July 1960, pp. 23–4.
'Labour and Culture', *New Epoch*, May 1960. Not seen. Source: *Tribune*, 13 May 1960, p. 2.
'Lawrence and Tolstoy', *Critical Quarterly* 2 (1960), pp. 33–9.
'London Letter: The New British Left', *Partisan Review* 27 (1960), pp. 341–7.
'The Magic System', *New Left Review*, no. 4 (1960), pp. 27–32. Reprinted in *Problems in Materialism and Culture*.
'Oxford Ibsen', review of *Ibsen: Volume VI*, tr. and ed. J. W. McFarlane, *New Statesman*, vol. 60, 24 September 1960, pp. 447–8.
'A Practical Critic', review of *The Truest Poetry*, by Laurence Lerner, *New Statesman*, vol. 59, 5 March 1960, pp. 338–9.
'Working Class Attitudes', Richard Hoggart and Raymond Williams, *New Left Review*, no. 1 (1960), pp. 26–30.

1961

'The Achievement of Brecht', *Critical Quarterly* 3 (1961), pp. 153–62.
'The Common Good', *Adult Education* 34 (1961), pp. 192–9.
'Definition of Culture' [Comments by Kingsley Amis, Frank Kermode, Raymond Williams, Edward Shils on *Socialism and Culture*, by Richard Wollheim], *New Statesman*, vol. 61, 2 June 1961, pp. 880–4.
'New English Drama', *Twentieth Century* 170 (1961), pp. 169–80. Reprinted in *The Pelican Guide to English Literature*, vol. 7.
'The Figure in the Rug', review of *Somerset Maughan*, by Richard Cordell, *New Statesman*, vol. 62, 7 July 1961, pp. 20–1.
'The Future of Marxism', *20th Century* 170 (1961), pp. 128–42.
'Hope Deferred', review of performance of 'Waiting for Godot', *New Statesman*, vol. 61, 19 May 1961, p. 802.
'My Performances', On the Memoirs of Thomas Bewick, *New Statesman*, vol. 62, 8 December 1961, pp. 892–3.
'Shame the World', on a performance of 'The Visions of Simone Machard', by Brecht, *New Statesman*, vol. 69, 9 June 1961, pp. 932–3.
'Thoughts on a masked stranger', review of *Between Past and Future*, by Hannah Arendt, *Kenyon Review* 23 (1961), pp. 698–702.
'Three-Quarters of a Nation', review of *English for Maturity*, by David Holbrook, *New Statesman*, vol. 61, 3 March 1961, p. 351.
'Virtuous Circle', review of *The Story of Fabian Socialism*, by Margaret Cole, *The Listener*, vol. 66, 30 November 1961, pp. 933–4.
'Work and Leisure', *The Listener*, vol. 65, 25 May 1961, pp. 926–7.

144   *A Raymond Williams Bibliography*

'A Dialogue on Tragedy', *New Left Review*, nos 13/14 (1962), pp. 22–35.

'The deadlock', *Encounter* 18, no. 1 (1962), pp. 14–15.

'Fiction and Delusion: A note on *Auto-da-Fe*, by Elias Canetti', *New Left Review*, no. 15 (May-June 1962), pp. 103–6.

'From Scott to Tolstoy', review of *The Historical Novel*, by Georg Lukács, *The Listener*, 8 March 1962, pp. 436–7.

'Into the Wilderness', review of *The Popular Novel in England 1770–1800*, by J. M. S. Tompkins, *New Statesman*, vol. 63, 2 March 1962.

'Strong Feelings', review of *The New Radicalism*, by Brian Magee, *The Listener*, vol. 68, 4 October 1962, pp. 529–30.

Review of *Llareggub Revisited*, by David Holbrook, *The Listener*, vol. 67, 12 April 1962, pp. 651–2.

'To the North', review of *Ibsen and Strindberg*, by F. L. Lucas, *The Listener*, vol. 67, 17 May 1962, pp. 868–70.

'Sensible People', review of *Learning and Living, 1790–1960*, by J. F. C. Harrison, *New Statesman*, vol. 63, 5 January 1962, pp. 21–2.

'Strindberg and the New Drama in Britain', *Le Theatre dans le Monde/World Theatre* 11, no. 1 (1962), pp. 61-.

'Television in Britain', *The Journal of Social Issues* 18, no. 2 (1962), pp. 6–15.

1963

'Books', *On Human Unity*, by E. E. Hirschmann, in reply to a question about what books had been neglected or undervalued in the last five years, *Twentieth Century* 172 (1963), p. 137.

'From Hero to Victim: Notes on the development of liberal tragedy', *New Left Review*, no. 20 (1963), pp. 54–68.

'Going into Europe', *Encounter* 20 (March 1963), p. 68.

'Minor Ibsen', review of *The Oxford Ibsen* Volume Two (The Vikings at Helgeland, Love's Comedy, The Pretenders), ed. J. W. McFarlane, *The Cambridge Review* 84 (19 January 1963), pp. 195, 197.

'Radical History', review of *The Making of the English Working Class*, by E. P. Thompson, *The Listener*, vol. 70, 5 December 1963, pp. 938–9.

'Liberal Breakdown', review of *The Free Spirit*, by C. B. Cox, *The Listener*, vol. 69, 30 May 1963, pp. 926–9.

Review of *The Meaning of Contemporary Realism*, by Georg Lukács, *The Listener*, vol. 69, 28 February 1963.

'Tolstoy, Lawrence, and Tragedy', *Kenyon Review* 25 (1963), pp. 633–50.

'Tragic despair and revolt', *Critical Quarterly* 5 (1963), pp. 103–15. Advance chapter of *Modern Tragedy*.

'Tragic resignation and sacrifice', *Critical Quarterly* 5 (1963), pp. 5–19. Advance chapter of *Modern Tragedy*.

'What kind of education', *The Listener*, vol. 70, 18 July 1963, p. 91.

1964

'From Hero to Victim: Ibsen, Miller and the Development of Liberal Tragedy', *Studies on the Left* 4, no. 2 (1964). pp. 83–97. Edited from *New Left Review*; to appear in *Modern Tragedy*.
'La gauche britannique', *Esprit* 32 (1964), pp. 581–92.
'Labour's cultural policy', *Views*, no. 5 (1964), pp. 40–44.
'Prelude to Alienation', *Dissent* 11 (1964), pp. 303–15. Reprinted in *Stand* vol. 7, no. 4 (1965), pp. 36–44. On Blake.
'Social Criticism in Dickens: Some problems of method and approach', *Critical Quarterly* 6 (1964), pp. 214–27. See also correspondance with J. C. Maxwell, p. 373.
'A Structure of Insights', review of *The Gutenberg Galaxy*, by Marshall McLuhan, *University of Toronto Quarterly*, April 1964. Reprinted in *McLuhan: Hot and Cold*, edited by Gerald E. Stearn, 1967.
'Thomas Hardy', *Critical Quarterly* 6 (1964), pp. 341–51.

1965

'The British Left', *New Left Review*, no. 30 (March-April 1965), pp. 18–26. From *Esprit*.
'Other Views' [Labour in Britain], *Views*, no. 7 (1965), pp. 13–15.
'Tragic Inquiry', review of *Greek Tragedy and the Modern World*, by Leo Aylen, *The Spectator*, 8 January 1965, p. 46.
'Why I am Marching: You Can't Have It Both Ways–The Bomb *and* Democracy', *Sanity*, April 1965, p. 6.
'What is the Future of the Left', *Sanity*, April 1965, p. 9.

1966

'New Left Catholics', *New Blackfriars*, vol. 48, November 1966, pp. 74–7.

1967

'Literature and rural society', *The Listener*, vol. 78, 16 November 1967, pp. 630–2. From the Third Programme.
'Literature and the City', *The Listener*, vol. 78, 23 November 1967, pp. 653–6. From the Third Programme.

1968

'How television should be run', *The Listener*, vol. 80, 11 July 1968, pp. 33–5.
'Pastoral and counter-pastoral', *Critical Quarterly* 10 (1968), pp. 277–90. To be published in *The Country and the City*.
'Why do I demonstrate?', *The Listener*, vol. 79, 25 April 1968, pp. 521–3. From a talk broadcast on the Third Programme.

1969

'Crisis in communications: A new mood of submission', *The Listener*, vol. 82, 31 July 1969, pp. 138, 140. Reprinted in *Problems in Materialism and Culture*.
'The Knowable Community in George Eliot's Novels', *Novel* 2 (1969), pp. 255–68. To appear in a different form in *The Country and the City*.
'National Convention of the Left: Why CND must be there', *Sanity*, March 1969, p. 6.
'On Reading Marcuse', review of *Negations*, by Herbert Marcuse, *The Cambridge Review* 90 (30 May 1969), pp. 366–8. Reprinted in *The Cambridge Mind* ed. E. Homberger et al., Boston, Little, Brown, 1970.
'Dramatic changes', review of *The English Drama, 1485–1585*, Oxford History of English Literature, by F. P Wilson; *Shakespeare's Dramatic Heritage*, by Glynne Wickham, *The Listener*, 24 April 1969, pp. 582–3.

1970

'An experimental tendency', *The Listener*, vol. 84, 3 December 1970, pp. 785–6.
'A Hundred Years of Culture and Anarchy', *The Spokesman*, no. 8, December 1970, pp. 3–5. From a talk in April 1969. Reprinted in *Problems in Materialism and Culture*.
'Ideas of nature', *Times Literary Supplement*, 4 December 1970, pp. 1419–21. Reprinted in *Problems in Materialism and Culture*.
'The Intellectual in Politics', *The Spokesman*, no. 3 (May 1970), pp. 3–5.
'The popularity of the press', *The Listener*, vol. 84, 15 October 1970, pp. 508–9. From Radio 3.
'Shadowing Orwell', *The Listener*, vol. 84, 13 August 1970, p. 218.

1971

'Dutschke and Cambridge', *Cambridge Review* 92, 29 January 1971, pp. 94–5. See also two statements, pp. 95–6.
'Going into Europe–Again?, *Encounter* 36 (June 1971), p. 13.
'In praise of films,' *The Listener*, vol. 85, 20 May 1971, p. 633–5. From Radio 3.
'Literature and Sociology: In memory of Lucien Goldmann', *New Left Review*, no. 67 (1971), pp. 3–18.
'On and from any shore', review of *The Penguin Book of Socialist Verse*, ed. Alan Bold, *Stand* 12, no. 2 (1971), pp. 35–7.
'Radical Intellectuals', review of *Fellow Travellers*, by T. C. Worsley, *The Listener*, vol. 85, 24 June 1971, p. 821.
'Raymond Williams thinks well of the Open University', *The Listener*, vol. 86, 14 October 1971, pp. 507–8.

1972

'Lucien Goldmann and Marxism's alternative tradition', *The Listener*, vol. 87,

23 March 1972, pp. 375–6. From Radio 3.

'Social Darwinism', *The Listener*, vol. 88, 23 November 1972, pp. 696–700. Radio 3. One of a series of lectures at the ICA.

'What happened at Munich', *The Listener*, vol. 88, 14 September 1972, pp. 321–2. Reprinted in *Raymond Williams on Television*.

1973

'Base and Superstructure in Marxist Cultural Theory', *New Left Review*, no. 82 (1973), pp. 3–16. German translation as 'Materialistische Literaturtheorie IX', *Alternative* 101 (April 1975), pp. 77–91.

'How we lost the world we never had: the country and the city in history', introduction by Leo Marx, *Royal Institute of British Architects Journal* 80 (1973), pp. 421–31.

'Images of Solzhenitsyn', review of *Ten Years after Ivan Denisovich*, by Zhores Medvedev; *Candle in the Wind*, by Alexander Solzhenitsyn, *The Listener*, vol. 90, 29 November 1973, pp. 750–1.

'Views', *The Listener*, vol. 89, 7 June 1973, pp. 744–5. Reprinted in *Raymond Williams on Television*.

1974

'Communication as Cultural Science', *Journal of Communication* 24 (Summer 1974), pp. 17–25. Reprinted in *Approaches to Popular Culture*, ed. C. W. E. Bigsby, London, Arnold, 1976.

'The English Language and the English Tripos', *Times Literary Supplement*, 15 November 1974, pp. 1293–4.

'On High and Popular Culture', *New Republic*, vol. 171, 23 November 1974, pp. 13–16. Reprinted in *Cambridge Review* (1975).

'Pastoral Versions', review of *Rural Discontent in 19th-Century Britain*, by J. P. D. Dunbabin; *Land and Industry: The Landed Estate and the Industrial Revolution*, ed. J. T. Ward and R. C. Wilson, *New Statesman*, vol. 88, 27 September 1974, pp. 428–9.

1975

'On High and Popular Culture', *Cambridge Review*, vol. 96 (May 1975), pp. 126–9. Reprinted from *The New Republic* (1974).

'The Referendum Choice', *New Statesman*, vol. 89, 30 May 1975, p. 719.

'Variations on a Welsh Theme: On Aspects of the Welsh "Fixation on the Past" '. *The Listener*, vol. 94, 2 October 1975, pp. 429–30.

1976

'The Bomb and Democracy–you can't have it both ways', *Sanity*, November 1976, pp. 10. Reprinted from *Sanity*, April 1965 as part of a special issue to celebrate CND programme on BBC-2.

'Contemporary Drama and Social Change in Britain', *Revue des Langues Vivantes* 42 (1976), pp. 624–31.

'The Cultural Contradictions of Capitalism', review of the book by Daniel Bell, *The New York Times Book Review*, 1 February 1976, p. 3.

'Developments in the sociology of Culture', *Sociology* 10 (1976), pp. 497–506. Prepared for the BSA Annual Conference, 1975.

'Legal? Decent? Honest? Truthful?–an argument about advertising', *The Listener*, vol. 96, 16 September 1976, pp. 331–2.

'Notes on Marxism in Britain since 1945', *New Left Review* 100 (1976–7), pp 81–94.

1977

'The fiction of reform', *Times Literary Supplement*, 25 March 1977, pp. 330–1.

'The Growth and Role of the Mass Media', *International* 3, no. 3 (1977), pp. 3–6. Reprinted as 'The Role of the mass media: a discussion', *Wedge* 1 (1977). In *Media, Politics and Culture*, ed. C. Gardner (Macmillan, 1979).

'A Lecture on Realism', *Screen* 18, no. 1 (1977), pp. 61–74.

'The paths and pitfalls of ideology as an ideology', *Times Higher Education Supplement*, 10 June 1977, p. 13.

Review of *English Jacobin Novel*, by G. Kelly, *Times Literary Supplement*, 25 March 1977, pp. 330–1.

'The Role of the Mass Media', *Wedge*, no. 1 (1977), pp. 33–8.

'The Social Significance of 1926', *Llafur* 2, no. 2 (1977), pp. 5–8.

'The Sociology of Culture', *Gulliver: German-English Yearbook* 2 (1977), pp. 49–53.

'Speak for England,' review of *An Oral History of England: 1900–1975*, compiled by Melvyn Bragg, *The New York Times Book Review*, 27 February 1977, p. 3.

1978

'Commitment', *Stand* 20, no. 3 (1978), pp. 8–11.

'A man confronting a very particular kind of mystery' [On the death of F. R. Leavis], *Times Higher Education Supplement*, 5 May 1978, p. 10.

'Problems of Materialism', *New Left Review* 109 (1978), pp. 3–17.

'Utopia and Science-Fiction', *Science-Fiction Studies* 5 (1978), pp. 203–14. Reprinted in *Problems in Materialism and Culture*.

1979

'The Arts Council', *Political Quarterly* 50 (1979), pp. 157–71.

1980

'Beyond actually existing socialism', *New Left Review*, no. 120 (1980), pp. 3–19. Reprinted in *Problems in Materialism and Culture*.

'From Communism to Marxism', review of *Marxism: For and Against*, by R. L. Heilbroner, *New York Times Book Review*, 13 April 1980, p. 11.

'Gravity's Python', review of *From Fringe to Flying Circus*, by Roger Wilmut, *London Review of Books* 2, no. 23, 4–17 December 1980, p. 14.

A Raymond Williams Bibliography 149

'Isn't the news terrible?', review of *More Bad News*, Glasgow University Media Group; *The Whole World is Watching*, by Todd Gitlin, *London Review of Books* 2, no. 13, 3–16 July 1980, pp. 6–7.

'Pierre Bourdieu and the sociology of culture: an introduction', by Nicholas Garnham and Raymond Williams, *Media, Culture and Society* 2 (1980), pp. 209–23. Reprinted in *Media, Culture and Society* (1986).

'The Politics of Nuclear Disarmament', *New Left Review*, no. 124 (1980), pp. 25–42. Reprinted in *Exterminism and Cold War*, London, New Left Books, 1982.

'The Role of the Literary Magazine', *Times Literary Supplement*, 6 June 1980, p. 637.

'The Writer: Commitment and Alignment', *Marxism Today*, June 1980, pp. 22–5. Marx memorial Lecture, March 1980.

1981

'An Alternative Politics', *Socialist Register* (1981), pp. 1–10.

'Die Politik der atomaren Abrustung', *Das Argument*, no. 127 (May-June 1981), pp. 352–66. From *New Left Review*, no. 124 (1980).

'English Brecht', review of *Collected Plays*, vols. V and VI, *London Review of Books* 3, no 13, 16 July–5 August 1981, pp. 19–20.

'Ideas and the labour movement', *New Socialist* no. 2, November/ December 1981, pp. 28–33.

'Marxism, Structuralism and Literary Analysis', *New Left Review*, no. 129 (1981), pp. 51–66. Reprinted in *Writing in Society*.

Review of *George Orwell, A Life*, by Bernard Crick, *Marxism Today*, June 1981, pp. 28–9.

'Talking to Ourselves', *The Cambridge Review* 102 (27 April 1981), pp. 160–4.

'Their bark may well be lost, if it is not tempest tossed', *Guardian*, 24 January 1981, p. 11. On Cambridge English and the MacCabe dispute.

1982

'Democracy and parliament', *Marxism Today* 26, no. 6 (June 1982), pp. 14–21. Socialist Society pamphlet, 1982.

'Distance', *London Review of Books*, 17–30 June 1982, pp. 19–20.

'How to be the arrow, not the target', *Irish Broadcasting Review*, no. 15 (1982), pp. 16–21. From an address to the Festival of Film and Television in the Celtic Countries, Wexford, March 1982.

1983

'Cambridge English and Beyond', *London Review of Books* 5, no. 12, 7–20 July 1983, pp. 3–8. Reprinted in *Writing in Society*.

'Problems of the Coming Period', *New Left Review*, no. 140 (1983), pp. 7–18. Talk for the Socialist Society, May 1983.

'The Red and the Green', review of *Socialism and Survival*, by Rudloph Bahro and *Capitalist Democracy in Britain*, by Ralph Miliband; *Socialist Register*

1982, ed. Martin Eve and David Musson, *London Review of Books* 5, no. 2, 3–16 February 1983, pp. 3, 5.

'The Robert Tressel Memorial Lecture, 1982', *History Workshop*, no. 16 (Autumn 1983), pp. 74–82.

1984

'Nineteen Eighty Four in 1984', *Marxism Today*, January 1984, pp. 12–16. Reprinted in *Monthly Review* 36, no. 7 (December 1984), pp. 13–28. From 1984 edition of *Orwell*.

'Splits, pacts and coalitions', *New Socialist*, no. 16, March/April 1984, pp. 31–5. Reprinted in *The Future of the Left*, ed. J. Curran, Cambridge, Polity Press and New Socialist 1984.

1985

'Community', review of *The Taliesin Tradition: A Quest for the Welsh Identity*, by Emyr Humphries; *Jones: A Novel*, by Emyr Humphreys; *Wales! Wales?*, by Dai Smith; *The Matter of Wales: Epic Views of a Small Country*, by Jan Morris, *London Review of Books*, vol. 7, no. 1, 24 January 1985, pp. 14–15.

'Mining the meaning: Key words in the miners' strike', *New Socialist*, no. 25, March 1985, pp. 6–9.

'Ruskin among others', review of *John Ruskin: The Early Years*, by Tim Hilton, *London Review of Books* 7, 20 June 1985, p. 18.

'Torches for Superman', review of *By the Open Sea*, by August Strindberg, tr. Mary Sandbach; *August Strindberg*, by Olaf Lagercrantz, tr. Anselm Hollo; *Strindberg: a Biography*, by Michael Meyer, *London Review of Books*, vol. 7, 21 November 1985, pp. 17–18.

'Walking backwards into the future', *New Socialist*, no. 27, May 1985, pp. 21–3.

1986

'Towards Many Socialisms', *Socialist Review*, no. 85 (January–February 1986), pp. 45–65, paper delivered at Roundtable '85, 'Socialism on the Threshold of the Twenty-first Century', held at Cavtat, Yugoslavia, 21–6 October, 1985. Reprinted in *Socialism on the Threshold of the Twenty-first Century* (Verso Books, forthcoming).

'Desire', review of *Landscape for a Good Woman: A Story of Two Lives*, by Carolyn Steedman, *London Review of Books*, vol. 8, 17 April 1986, pp. 8–9.

'The Uses of Cultural Theory', *New Left Review* 158 (July/August 1986), pp. 19–31.

1987

'The Future of English', *News From Nowhere*, no. 3 (May 1987), pp. 14–25. Talk for Oxford English Limited, 28 January 1987.

'Past Masters', review of *Joachim of Fiore and the Myth of the Eternal Evangel in the 19th Century*, by Marjorie Reeves and Warwick Gould; *Beauty and Belief: Aesthetics and Religion in Victorian Literature*, by Hilary Fraser; *The Correspondance of John Ruskin and Charles Elliot Norton*, ed. John Bradley and Ian Ousby, *London Review of Books*, vol. 9, no. 12, 25 June 1987, pp. 13–14.

1988

'Art: Freedom as Duty', *Planet*, 68 (April/May 1988), pp. 7–14. Lecture to a 1979 conference organized by the Extra-Mural Department at UCW Aberystwyth and the Welsh Arts Council.

'The Importance of Community', *Radical Wales*, no. 18 (Summer 1988), pp. 16–20. A lecture to the 1977 Plaid Cymru Summer School, Llandudno.

7 *Book reviews in the* Guardian

[Reprint in *The Manchester Guardian Weekly* in brackets]

'The reaction to Coleridge', review of *Coleridge the Visionary*, by J. B. Beer, 17 July 1959, p. 4. [23 July 1959, p. 10]

'Messages from a spiritual storm-centre', review of *Collected Letters of Samuel Coleridge* vols 3 and 4, edited by E. L. Griggs, 11 September 1959, p. 6.

'Fiction and ideas: the case of George Eliot', review of *The Novels of George Eliot*, by Jerome Thrale, 9 October 1959, p. 6. ['Ideas and the novelist', 15 October 1959, p. 10]

'Views from the ante-rooms of power', review of *The Spare Chancellor*, by Alister Buchan, 16 October 1959, p. 9.

'The clerk without a church', review of *The Life of John Middleton Murray*, by F. A. Lea, 6 November 1959, p. 8. ['Reassembling a writer', 12 November 1959, p. 11]

'The hallmarks of American', review of *American Critical Essays, Twentieth Century*, edited by Harold Beaver, 27 November 1959. ['American critical writing', 3 December 1959, p. 10]

'A thinker in politics', review of *Coleridge: Critic of Society*, by John Colmer, 11 December 1959, p. 6. ['A thinker in politics', 24 December 1959, p. 10]

'Children and writers,' review of *Young Writers, Young Readers*, edited by Boris Ford, 15 January 1960, p. 8.

'Shelley and science', review of *Shelley, his Thought and Work*, by Desmond King-Hale, 12 February 1960, p. 8.

'The Western literary heritage', review of *Literature and Western Man*, by J. B. Priestly, 19 February 1960, p. 7. ['Western literary heritage', 25 February 1959, p. 10]

'The roots of education', review of *Studies in the History of Education*, 1780–1870, by Brian Simon, 14 April 1960, p. 10.

'The necessary general view', review of *Studies in American Culture*, ed. Joseph J. Kwiat and Mary C. Turpie, 13 May 1960, p. 6. ['Taking the broad view', 19 May 1960, p. 10]

'Commentary on critics', review of *The Chartered Mirror*, by John Holloway, 27 May 1960, p. 9. [2 June 1960, p. 11]

'Common-sense romanticism', review of *Image and Experience*, by Graham Hough, 17 June 1960, p. 6.

152   *A Raymond Williams Bibliography*

'Mr. Winters and Professor X', review of *In Defence of Reason*, by Yvor Winters, 1 July 1960. [7 July 1960, p. 11]

'A scrapbook of reflections', review of *For Love or Money*, by Richard Rees, 12 August 1960, p. 5. [18 August 1960, p. 11]

'Literary and historical', review of *Critical History of English Literature*, by David Daiches, 23 September 1960, p. 8. [29 September 1960, p. 10]

'The uses of biology', review of *Darwin and Butler: Two versions of evolution*, by Basil Wiley, 30 September 1960, p. 8.

'Creative resources', review of *The Creative Vision: Modern European Writers on Their Art*, ed. Haskell M. Block and Herman Salinger, 25 November 1960, p. 9.

'Eliot and belief', review of *T. S. Eliot and the Idea of Tradition*, by Sean Lucy; *The Plays of T. S. Eliot*, by D. E. Jones, 9 December 1960, p. 6. ['The problem of T. S. Eliot', 15 December 1960, p. 11]

'A version of realism,' review of *Realism and Imagination*, by Joseph Chiari, 23 December 1960, p. 5. [29 December 1960, p. 10]

'Orpheus and Darwin', review of *The Orphic Voice*, by Elizabeth Sewell, 10 February 1961, p. 6.

'Patterns in literature', review of *Some Mythical Elements in English Literature*, by E. M. W. Tillyard, 24 February 1961, p. 9. ['Centres of reference', 2 March 1961, p. 10]

'Creators and consumers', review of *Brecht*, by Ronald Gray; *Ionesco*, by Richard N. Coe, 24 March 1961, p. 15. [30 March 1961, p. 10]

'The recovery of Hardy', review of *Thomas Hardy*, by Douglas Brown, 28 April 1961, p. 8. ['Hardy rehabilitated', 4 May 1961, p. 11]

'The human footnote', review of *Edith Simcox and George Eliot*, by K. A. McKenzie, 26 May 1961, p. 7. [1 June 1961, p. 11]

'Writers and "the writer"', review of *The Writer's Dilemma*, ed. Times Literary Supplement, 9 June 1961, p. 8. [15 June 1961, p. 10]

'Universal brotherhood', review of *On Human Unity*, by E. E. Hirschmann, 30 June 1961, p. 7. ['A reaffirmation of brotherhood', 6 July 1961, p. 10]

'Lessons of the masters', review of S. Gorley Putt on F. R. Leavis and C. P. Snow in *Essays and Studies, 1961*, 7 July 1961. [13 July 1961, p. 12]

'Literature and society: Raymond Williams replies to Donald Davie', 11 August 1961. A response to Davie, 'Towards a New Aestheticism?, in the *Guardian*, 21 July 1961, p. 7.

'The end of a mimic', review of *The Old Man at the Zoo*, by Angus Wilson, 29 September 1961, p. 7. [5 October 1961, p. 11]

'Critical Pelican', review of *The Modern Age*, The Pelican Guide to English Literature, vol. 7, ed. Boris Ford, 6 October 1961, p. 6.

'The art of a moralist', review of *The Art of George Eliot*, by W. J. Harvey, 20 October 1961, p. 6. [26 October 1961, p. 11]

'The meaning of tragedy', review of *The Death of Tragedy*, by George Steiner, 10 November 1961, p. 7.

'Experiment in reading', review of *An Experiment in Criticism*, by C. S. Lewis, 15 December 1961, p. 7.

'Looking around Utopia', review of *Heavens Below – Utopian Experiments in*

England, 1560–1960, by W. H. G. Armytage, 5 January 1962, p. 5. [11 January 1962, p. 10]

'Critic on top', review of *The Function of Criticism*, by Yvor Winters, 9 March 1962, p. 6. ['The crack of the critical whip', 15 March 1962, p. 11]

'Letters from Lawrence', review of *The Collected Letters of D. H. Lawrence*, ed. Harry T. Moore, 2 vols, 23 March 1962, p. 8. [29 March 1962, p. 11]

'Island story', review of *Island*, by Aldous Huxley, 30 March 1962, p. 6. ['Island experiment', 5 April 1962, p. 10]

'A matter of judgement', review of *Puzzles and Epiphanies*, by Frank Kermode, 11 May 1962, p. 6. [17 May 1962, p. 10]

'A continuing dialogue', review of paperback editions of *A Modern Symposium*, by Lowes Dickinson, introduced by E. M. Forster; *Notes towards the definition of culture*, by T. S. Eliot; *Literature, Popular Culture and Society*, by Leo Lowenthal; *The House of Intellect*, by Jacques Barzun; *The Captive Mind*, by Czeslaw Milosz, 15 June 1962, p. 7.

'Meanings of romantic', review of *Classic, Romantic and Modern*, by Jacques Barzun, 24 August 1962, p. 4. ['In defence of romanticism', 30 August 1962, p. 10]

'Nightmare and normality', review of *The Dark Comedy*, by J. L. Styan, 5 October 1962, p. 13. [11 October 1962, p. 10]

'Self and place', review of *Living in Croesor* by Philip O'Connor, 26 October 1962, p. 6.

'Stratford swans or what?', review of *Contemporary Theatre*, ed. J. R. Brown and B. Harris, 30 November 1962, p. 9. [6 December 1962, p. 11]

'Books of the year', the most interesting books of 1962; reissue of *Auto-da-Fe*, by Elias Canetti; translation of *The Historical Novel*, by Georg Lukács; *The Politics of Oil*, by Robert Engler, 21 December 1962, p. 8.

'A philosophy of emotion', review of *Philosophical Sketches*, by Suzanne Langer, 28 December 1962, p. 6. [3 January 1963, p. 10]

'Contemporary', review of *Contemporaries*, by Alfred Kazin, 1 February 1963, p. 7. ['The mask of orthodoxy', 7 February 1963, p. 10]

'Monumental history', review of *English Literature 1789–1815*, by W. L. Renwick, 15 February 1963, p. 7. ['One kind of history', 21 February 1963, p. 11]

'An effect of alienation', review of *The Public Happiness*, by August Heckscher, 29 March 1963, p. 7. [4 April 1963, p. 11]

'Pulp pioneers', review of *Fiction for the Working Man 1830–1850*, by Louis James, 27 September 1963, p. 8. ['Pulp pioneers', 3 October 1963, p. 10]

'Literature and conviction', review of *The Dream and the Task*, by Graham Hough; *Logic and Criticism*, by William Righter; *Experience into Words*, by D. W. Harding, 11 October 1963, p. 9. ['Literature and morals', 17 October 1963, p. 11, first two books only]

'Scrutiny', review of *Scrutiny*, vols 1–20, 25 October 1963, p. 9

'The Dickens argument', review of *Dickens and Education*, by Philip Collins, 22 November 1963, p. 6.

'Shaw and others', review of *Shaw and the Nineteenth Century Theatre*, by Martin Meisel; *The Drama of Chekhov, Synge, Yeats and Pirandello*, by F. L. Lucas,

3 January 1964, p. 6. ['Bernard Shaw and others', 9 January 1964, p. 11]

'Gracious mean', review of *The Age of Equipoise*, by W. L. Burn, 24 January 1964, p. 7.

'Ceremony for a radical', review of *The Radical Tradition*, by R. H. Tawney, 21 February 1964, p. 8. ['Politics and the quality of life', 27 February 1964, p. 10]

'A human abstract', review of *Science: The Glorious Entertainment*, by Jacques Barzun, 15 May 1964, p. 8.

'The rhetoric of death', review of *The Mortal No: Death and the Modern Imagination*, by Frederick J. Hoffman, 12 June 1964, p. 7. ['Rhetoric of death', 18 June 1964, p. 10]

'Strange ideology', review of *John Addington Symonds: A Biography*, by Phyllis Grosskurth, 3 July 1964, p. 7. ['A deviant ideology', 9 July 1964, p. 11]

'The believers', review of *The Unbelievers*, by A. O. J. Cockshut, 10 July 1964, p. 8. [16 July 1964, p. 10]

'Sincerity', review of *Wordsworth and the Poetry of Sincerity*, by David Perkins, 28 August 1964, p. 7.

'Edwardian illusion', review of *Edwardian England 1901–1914*, edited by Simon Nowell-Smith, 9 October 1964, p. 9. [15 October 1964, p. 11]

'Not public enough', review of *Corridors of Power*, by C. P. Snow, 6 November 1964, p. 8. ['Public and private lives', 12 November 1964, p. 10]

'Professional writer', review of *The Profession of English Letters*, by J. W. Saunders, 27 November 1964, p. 13. ['Writing to live', 3 December 1964, p. 11]

'Creative power', review of *Power in Men*, by Joyce Cary, 11 December 1964. ['Creative energy', 17 December 1964, p. 11}

'Workers College', review of *The Central Labour College*, by William W. Craik, 1 January 1965, p. 6.

'Early Dickens', review of *The Letters of Charles Dickens*, vol. 1, 1820–39 ed. Madeline House and Graham Storey; *Dickens from Pickwick to Dombey*, by Stephen Marcus, 5 February 1965. ['Dickens and his day', 11 February 1965, p. 10]

'The uses of France', review of *The View of France from Arnold to Bloomsbury*, by Christophe Campos; *A Comparative View of French and British Civilization 1850–1870*, by F. C. Green, 26 March 1965, p. 9. ['Looking across to France', 8 April 1965, p. 10]

'Exploration and commitment', review of *Further Explorations*, by L. C. Knights, 9 April 1965, p. 15.

'Conservative values', review of *Education and Values*, by G. H. Bantock, 23 April 1965, p. 9. ['A conservative view of education', 29 April 1965, p. 10]

'Old year letter', review of *New Year Letter*, by W. H. Auden, 21 May 1965, p. 9.

'Articles as books and books as articles', review of *A Sad Heart at the Supermarket*, by Randall Jarrell; *Doings and Undoings*, by Norman Podhoretz, 11 June 1965, p. 8.

'A liberal critic', review of *A Vision of Reality*, by Frederick Grubb, 2 July 1965, p. 7.

'Revolt and conformity', review of *The Theatre of Revolt*, by Robert Brustein, 9 July 1965, p. 7.

'Ideas in politics', review of *The Pursuit of Certainty*, by Shirley Robin, 24 September 1965.

'Cauldwell', review of *The Concept of Freedom*, by Christopher Cauldwell; *Poems*, by Christopher Cauldwell, 12 November 1965, p. 9. ['A young man's papers', 18 November 1965, p. 11]

'The world we have changed', review of *The World We Have Lost*, by Peter Laslett, 19 November 1965, p. 8. [25 November 1965, p. 10]

'A critic in action', review of *Writers and Politics*, by Conor Cruise O'Brien, 26 November 1965, p. 13. [2 December 1965, p. 11]

'A laurel for Hardy', review of *Thomas Hardy: The Will And The Way*, by Roy Morrell; *Hardy of Wessex*, by Carl J. Weber; *The Dynasts*, by Thomas Hardy, 10 December 1965, p. 6. ['Learning about Hardy', 16 December 1965, p. 10]

'Beyond liberalism', review of *Beyond Culture*, by Lionel Trilling, 15 April 1966, p. 8. [21 April 1966, p. 10]

'Chronicles', review of *The Beginners*, by Dan Jacobsen, 27 May 1966, p. 7. [9 June 1966, p. 11]

'Tolstoy in England', review of *Tolstoy and the Novel*, by John Bayley, 21 October 1966, p. 7.

'Any old myths?', review of *The Primal Curse: the myth of Cain and Abel in the theatre*, by Honor Matthews, 13 January 1967, p. 7.

'Coleridge today', review of *Coleridge: The Work and the Relevance*, by William Walsh, 24 February 1967, p. 7.

'William Morris', review of *The Work of William Morris*, by Paul Thompson, 3 March 1967, p. 7.

'Fenland people', review of *Fenland Chronicle*, by Sybil Marshall, 31 March 1967, p. 9.

'Novels and ideas', review of *Sartre: Romantic Rationalist*, by Iris Murdoch, 12 May 1967, p. 8. ['Novels, politics and ideas', 18 May 1967, p. 11]

'Hardy in public', *Thomas Hardy's Personal Writings*, edited by Harold Orel, 19 May 1967, p. 7. [25 May 1967, p. 10]

'Father knew George Orwell', review of *The Crystal Spirit: A Study of George Orwell*, by George Woodcock, 26 May 1967, p. 7. [1 June 1967, p. 10]

'Radical landmarks', review of *The Autobiography of Samuel Bamford, Vol. 1, Early Days; Vol. 2, Passages in the Life of a Radical*, ed. W. H. Chaloner; *The Autobiography of a Working Man*, by Alexander Somerville with a preface by Brian Behan, 7 July 1967, p. 5.

'Never trust the critic', review of *'Anna Karenina' and Other Essays*, by F. R. Leavis, 1 December 1967, p. 9. ['The critic and the tale', 7 December 1967, p. 11]

'Another Pheonix', review of *Pheonix II*: Uncollected, unpublished and other prose works by D. H. Lawrence, ed. Warren Roberts and Harry T. Moore, 19 January 1968, p. 7. ['From the Lawrence ashes', 25 January 1968]

'Talking to intellectuals', review of *Intellectuals Today: Problems in a Changing*

Society, by T. R. Fyvel, 1 March 1968, p. 7. [7 March 1968, p. 10]

'The left in the thirties', review of *The Left Review*, October 1934 – May 1938, reprinted in eight volumes in the series English Little Magazines, 22 March 1968, p. 9.

'A choice of worlds', review of *The Ordinary Universe: Soundings in Modern Literature*, by Dennis Donoghue, 5 July 1968, p. 7. ['The man who bites the coins', 11 July 1968, p. 11]

'How we see suffering', review of *Cancer Ward*, by Alexander Solzhenitsyn, 20 September 1968, p. 9. ['Complexities of pain and pity', 26 September 1968, p. 15]

'Blair to Orwell', review of *Collected Essays, Journalism and Letters of George Orwell*, 4 vols, by George Orwell, 4 October 1968, p. 6. ['From Blair to Orwell', 10 October 1968, p. 14]

'Work on the human voice', review of *The First Circle*, by Alexander Solzhenitsyn, 15 November 1968, p. 6. ['Solzhenitsyn's courage', 21 November 1968, p. 14]

'The need for Sartre', review of *The Philosophy of Jean-Paul Sartre*, ed. and introduced by Robert Denoon Cumming, 29 November 1968, p. 11.

'Air or nothing', review of *Experiment in Autobiography*, by H. G. Wells, 24 January 1969, p. 7. ['A case of air or nothing', 30 January 1969, p. 14]

'A report on suffering', review of *Cancer Ward, Part Two*, by Alexander Solzhenitsyn, 9 March 1969, p. 9. [20 March 1969, p. 14]

'Spender on students', review of *The Year of the Young Rebels*, by Stephen Spender, 17 April 1969, p. 9. ['Mr. Spender and the students', 24 April 1969, p. 14]

'For and against Mill', review of *Mill: A Collection of Critical Essays*, ed. J. B. Schneewind, 12 June 1969, p. 9. ['Our liberal friend', 19 June 1969, p. 15]

'On structures', review of *Conversations with Claude Levi-Strauss*, by G. Charbonnier, tr. by J. Weightman and D. Weightman, 26 June 1969, p. 9.

'Getting the inside story', review of *The Right to Know: The Rise of the World Press*, by Francis Williams, 3 July 1969, p. 9. ['Getting outside the inside story', 10 July 1969, p. 14.]

'Black and White', review of *Murderous Angels*, by Conor Cruise O'Brien, 10 July, p. 7. [17 July 1969, p. 18]

'Coleridge as The Friend', review of *The Friend*, by S. T. Coleridge, edited by Barbara E. Rooke, 7 August 1969, p. 5. [14 August 1969, p. 18]

'Romantic revival', review of *Romanticism*, edited by John B. Halstad, 21 August 1969, p. 7. [28 August 1969, p. 18.]

'Provocations', review of *Shaw – 'The Chucker-Out'*, by Allan Chappelow, 18 September 1969, p. 9. ['No ordinary playwright', 17 September 1969, p. 19.

'In the city of apples', review of *The Keeper of Antiquities*, by Yury Dombrovsky, tr. Michael Glenny, 23 October 1969, p. 9. ['City of apples', 1 November 1969, p. 18.]

'Changing the terms of reason', review of *American power and the new mandarins*, by Noam Chomsky, 30 October 1969, p. 8. ['The moments of decision', 8 November 1969, p. 16.]

'Dickens at 157', review of *The Uncollected Writings of Charles Dickens: Household Words, 1850–1859*, ed. Harry Stone; *The Letters of Charles Dickens, Volume Two, 1840–1841* ed. Madelaine House and Graham Storey; *Charles Dickens, 1812–1870, A Centenary Volume*, ed. E. W. F. Tomlin, 20 November 1969, p. 8.

'The ruling class', review of *The English Ruling Class*, ed. W. L. Guttsman, 27 November 1969, p. 10. ['The class apart', 6 December 1969, p. 18]

'A refusal to be resigned', review of *English Literature in Our Time and the University*, by F. R. Leavis, 18 December 1969, p. 7.

'Beyond protest', review of *The Limits of Protest*, by Peter Buchman, 8 January 1970.

'Masters and others', review of Fontana Modern masters series, ed. Frank Kermonde: *Camus*, by Conor Cruise O'Brien; *Fanon*, by David Caute; Levi-Strauss, by Edmond Leach; *Marcuse*, by Alister MacIntrye; *Guevara*, by Andrew Sinclair, 15 January 1970, p. 9. ['Mixed bag', 24 January 1970, p. 19]

'Practical critic', review of *Speaking to Each Other*, vol. 1, About Society; vol. 2, About Literature, by Richard Hoggart, 26 February 1970. ['Keeping up with Hoggart', 7 March 1970, p. 18]

'Young Brecht', review of *Bertolt Brecht: Collected Plays*, vol. 1, 1918–23, ed. John Willet and Ralph Manheim, 22 April 1970, p. 9. [9 May 1970, p. 19]

'Dickens celebrations', review of *The World of Charles Dickens*, by Angus Wilson; *Inimitable Dickens*, by A. E. Dyson; *Dicken's England*, by Michael and Mollie Hardwick, 28 May 1970, p. 15. ['The Dickens Celebrations', 6 June 1970, p. 18]

'Violence and confusion', review of *On Violence*, by Hannah Arendt, 25 June 1970, p. 14 ['Violence defined', 4 July 1970, p. 18]

'Report in repertory', review of *Brief Chronicles: Essays on Modern Theatre*, by Martin Esslin, 2 July 1970, p. 9. [11 July 1970, p. 18]

'Notes on a campaign'. Review of *Fears of Fragmentation*, by Arnold Wesker, 16 July 1970.

'Theory and practice', review of *A Theory of Communication*, by Philip Hobsbaum, 3 September 1970, p. 7.

'Myth and intimations', review of *The Rape of Tamar*, by Dan Jacobson, 1 October 1970, p. 9.

'Teletalk', review of *The New Priesthood: British Television Today*, by Joan Bakewell and Nicholas Garnham, 5 November 1970, p. 9.

'A power to fight', review of *The Stubborn Structure: Essays on Criticism and Society*, by Northrop Frye, 12 November 1970, p. 9.

'Varieties of protest', review of *Protest and Discontent*, edited by Bernard Crick and William A. Robson, 26 November 1970, p. 12.

'Open change', review of *Industrialization and Culture, 1830–1914*, ed. Christopher Harvie, Graham Martin and Aaron Scharf, 31 December 1970, p. 7.

'Working class politics', review of *Respectable Radical: George Howell and*

Victorian Working Class Politics, by F. M. Leventhal; *The Decline of Working Class Politics*, by Barry Hindess, 28 January 1971, p. 7. [6 February 1971, p. 16]

'Socialism active and passive', review of *History and Class Consciousness*, by Georg Lukács; Solzhenitsyn, by George Lukacs, 25 February 1971, p. 8.

'Good societies', review of *The Good Society. A book of readings*, ed. Anthony Arblaster and Stephen Lukes, 13 May 1971, p. 9. [22 May 1971, p. 18]

'Who speaks for Wales', review of *The Welsh Extremist: A Culture in Crisis*, by Ned Thomas, 3 June 1971.

'Labour and/or socialism', review of *The Crisis of British Socialism*, by Ken Coates, 1 July 1971, p. 9. ['The shame of the sixties', 10 July 1971, p. 18]

'Reading Carlyle', *Thomas Carlyle: Selected Writings*, ed. Alan Shelston; *Thomas Carlyle: Critical heritage*, ed. Jules Paul Seigel; *The Carlyles*, by John Stewart Collis, 18 November 1971, p. 11. [27 November 1971, p. 25]

'Radical categories', review of *Radical Man*, by Charles Hampden-Turner, 9 December 1971, p. 8. [27 January 1972]

'The novel and the people', *Working-Class Stories of the 1890s*, ed. P. J. Keating; *The Working-Classes in Victorian Fiction*, by P. J. Keating, 30 December 1971, p. 13. [8 January 1972]

'General studies?', review of *The Twentieth Century Mind: Vol. 1: 1900–1918*, ed. C. B. Cox and A. E. Dyson, 20 January 1972, p. 11.

'Beyond social abstractions', review of *Beyond Freedom and Dignity*, by B. F. Skinner, 9 March 1972, p. 14.

'Open-circuit television', review of *Television and the People: a program for democratic participation*, by Brian Groombridge, 27 April 1972, p. 14. [6 May 1972, p. 22]

'Suspecting the left', review of *The Suspecting Glance*, by Conor Cruise O'Brien, 8 June 1972, p. 16. ['Illiberal reactions', 17 June 1972, p. 23]

'Creative quarrelling?', review of *Nor Shall My Sword: Discourses on pluralism, compassion, and social hope*, by F. R. Leavis, 13 July 1972, p. 14. [29 July 1972, p. 22]

'Russia betrayed', review of *August 1914*, by Alexander Solzhenitsyn, tr. Michael Glenny, 21 September 1972, p. 14. [30 September 1972, p. 22]

'Stand up for what?', review of *The Obscenity Report*, introduced by John Trevelyn, preface by Maurice Girodias; *Pornography: The Longford Report*; *The Case against Pornography*, ed. David Holbrook, 28 September 1972, p. 16. [7 October 1972, p. 29]

'A radical miscellany', review of *Radical Perspectives in the Arts*, ed. Lee Baxindall, 26 April 1973, p. 26. ['The Marx Arts', 5 May 1973, p. 26]

'No wealth but life', review of *Interpretations and Forecasts, 1922–1972*, by Lewis Mumford, 23 August 1973, p. 9. ['The other Mumford', 1 September 1973, p. 23]

'A city and its writers', review of *Charles Baudelaire: A Lyric Poet in the Era of High Capitalism*, by Walter Benjamin, tr. Harry Zohn, 30 August 1973, p. 12. ['Baudelaire's Paris', 8 September 1973, p. 22]

'Against monopoly', review of *Tools for Conviviality*, by Ivan D. Illich, 27 September 1973, p. 11.

'Systems of error', review of *For Reasons of State*, by Noam Chomsky; *The Backroom Boys*, by Noam Chomsky; *Problems of Knowledge and Freedom*, by Noam Chomsky, 1 November 1973, p. 11.

'Radical Blake', review of *The Notebook of William Blake: A photographic and typographic facsimile*, ed. David V. Erdman; *The 'Heaven' and 'Hell' of William Blake*, by G. R. Sabri-Tabrizi, 29 November 1973, p. 15.

'Developing what?', review of *Education For Liberation*, by Adam Curle, 27 December 1973, p. 7. [12 January 1974, p. 24]

'The Frankfurt School', review of *The Dialectical Imagination*, by Martin Jay; *Aspects of Sociology*, by Frankfurt Institute for Social Research, with a preface by Max Horkheimer and Theodor Adorno; *Negative Dialectics*, by Theodor Adorno, tr. E. B. Ashton; *The Jargon of Authenticity*, by Theodor Adorno, tr. Knut Tarnowski and Frederick Will, 14 February 1974, p. 14. [26 January 1974, p. 23]

'Knots of socialism', review of *The Socialist Register 1973*, ed. Ralph Miliband and John Saville, 14 February 1974, p. 14. [23 February 1974, p. 24]

'Who are the intellectuals?', review of *Between Existentialism and Marxism*, by Jean-Paul Sartre; *Sartre*, by Hazel E. Barnes; *Camus and Sartre*, by Germaine Bree, 25 April 1974, p. 17.

'Working lives', review of *Useful Toil: Autobiographies of Working People from the 1820s to the 1920s*, ed. John Burnett, 13 June 1974, p. 9.

'Shelley plain', review of *Shelley: The Pursuit*, by Richard Holmes; *Shelley*, selected by Kathleen Raine, 25 July 1974, p. 9. [3 August 1974, p. 21]

'In the great tradition', review of *The Great Web: the form of Hardy's major fiction*, by Ian Gregor; *Thomas Hardy and History*, by R. J. White, 8 August 1974, p. 9. [17 August 1974, p. 22]

'Vindication of a radical', review of *The Life and Death of Mary Wollstonecraft*, by Claire Tomalin, 5 September 1974, p. 14. [14 September 1974, p. 22]

'When myth meets myth', review of *The Eating of the Gods: An Interpretation of Greek tragedy*, by Jan Kott, 10 October 1974, p. 16 [19 October 1974, p. 20]

'Is there anything wrong?', review of *The Socialist Idea: A Reappraisal*, ed. Leszek Kolakowski and Stuart Hampshire, 28 November 1974, p. 11. ['Defining socialism', 7 December 1974, p. 18]

'What the papers don't say', review of *Newspaper Money: Fleet Street and the search for the Affluent Reader*, by Fred Hirsch and David Gordon; *Paper Voices: The Popular Press and Social Change*, by A. C. H. Smith, with Elizabeth Immirzi and Trevor Blackwell, 22 May 1975, p. 14. [31 May 1975, p. 17]

'A little more on Hardy', review of *Desperate Remedies; A Pair of Blue Eyes; The Hand of Ethelberts; A Laodicean; Two on a Tower; The Well-Beloved* (New Wessex Edition), by Thomas Hardy; *Thomas Hardy: The Forms of Tragedy*, by Dale Kramer; *Thomas Hardy: An Illustrated Biography*, by Timothy O'Sullivan; *The Genius of Thomas Hardy*, ed. Margaret Drabble, 5 February 1976, p. 7. [15 February 1976, p. 21]

'Only yesterday', review of *The Left in Britain, 1956–1968*, by David Widgery, 12 February 1976, p. 12. ['Left with nothing to celebrate', 22 February 1976, p. 21]

'The anger of exile', review of *Lenin in Zurich*, by Alexander Solzhenitsyn, tr. H. T. Williams, 22 April 1976, p. 9. [9 May 1976, p. 22]

'Meanings of dialectic', review of *Critique of Dialectical Reason*, by Jean-Paul Sartre, tr. Alan Sheridan, 20 January 1977, p. 14.

'All power to the poem', review of *The Spiral Ascent, a trilogy*, by Edward Upward, 28 July 1977, p. 9. ['Power to the poem', 7 August 1977, p. 22]

'A radical perspective', review of *Milton and the English Revolution*, by Christopher Hill, 6 October 1977, p. 9. [16 October 1977, p. 21]

'Politics and letters', review of *Edmund Wilson: Letters on Literature and Politics, 1912–1972*, ed. Elena Wilson, 17 November 1977, p. 10. [1 January 1978, p. 22]

'Enduring ghost', review of *Ibsen: A Dissenting View*, by Ronald Gray, 8 December 1977, p. 10.

'The Englishness of Chaucer', review of *The Life and Times of Chaucer*, by John Gardner, 5 January 1978, p. 7. [15 January 1978, p. 22]

'Rural yet shrewd', review of *The Older Hardy*, by Robert Gittings; *An Essay on Hardy*, by John Bayley, 9 March 1978, p. 11. [19 March 1978, p. 22]

'Explaining the word', review of *Aesthetics and Politics*, ed. New Left Books, 23 March 1978, p. 11.

'The link in Tolstoy', review of *Tolstoy's Letters*, ed. in two volumes by R. F. Christian, 20 April 1978, p. 9. [30 April 1978, p. 22]

'Most generally known', review of *Samuel Johnson*, by W. Jackson Bate, 18 May 1978, p. 10. ['A life of Johnson', 28 May 1978, p. 22]

'The black domain', review of *The Merthyr Rising*, by Gwyn A. Williams, 8 June 1978. ['Black domain', 18 June 1978, p. 22]

'The yapping pack', review of *The Policics of Information*, by Anthony Smith, 3 August 1978, p. 7.

'A call to struggle', review of *The Moment of Scrutiny*, by Francis Mulhern, 17 May 1979, p. 9.

'Dreams and sea', review of *Conrad in the Nineteenth Century*, by Ian Watt, 29 May 1979, p. 16.

'The book of Governors', review of *Governing the BBC*, by Asa Briggs, 29 November 1979, p. 10. [23 December 1979, p. 14]

'Lawrence in the '80s', review of *D. H. Lawrence Country*, by Roy Spencer; *The Life of D. H. Lawrence*, by Keith Sagar, 28 February 1980, p. 7. [9 March 1980, p. 21]

'The Greeks in England', review of *The Victorians and Ancient Greece*, by Richard Jenkyns, 7 August 1980, p. 9. [24 August 1980, p. 22]

'Life on the other side of the tracks', review of *The Railway Workers, 1840–1970*, by Frank McKenna, 16 October 1980, p. 9. [26 October 1980, p. 21]

'The little green book', review of *Edward Carpenter 1844–1929*, by Chushichi Tsuzuki, 20 November 1980, p. 18.

'Straddling the chasm', review of *Mediations: Essays on Brecht, Beckett, and the Media*, by Martin Esslin, 29 January 1981, p. 7.

'1956 and all that', review of *In Anger: Culture in the Cold War, 1945–60*, by Robert Hewison, 2 April 1981, p. 11.

'A future for Europe?', review of *The Dynamics of European Nuclear Disarmament*, by Alva Mydral et al., 13 August 1981, p. 12.

'Writers' reading in 1981', 10 December 1981, p. 14. Eleven *Guardian* writers and readers recall the books that have meant the most to them during the year. [27 December 1981, p. 22]

'Close friends', review of *A Memoir of D. H. Lawrence (The Betrayal)*, by G. H. Neville, 14 January 1982, p. 16. [24 January 1982]

'The reasonable Englishman', review of *An English Temper*, by Richard Hoggart, 8 April 1982, p. 16.

'Danger: intellectuals!', review of *The Transformation of Intellectual Life in Victorian England*, by T. W. Heyck; *Fabianism and Culture*, by Ian Britain, 1 July 1982, p. 8. [11 July 1982, p. 21]

'Putting the Welsh in their place', review of *The Welsh in Their History*, by Gwyn A. Williams, 9 September 1982, p. 8. [19 September 1982, p. 21]

'Movement of faith', review of *The Critic as Anti-Philosopher*, by F. R. Leavis, 11 November 1982, p. 10. [21 November 1982, p. 22]

'Generations out of joint', review of *A Margin of Hope*, by Irving Howe, 10 March 1983, p. 10. [20 March 1983, p. 22]

'The new morality', review of *Eve and the New Jerusalem*, by Barbara Taylor, 17 March 1983, p. 16.

'Ours and not ours,' review of *The World, the Text and the Critic*, by Edward Said, 8 March 1984, p. 10.

'The politics of poverty', review of *The Idea of Mass Poverty: England in the Early Industrial Age*, by Gertrude Himmelfarb, 5 April 1984, p. 18.

'The resonance of Antigone', review of *Antigone*, by George Steiner, 20 July 1984, p. 14.

'Feeling the draft', review of *Mr. Noon*, by D. H. Lawrence, ed. Lindeth Vasey, 13 September 1984, p. 20. [23 September 1984, p. 21]

'Two faces of liberalism', review of *The Rise and Decline of Western Liberalism*, by Anthony Arblaster; *An End to Allegiance*, by Geoffrey Sampson, 11 October 1984, p. 20. [21 October 1984, p. 21]

'Had your letter, yesterday', review of *The Letters of D. H. Lawrence*, Vol. 3, 1916–21, ed. James T. Boulton and Andrew Robertson, 29 November 1984, p. 13.

'The shadow of the dragon', review of *When was Wales?*, by Gwyn A. Williams; *Wales: A History*, by Winford Vaughan-Thomas, 24 January 1985, p. 20.

'The literary civil war', review of *Writing and Revolution in 17th Century England*, vol. 1 of the collected essays of Christopher Hill, 11 April 1985, p. 21.

'Lawrence's century', review of *D. H. Lawrence and Tradition*, ed. Jeffrey Meyers; *D. H. Lawrence: Life into Art*, by Keith Sager; *Flame into Being: the Life and Work of D. H. Lawrence*, by Anthony Burgess, 19 September 1985, p. 10.

'The better half of Lev Tolstoy', Review of *The Diaries of Sofia Tolstaya*, tr. Cathy Porter; *Tolstoy's Diaries*, tr. R. F. Christian, 28 November 1985, p. 11.

'Clare's voices' review of *The Letters of John Clare*, ed. Mark Storey, 13 February 1986, p. 21.

'A Welsh companion', review of *The Oxford Companion to the Literature of Wales*, ed. Meic Stephens, 27 February 1986, p. 23.

'Elites and loyalties', review of *The Red and the Blue: Intelligence Treason, and the Universities*, by Andrew Sinclair, 19 June 1986, p. 21. [29 July 1986, p. 21]

'How Bloomsbury contrived to borrow time', review of *Victorian Bloomsbury: the early literary history of the Bloomsbury Group*, vol. 1, by S. P. Rosenbaum, 20 February 1987, p. 13.

'The word and the dictator', review of *I The Supreme*, by Augusto Roa Bastos, 13 March 1987, p. 13.

'A novel out of this world', review of *Women in Love*, by D. H. Lawrence, ed. David Farmer; *The Letters of D. H. Lawrence*, vol. IV, 1921–24, ed. Warren Roberts, James T. Boulton and Elizabeth Mansfield, 22 May 1987, p. 13.

'Doing despair', review of *Vladimir's Carrot: Modern Dance and the modern imagination*, by John Peter; *The Field of Drama*, by Martin Esslin, 17 July 1987, p. 13.

8 *Articles in* Tribune

'Man on the run from himself', 27 March 1959, p. 13. See letter from Frederick Harper, 27 April 1959, p. 4.

'Investigator, first investigate yourself!', review of *Britain Revisited*, by Tom Harrison, 21 April 1961, pp. 6–7.

'Sociology's range', review of *Ideology and Society*, by Donald Macrea, 4 August 1961, p. 9.

'Culture and Labour', letter, 14 August 1964, p. 2.

'R. H. Tawney', Voices of Socialism series, 1 January 1965, p. 13. See letter from David Elstein, 15 January 1965, p. 2.

'Tawney's Christianity', letter, 22 January 1965, p. 2.

'We are starting to use our own voices!', 5 March 1965, pp. 1, 6.

'Communications: Just what is Labour's policy for radio?', 18 February 1966, p. 8. See letter from J. R. Grierson, 4 March 1966, p. 11.

'Policy for radio', letter, 11 March 1966, p. 11.

'Oxbridge *Their* Oxbridge', 3 June 1966, p. 6. Invited comment with Stephen Lukes and John Saville on the Franks Report on British Universities.

'Expulsion of Ken Coates', letter with others, 23 September 1966, p. 8.

'The future of broadcasting: what happens after the "pirates" walk the plank?', 7 October 1966, p. 9.

' "Bemused liberalism" from Hugh Jenkins', 21 October 1966, p. 6. See letters from Ronan O'Rahilly and Brian Blain, 14 October 1966.

'Communications put in order', letter, 2 December 1966, p. 8.

'May Day Manifesto 1967', 28 April 1967, p. 5. See letter from John Sheridan, 26 May 1967, p. 9.

'May Day Manifesto', letter, 2 June 1967, p. 8.

'Commercial radio: the thin edge of the wedge?', 2 August 1968, pp. 6–7.

'A National Convention of the Left', 28 March 1969, p. 5.

9 Articles on politics in Britain in The Nation

'The culture of politics', vol. 188, 3 January 1959, pp. 10–12.
'The British elections', vol. 199, 28 September 1964, pp. 154–7.
'Letter from Britain' vol. 203, 4 July 1966, pp. 18–19. See correction, p. 90.
'Significance of economic–political crisis; illusions lost', vol. 203, 5 September 1966, pp. 185–7.
'Affluence after anger: on the development of the British "cultural generation" of the 1950's', vol. 203, 19 December 1966, pp. 676–7.
'Britain's press crisis; trend to monopoly', vol. 204, 10 April 1967, pp. 466–7.
'The Catholic crisis: tension between hierarchy and reformers', vol. 205, 17 July 1967, pp. 51–2.
'Socialism's crisis of theory', vol. 206, 26 February 1968, pp. 274–6.
'Great Britain: saying "no" to the Labour Party', vol. 210, 15 June 1970, pp. 710–12.
'Downhill to Dutschke' vol. 212, 15 February 1971, pp. 210–12.
'The Liberals move up fast; Britain's third party', vol. 217, 29 October 1973, pp. 432–4.
'Crisis in Britain: reality behind the appearance', vol. 218, 19 January 1974, pp. 73–4.
'British elections: muddling through to hope', vol. 218, 23 March 1974, pp. 359–61.
'The size of the crisis: Britain after the election', vol. 219, 2 November 1974, pp. 428–30.
'The impossible society: Britain needs a New Left', vol. 220, 28 June 1975, pp. 780–2.
'Structural unemployment: Britains' small deal', vol. 222, 20 March 1976, pp. 330–2.

See section 6 for book review in The Nation, 1959.

10 Television column in The Listener

All of these columns are reprinted in *Raymond Williams on Television*, ed. A. O'Connor, Toronto, Between The Lines, 1988; London and New York, Routledge, 1989.
'As we see others', 1 August 1968, pp. 154–5.
'Private worlds', 12 September 1968, pp. 346–8.
'Shoot the Prime Minister', 10 October 1968, p. 483.
'The miner and the city', 7 November 1968, p. 623.
'A moral rejection', 5 December 1968, pp. 771–2.
'A new way of seeing', 2 January 1969, pp. 27–8.
'Persuasion', 30 January 1969, pp. 155.
'To the last word: on *The Possessed*', 20 February 1969, pp. 248–9.
'Personal relief time', 20 March 1969, p. 399.
'A noble past', 17 April 1969, p. 543.
'Combined operations', 15 May 1969, p. 697. Reprinted in *Communications*, 3rd edn.

'Based on reality', 12 June 1969, pp. 838–9.
'Watching from elsewhere', 10 July 1969, pp. 59–60.
'Crimes and crimes', 21 August 1969, p. 235. Reprinted in *A Listener Anthology*, ed. K. Miller, London, BBC, 1970.
'Death wish in Venice', 4 September 1969, pp. 322–3.
'Science, art and human interest', 2 October 1969, pp. 462–3.
'Pitmen and pilgrims', 30 October 1969, p. 611.
'Most doctors recommend', 27 November 1969, pp. 770–1.
'A bit of a laugh, a bit of glamour', 25 December 1969, p. 903.
'Brave Old World', 22 January 1970, pp. 126–7.
'The green language', 19 February 1970, pp. 259–60.
'The best things in life aren't free', 19 March 1970, pp. 386–7.
'There's always the sport', 16 April 1970, pp. 522–3.
'Going places', 7 May 1970, pp. 626–7.
'Against adjustment', 4 June 1970, pp. 770–1.
'Back to the world', 2 July 1970, p. 27.
'ITV's domestic romance', 30 July 1970, pp. 159–60. Reprinted in Communications, 3rd edn.
'Breaking out', 27 August 1970, pp. 286–7.
'Between us and chaos', 24 September 1970, pp. 432–3.
'The decadence game', 22 October 1970, pp. 557–8.
'A very late stage in bourgeois art', 12 November 1970, pp. 678–9.
'Galton and Simpson's *Steptoe and Son*', 17 December 1970, pp. 854–5.
'Being serious', 14 January 1971, pp. 60–1.
'Billy and Darkly', 11 February 1971, p. 188.
'Programmes and sequences', 11 March 1971, pp. 314–15. Reprinted in *Communications*, 3rd edn.
'Remembering the thirties', 8 April 1971, pp. 463–4.
'Open teaching', 6 May 1971, pp. 594–5.
'Terror', 3 June 1971, pp. 731–2.
'Cowboys and missionaries', 1 July 1971, p. 27.
'Careers and jobs', 29 July 1971, pp. 155–6.
'China-watching', 26 August 1971, p. 281.
'An English autumn', 23 September 1971, pp. 423–4.
'Judges and traitors', 21 October 1971, pp. 552.
'Sesame Street', 18 November 1971, pp. 700.
'Three documentaries', 16 December 1971, p. 850.
'Raymond Williams writes that free speech is being curtailed, and in ways that are not generally understood', 13 January 1972, pp. 60–1. See reply from Noel Annan, 3 February 1972, pp. 131–3.
'Culture', 10 February 1972, pp. 191.
'Old times and new', 16 March 1972, pp. 351–2.
'Hardy annuals', 6 April 1972, pp. 463.
'Where does Rozanov come in?', 4 May 1972, pp. 599–600.
'The golden lotus', 1 June 1972, pp. 739–40.
'Hassle', 27 July 1972, p. 124.

'Natural breaks', 24 August 1972, pp. 251–2. Reprinted in *Communications*, 3rd edn.
'Ad hominem', 14 September 1972, pp. 347–8.
'Versions of Webster', 19 October 1972, pp. 515.
'Intellectual superiority', 16 November 1972, pp. 684–5.
'Why the BBC is like Monty Python's Flying Circus?', 14 December 1972, pp. 839–40.
'The top of the laugh', 10 January 1974, pp. 58–9.
'Isaac's urges', 31 January 1974, p. 155.

Williams's other contributions to *The Listener* are listed in section 6.
For a column on American television see 'Views', *The Listener* (1973).

11 Book reviews in New Society

'Mill, Arnold and the Zeitgeist', review of *Matthew Arnold and John Stewart Mill*, by Edward Alexander, 10 June 1965, pp. 31–2.
'The achievement of Balzac', review of *Prometheus*, by Andre Maurois. 4 November 1965, pp. 28–9.
'The pain of industrial relations', review of *It Was Not in the News*, by Max Cohen, 2 December 1965, pp. 33–4.
'A critic in business', review of *The Collected Works of Walter Bagehot*, vols 1 and 2, ed. Norman St John-Stevas, 6 January 1966, pp. 23–4.
'Ordinary letters', review of *The letters of Mrs. Gaskell*, ed. J. A. V. Chapple and Arthur Pollard, 1 December 1966, pp. 843–4.
'Shifting barriers', review of *Class*, ed. Richard Mabey, 2 March 1967, pp. 324–5.
'A Northampton family', review of *The Underprivileged*, by Jeremy Seabrook, 27 April 1967, p. 621.
'Cambridge reforms', review of *The Revolution of the Dons: Cambridge and Society in Victorian England*, by Sheldon Rothblatt, 8 February 1968, p. 204.
'Against academic orthodoxy', review of *The Dissenting Academy*, ed. Theodore Roszak, 4 April 1968, p. 507.
'Up north', review of *Working Class Community*, by Brian Jackson, 25 April 1968, pp. 611–12.
'Secondary stuff', review of *The Victorian Debate*, by Raymond Chapmen, 25 July 1968, pp. 134–5.
'Man of letters', review of *The Rise and Fall of the Man of Letters*, by John Gross, 22 May 1969, p. 809.
'Beyond words', review of *The Sociology of Literature*, by Diana T. Laurenson and Alan Swingswood, 24 August 1972, p. 404.
'Television and the mandarins', on the Annan Report, *The Future of Broadcasting*, 31 March 1977, pp. 651–2. See letters 14 April 1977, p. 79; 21 April 1977, p. 131.
'French connection', review of *Reproduction in Education, Society and Culture*, by

Pierre Bourdieu and Jean-Claude Passeron; *Society, State and Schooling*, ed. Michael F. D. Young and Geoff Whitty, 5 May 1977, pp. 239–40.

'Class of the conscious', review of *Cultural Creation in Modern Society*, by Lucien Goldmann; *Lukács and Heidegger: towards a new philosophy*, by Lucien Goldmann, 5 January 1978, pp. 26–7.

'A book at bedtime', review of *Fiction and the Fiction Industry*, by J. A. Sutherland, 4 May 1978, pp. 264–5.

' "The god that failed" all over again', review of *Main Currents of Marxism*, 3 vols., by Leszek Kolakowski, 23 November 1978, pp. 469–70. See correction 30 November 1978, pp. 533.

'What is anti-captialism?', review of *Georg Lukács – From Romanticism to Bolshevism*, by Michael Lowy, 24 January 1980, pp. 189–90.

'The popularity of melodrama', review of *Performance and Politics in Popular Drama*, ed. David Bradby, Louis James and Bernard Sharratt, 24 April 1980, pp. 170–1.

'Realism again', review of *Essays on Realism*, by Georg Lukács, 20 November 1980, pp. 381–2.

'Radical drama', review of *Stages in the Revolution: political theatre in Britain since 1968*, by Catherine Itzin, 27 November 1980, pp. 432–3.

'The rise of the careerist intelligentsia', review of *Teachers, Writers, Celebrities: the Intellectuals of Modern France*, by Regis Debray, tr. David Macey, 21 May 1981, pp. 322–3.

'The man who shifted against the tide', review of *William Cobbett: the poor man's friend*, by George Spater, 29 April 1982.

'The need to get beyond the past', review of *Destiny Obscure: autobiographies of childhood, education and family from the 1820s to the 1920s*, by John Burnett; *Working Class Childhood: an oral history*, by Jeremy Seabrook, 7 October 1982, pp. 37–8.

'The estranging language of post-modernism', review of *The Naked Artist*, by Peter Fuller; *Aesthetics after Modernism*, by Peter Fuller, 16 June 1983, pp. 439–40.

'Double Default', review of *Dockers and Detectives*, by Ken Worpole, 5 January 1984, pp. 17–18.

'Goodbye to Sartre', review of *Adieux: a farewell to Sartre*, by Simone de Beauvoir, tr. Patrick O'Brien, 21 June 1984, pp. 470–1.

'The Collier's Letter', review of *The Literature of Labour: 200 years of working class writing*, by H. Gustav Klaus, 28 February 1985, pp. 335–6.

'Signs of the time', review of *The Grain of the Voice*, by Roland Barthes, tr. Linda Coverdale, 11 October 1985, p. 65.

'West of Offa's Dyke', review of *Wales: The Imagined Nation*, ed. Tony Curtis, 4 July 1986,

12 Published interviews

'Two interviews with Raymond Williams', *Red Shift* [Cambridge] (1977), no. 2, pp. 12–17; no. 3, pp. 13–15.

'Making It Active', an interview with Ken Worpole, *The English Magazine*, no. 1 (Spring 1979), pp. 4–7.

'Raymond Williams: building a socialist culture', interview with Dave Taylor, *The Leveller*, 24 (March 1979), pp. 25–7.

'Television and Teaching: An Interview with Raymond Williams', *Screen Education*, no. 31 (Summer 1979), pp. 5–14. Reprinted in *Raymond Williams on Television*.

'The Labour Party and Beyond', an interview with Raymond Williams, by Peter Anderson and Martin Steckelmacher, *Revolutionary Socialism*, no. 5 (Summer 1980), pp. 3–7.

'This Sadder Recognition', Sue Aspinal talks to Raymond Williams about *So That You Can Live*, *Screen*, vol. 23, nos 3–4 (September/ October 1982), pp. 144–52.

'Nationalisms and Popular Socialism: Phil Cooke talks to Raymond Williams', *Radical Wales*, no. 2 (Spring 1984), pp. 7–8.

'An Interview with Raymond Williams', Stephen Heath and Gillian Skirrow, in *Studies in Entertainment: Critical Approaches to Mass Culture*, ed. Tania Modleski, Bloomington and Indiana, Indiana University Press, 1986, pp. 3–17.

'The practice of possibility', an interview with Terry Eagleton, *New Statesman*, 7 August 1987, pp. 19–21.

'People of the Black Mountains', John Barnie interviews Raymond Williams, *Planet*, 65 (October/November 1987), pp. 3–13.

13 Letters to newspapers

On railway accidents, letter to *The Times*, 28 July 1955.
On nationalized industries, letter to *The Times*, 30 November 1956.
On subsistence, letter to *The Times*, 5 July 1957.
On nuclear policy, letter to *The Times*, 10 September 1964.
On Vietnam, letter with others to *The Times*, 23 July 1966.
On National Extension College, letter with others to *The Times*, 28 December 1966.
On Pakistan guerrillas, letter to *The Times*, 3 November 1971.
On the future of the UN, letter with others from the Bertrand Russell Peace Foundation in *Manchester Guardian Weekly*, 11 January 1987, p. 2.

14 Williams as editor

Journals

Cambridge University Journal Student newspaper. Williams was editor from April to June 1940.

Outlook Published in Cambridge. Williams was an editor for 1941. Similar in format to *Penguin New Writing*.

Twentyone Weekly newspaper of the 21st Anti-Tank Regiment, Royal Artillary. Printed at Pinneberg, Germany. Williams was editor, April–October 1945.

The Critic
Politics & Letters
The Critical Quarterly
New Left Review
The Week   Williams described as a 'sponsor'.
The Spokesman
Constituency bulletin for Cambridgeshire Labour Party. With Joy Williams.
   Some time between 1961 and 1966.
Literature and History   Editorial advisor.
Media, Culture and Society   Editorial board.

Books in series

The New Thinkers Library. Published in London by C. A. Watts & Co.
   Williams was General Editor 1962–70.
Communications and Culture series. Macmillan. Editorial board.
Marxist Introductions. Oxford University Press.
English Literature in History series. General editor.
Communications series. Fontana.

Works about Raymond Williams

15   Select Bibliography on Williams

Amis, Kingsley, 'Martians Bearing Bursaries', *The Spectator*, 27 April 1962, pp.
   554–5. Review of *Communications*.
Barnett, Anthony, 'Raymond Williams and Marxism: A Rejoinder to Terry
   Eagleton', *New Left Review*, no. 99 (1976), pp. 47–64.
Barnett, Anthony, 'Towards a theory', *New Society*, 21 July 1977, pp. 145–6.
   Review of *Marxism and Literature*.
Bateson, F. W., *Manchester Guardian Weekly*, 22 February 1976. Review of
   Keywords.
Bayley, J., *New York Review of Books*, 8 October 1970, p. 8. Review of *The
   English Novel*.
Berman, Marshall, *New York Times Book Review*, 15 July 1973, pp. 1, 26–30.
   Review of *The Country and the City*.
Blackburn, Robin, 'Raymond Williams and the Politics of a New Left', *New
   Left Review* 168 (March/April 1988), pp. 12–22.
Briggs, Asa, 'Creative Definitions', *New Statesman*, vol. 61, 10 March 1961, pp.
   386–7.
Briggs, Asa, *Partisan Review*, vol. 45, no. 3 (1978). Review of *Television*.
Bryant, Anthony, 'The case of Raymond Williams', *The Insurgent Sociologist* 11
   (Spring 1982), pp. 89–97. Review of *Politics and Letters*.
Bryant, Bernard Anthony David, 'The New Left in Britain: the dialectic of
   rationality and participation', Ph.D. dissertation, London School of
   Economics, 1981. Chapter Nine, 'Raymond Williams and New Leftism'.
Burchfield, R.W., 'A Case of Mistaken Identity: Keywords', *Encounter* 46 (June
   1976), pp. 57–64. Review of *Keywords*.

Burgess, Anthony, 'A Very Tragic Business', *The Spectator*, 10 June 1966, p. 731. Review of *Modern Tragedy*.

Chanan, Michael, 'So that you can live (For Shirley)', *Framework* 18 (1982), pp 7–8.

Christgau, Robert, 'Living in a Material World: Raymond Williams' Long Revolution', *The Village Voice Literary Supplement*, no. 34, April 1985, pp. 1, 12–18.

Clifford, James, 'On Ethnographic Allegory', in *Writing Culture: The Poetics and Politics of Ethnography*, ed. James Clifford and George E. Marcus, Berkeley, University of California Press, 1986, pp. 113–15.

Connolly, Cyril, 'Precious Land', *Sunday Times*, 8 April 1973, p. 38. Review of *The Country and the City*.

Corrigan, Maureen, 'Raymond Williams: Only Connect', *Village Voice*, 29 May 1984, p. 47. Review of *Towards 2000*.

Corrigan, Philip, *Media, Culture and Society* 2 (1980), pp. 87–91. Review of *Politics and Letters*.

Corrigan, Philip, *border/lines* 1 [Toronto] (1984), pp. 38–9. Review of *Towards 2000*.

Cowling, Maurice, 'Mr. Raymond Williams', *The Cambridge Review*, 27 May 1961, pp. 546–51.

Davies, D. I., 'Pilgrim's Progress from Morris to Marx', *Canadian Forum*, August 1980, pp. 30–32. Review of *Politics and Letters*.

Davies, Ioan, *Stand* 5 (1961), pp. 61–4. Review of *The Long Revolution*.

Donoghue, Dennis, 'Examples', *London Review of Books*, 2–15 February 1984, pp. 20–22. Review of *Towards 2000*.

Eagleton, Terry, 'The Idea of a Common Culture', in *From Culture to Revolution*, ed. Terry Eagleton and Brian Wicker, London, 1968, pp. 35–57.

Eagleton, Terry, 'The English Novel', *The Spokesman*, nos 15/16 (August/September 1971).

Eagleton, Terry, 'Criticism and Politics: The Work of Raymond Williams', *New Left Review*, no. 95 (1976), pp. 3–23. Reprinted in his *Criticism and Ideology: A Study in Marxist Literary Theory*, London, New Left Books, 1976, pp. 21–43.

Eagleton, Terry, *The Function of Criticism: From The Spectator to Post-Structuralism*, London, Verso, 1984, pp. 108–15.

Eagleton, Terry, 'Stepping Out', *New Statesman*, 27 January 1984, pp. 21–2. Review of *Writing in Society*.

Eagleton, Terry, 'Resources for a Journey of Hope: The Significance of Raymond Williams', *New Left Review* 168 (March/April 1988), pp. 3–11.

Empson, William, 'Compacted Doctrines', *The New York Review of Books*, 27 October 1977, pp. 21–2. Review of *Keywords*.

Fairlie, Henry, *Encounter*, August 1962. Review of *Communications*.

Franco, Jean, 'Go with the flow: books on television', *Tabloid* 3 (Winter 1981), pp 35–41. Review of *Television*.

Friedman, Michael H., *Science and Society* 41 (1977), pp. 221–4. Review of *Keywords*.

Garnham, Nicholas, 'Raymond Williams, 1921–1988: A Cultural Analyst, A Distinctive Tradition', *Journal of Communication* 38 (1988), pp. 123–31.

Giddens, Anthony, 'Raymond Williams' long revolution', *Times Higher Education Supplement*, 14 December 1979, pp. 11–12. Reprinted in his *Profiles and Critiques in Social Theory*, Berkeley and Los Angeles, University of California, 1982, pp. 133–43.

Giddens, Anthony, 'The state of sociology', *Times Literary Supplement*, 27 February 1981, p. 215. Review of *Culture*.

Green, Michael, 'Raymond Williams and Cultural Studies', *Cultural Studies* 6 (1975), pp. 31–48.

Gregor, Ian, *Essays in Criticism* 9 (1959), pp. 425–30. Review of *Culture and Society*.

Gross, John, *New Statesman*, 4 May 1962. Review of *Communications*.

Grossberg, Lawrence, 'Strategies of Marxist Cultural Interpretation', *Critical Studies in Mass Communication* 1 (1984), pp. 400–2.

Grundy, Bill, 'State papers?', *The Spectator*, 26 April 1968, pp. 560–61. Review of *Communications*.

Hall, Stuart, 'Some Notes on the Long Revolution and the Example of the 1840's', *Unveröffentlicht* (1970).

Hall, Stuart, 'Cultural Studies: two paradigms', *Media, Culture and Society* 2 (1980), pp. 57–72.

Hall, Stuart, 'The Williams Interviews', *Screen Education*, no. 34 (1980), pp. 94–104. Review of *Politics and Letters*.

Hall, Stuart, 'Only Connect: the life of Raymond Williams', *New Statesman*, 5 February 1988, pp. 20–21.

Hampshire, Stuart, 'Unhappy Families', *New Statesman*, 29 July 1966, pp. 169–70. Review of *Modern Tragedy*.

Harding, D. W., 'The Single Culture', *The Spectator*, 10 October 1958, pp. 495–6. Review of *Culture and Society*.

Harrington, Michael, *Commonweal*, 4 December 1959, p. 294. Review of *Culture and Society*.

Hartley, Anthony, 'The Loaf and the Leaven', *Manchester Guardian*, 7 October 1958, p. 10. Review of *Culture and Society*.

Hartley, Anthony, 'Philistine to Philistine?', in *International Literary Annual 2*, ed. John Wain, London, John Calder, 1959, pp. 11–36.

Hartley, Anthony, 'The Intellectuals of England', *The Spectator*, 4 May 1962, pp. 577–81.

Heath, Stephen, 'Modern English Man', Presences series, *Times Higher Education Supplement*, 20 July 1984, p. 17.

Hewison, Robert, 'Collectively feeling', *Times Literary Supplement*, 27 February 1981, p. 239. Review of *Problems in Materialism and Culture*.

Hewison, Robert, *In Anger: British Culture in the Cold War 1945–60*, New York, Oxford University Press, 1981, pp. 160–200.

Hewison, Robert, *Too Much: Art and Society in the Sixties 1960–75*, London, Methuen, 1986, *passim*.

Higgins, John, 'Raymond Williams and the Problem of Ideology', in *Postmodernism and Politics*, ed. Jonathan Arac, Minneapolis, University of

Minnesota Press, 1986, pp. 112–22. Reprinted from *Boundary 2*, 11 (Fall/Winter 1982/3), pp. 145–54.

Hill, Christopher, *New Society*, 5 February 1976. Review of *Keywords*.

Hoggart, Richard, 'An Important Book', *Essays in Criticism* 9 (1959), pp. 171–9. Review of *Culture and Society*.

Hood, Stuart, *Guardian Weekly*, 8 June 1974, p. 21. Review of *Television*.

Hood, Stuart, 'In human contact', *Guardian Weekly*, 3 January 1982, p. 21. Review of *Contact*.

Hooker, Jeremy, 'A Dream of a Country: The Raymond Williams Triology', *Planet*, 49/50 (January 1980), pp. 53–61.

Howe, Irving, 'On Ideas of Culture', *The New Republic*, 2 February 1959, pp. 18–19; 9 February, pp. 23–4. Two-part review of *Culture and Society*.

Inglis, Fred, *Radical Earnestness: English Social Theory 1880–1980*, ch. 8, 'Culture and politics: Richard Hoggart, the *New Left Review* and Raymond Williams', Oxford, Martin Robertson, 1982.

Inglis, Fred, 'Innocent at home', *New Society*, 27 October 1983, pp. 158–60. Review of *Towards 2000*.

James, C. L. R., 'Marxism and the Intellectuals', in his *Spheres of Existence: Selected Writings*, Westport, Connecticut: Lawrence Hill and Co.; London: Allison and Busby, 1980, pp. 113–30. Originally written 1961.

Johnson, Richard, 'Three problematics: elements of a theory of Working-class culture', in *Working Class Culture: Studies in History and Theory*, ed. John Clarke et al., London, Hutchinson, 1979, pp. 201–37. For another version see his 'Histories of Culture/Theories of Ideology: Notes on an Impasse', in *Ideology and Cultural Production*, ed. Michele Barrett et al. London, Croom Helm, 1979.

Johnson, Richard, *Comment*, 15 September 1979. Review of *Politics and Letters*.

Kermode, Frank, review of *Culture and Society*, *Encounter*, 12 (January 1959), pp. 86–8.

Kermode, Frank, *Partisan Review*, vol. 29, no. 3 (1962). Review of *Border Country*.

Kermode, Frank, 'Tragedy and Revolution', *Encounter* 27 (August 1966), pp. 83–5. Review of *Modern Tragedy*.

Kettle, Arnold, 'Culture and Revolution: A Consideration of the Ideas of Raymond Williams and Others', *Marxism Today* 5 (1961), pp. 301–7.

Kettle, Arnold, *Red Letters* 6 (1977), pp. 71–3. Review of *Marxism and Literature*.

Kettle, Arnold, *Marxism Today* 23 (1979), pp. 28–9. Review of *Politics and Letters*.

Kettle, Arnold, 'Bernard Shaw and the New Spirit', in *Rebels and Their Causes*, ed. Maurice Cornford, Atlantic Highlands, N.J., Humanities Press, 1979, pp. 209–20.

Kiernan, V. G., 'Culture and Society', *New Reasoner* 9 (1959), pp. 74–83. Review of *Culture and Society*.

Klaus, Gustav H., 'Über Raymond Williams', in Raymond Williams, *Innovationen*, (1979), pp. 203–26.

Lange, Gerhard W., *Materialistische Kulturtheorie im Vergleich: Raymond*

Williams, Terry Eagleton und die deutsche Tradition, Munster, Lit Verlag, 1984.

Leavis, F. R., *Nor Shall My Sword*, London, Chatto and Windus, 1972, pp. 150–1.

Lerner, Laurence, 'Beyond Literature: Social Criticism versus Aesthetics', *Encounter* 41 (July 1973), pp. 62–5. Review of *The Country and the City*.

Liljegren, S. B., *Studia Neophilologica* 25 (1952–3), pp. 180–1. Review of *Drama From Ibsen to Eliot*.

Lockwood, Bernard, 'Four Contemporary British Working-Class Novelists: A thematic and critical approach to the fiction of Raymond Williams, John Braine, David Storey and Alan Sillitoe', Ph.D. dissertation, University of Wisconsin, 1966.

Luckett, Richard, 'A Marxist in town and country', *The Spectator*, 5 May 1973, pp. 554–5. Review of *The Country and the City*.

Macdonald, Dwight, 'Looking Backward', *Encounter* 16 (June 1961), pp. 79–84.

MacCabe, Colin, 'The end of literary criticism', *Guardian*, 26 January 1984, p. 12. Review of *Writing in Society*.

MacCabe, Colin, 'Class of '68,' in his *Theoretical Essays: Film, Linguistics, Literature*, Manchester, Manchester University Press, 1985, p. 20.

McGrath, John, 'The Theory and Practice of Political Theatre', *TQ (Theatre Quarterly)* 9 (1979), pp. 43–54.

McKeon, Michael, *Studies in Romanticism* 16 (Winter 1977), pp. 128–39. Review of *Keywords*.

Marcus, George E., 'Contemporary Problems of Ethnography in the Modern World System', in *Writing Culture: The Poetics and Politics of Ethnography*, ed. James Clifford and George E. Marcus, Berkeley, University of California Press, 1986, pp. 169–71.

Merrill, Michael, 'Raymond Williams and the Theory of English Marxism', *Radical History Review* 19 (1978–9), pp. 9–31.

Milner, Andrew, 'A Young Man's Death: Raymond Williams 1921–1988', *Thesis Eleven*, 20 (1988), pp. 106–18.

Morgan, Janet, 'Unquestioned questions', *Times Literary Supplement*, 4 November 1983, p. 1223. Review of *Towards 2000*.

Motterhead, Chris, *Screen Education* 14 (Spring 1975), pp. 35–8. Review of *Television*.

Mowat, C. L., 'The Education of Raymond Williams', *Critical Quarterly* 3 (1961), pp. 175–81. Review of *The Long Revolution* and *Border Country*.

Mulhern, Francis, 'Towards 2000, or News From You-know-where', *New Left Review*, no. 148 (November/December 1984), pp. 5–30. Review of *Towards 2000*.

Nairn, Tom, 'The Left Against Europe?', *New Left Review*, no. 75 (1972), pp. 106–8.

Nove, Alec, 'Struggling for the future', *Guardian*, 20 October 1983, p. 8. Review of *Towards 2000*.

O'Connor, Alan, 'Cultural Studies and Common Sense', *Canadian Journal of Political and Social Theory* 5 (1981), pp. 183–95.

O'Connor, Alan, 'Overlapping Worlds: The Circles of M. M. Bakhtin and Raymond Williams', in *Mikhail Mikhailovich Bakhtin: His Circle, His Influence*, papers presented at the International Colloquium, Queens University, 7–9 October, 1983. Department of French Studies, Queen's University, Kingston, Ontario, Canada.

Parrinder, Patrick, *Literature and History* 7 (1981), pp. 124–6. Review of *Politics and Letters*.

Parrinder, Patrick, 'The accents of Raymond Williams', *Critical Quarterly* 26 (1984), pp. 47–57.

Parrinder, Patrick, 'Pamphleteer's Progress', review of *The Functions of Criticism*, by Terry Eagleton, *London Review of Books*, 7 February 1985, pp. 16–17.

Parrinder, Patrick, 'Culture and Society in the 1980's', and 'Utopia and negativity in Raymond Williams', in his *The Failure of Theory: Essays on Criticism and Contemporary Fiction*, Brighton, Harvester, 1987, pp. 58–71, 72–84.

Parrinder, Patrick, 'Diary', *The London Review of Books*, 12 February 1988, p. 25.

Pechey, Graham, '*Scrutiny*, English Marxism, and the Work of Raymond Williams', *Literature and History*, vol. 11, no. 1 (Spring 1985), pp. 65–76.

Pfeil, Fred, 'Towards a portable Marxist Criticism: A Critique and Suggestion', *College English* 41 (1980), pp. 753–68.

Pittock, Malcolm, *Essays in Criticism* 9 (1959), pp. 430–32. Review of *Culture and Society*.

Pittock, Malcolm, 'The Optimistic Revolution', *Essays in Criticism* 12 (1962), pp. 82–91. Review of *The Long Revolution*.

Potter, Dennis, 'Unknown Territory', *New Left Review* 7 (January– February 1961), pp. 63–5. Review of *Border Country*.

Quinton, Anthony, 'The Quality of Living', *The Spectator*, 26 May 1961, pp. 761–2.

Rosenberg, Harold, 'The Threat of Culture', *The Nation*, 7 February 1959, pp. 121–2. Review of *Culture and Society*.

Rowbotham, Sheila, 'Picking up the pieces', *New Socialist*, no. 31, October 1985, p. 49. Review of the paperback edn. of *Towards 2000*.

Ryan, Alan, 'Feudal lord of culture and society', *New Society*, 20 September 1979, pp. 628–9. Review of *Politics and Letters*.

Ryan, Kiernan, 'Socialist Fiction and the Education of Desire: Mervyn Jones, Raymond Williams and John Berger', in *The Socialist Novel in Britain: Towards the Recovery of a Tradition*, ed. H. Gustav Klaus, Brighton, Sussex, Harvester Press, 1982, pp. 166–85.

Said, Edward, *Orientalism*, New York, Vintage, 1979.

Said, Edward, 'Reflections on Recent American "Left" Literary Theory', *boundary 2*, 8 (Fall 1979), pp. 11–30

Said, Edward, 'Traveling Theory', *Raritan* 1 (Winter 1982), pp. 41–67. Reprinted in his *The World, The Text, and The Critic*, Cambridge, Harvard University Press, 1983.

Said, Edward W., 'Raymond Williams, 1921–1988', *The Nation*, 5 March 1988, pp. 312, 314.

Sandall, Roger, 'When I hear the Word "Culture": From Arnold to Anthropology', *Encounter* 55 (October 1980), pp. 89–92. Review of *Politics and Letters*.

Scrivener, Michael, *Telos* 38 (Winter 1979–80), pp. 190–98. Review of *Marxism and Literature*.

Scruton, Roger, 'The Word in the World', *Times Literary Supplement*, 26 March 1976, p. 352. Review of *Keywords*.

Scruton, Roger, 'Raymond Williams', in his *Thinkers of the New Left*, London, Longman, 1985, pp. 54–65.

Sharratt, Bernard, 'Poisson: A modest review', in his *Reading Relations: Structures of Literary Production: A Dialectical Text/Book*, Brighton, Sussex, Harvester, 1982, pp. 35–40.

Siegmund-Schultze, Dorothea, 'Raymond Williams' Concept of Culture', *Zeitschrift fur Anglistik und Amerikanistik* 22 (1974), pp. 131–45.

Slater, David, 'Social Movements and a Recasting of the Political', in *New Social Movements and the State in Latin America*, ed. David Slater, Amsterdam, CEDLA, 1985, pp. 12–15.

Smith, Barry, 'A Historian's Comments upon *Culture and Society* and *The Long Revolution*', *The Melbourne Historical Journal* 8 (1969), p. 32.

Sparks, Colin, 'Raymond Williams, Culture and Marxism', *International Socialism* 9 (Summer 1980), pp. 131–44.

Spender, Stephen, *New York Review of Books*, 16 November 1972, p. 3. Review of *Orwell*.

Stedman Jones, Gareth, review of *Towards 2000* and *Wigan Pier Revisited*, by Beatrix Campbell, *Marxism Today*, July 1984, pp. 38–40.

Stein, Walter, 'Humanism and Tragic redemption', chapter 6 of *Criticism as Dialogue*, Cambridge, Cambridge University Press, 1969, pp. 183–246. On *Modern Tragedy*.

Thompson, E. P., 'The Long Revolution', *New Left Review*, no. 9 and no. 10 (May/June and July/August 1961), pp. 24–33, 34–9.

Thompson, E. P., 'A Nice Place to Visit', *New York Review of Books*, 6 February 1975, pp. 34–7. Review of *The Country and the City*.

Thompson, E. P.. 'Last Dispatches from The Border Country', *The Nation*, 5 March 1988, pp. 310–12.

Thompson, John O., 'Tragic Flow: Raymond Williams on Drama', *Screen Education*, no. 34 (Summer 1980), pp. 45–58.

Times Literary Supplement, 'The Weight of an Abstraction', 26 September 1958, p. 548. Review of *Culture and Society*. See letter from Williams, 3 October 1958, p. 561.

Times Literary Supplement, 'Notes Towards the Definition of What?', 10 March 1961, p. 147. Review of *The Long Revolution*.

Times Literary Supplement, 'A Time for Tragedy?', 11 August 1966, pp. 717–18. Review of *Modern Tragedy*, possibly by George Steiner.

Wain, John, 'The Coronation of the Novel', *The Listener*, 4 June 1970, pp. 755–6. Review of *The English Novel*.

Ward, J. P., *Raymond Williams*, Writers of Wales Series, University of Wales Press for the Welsh Arts Council, 1981.

Watkins, Evan, 'Raymond Williams and Marxist Criticism', *boundary 2*, 4 (1975–6), pp. 933–46.

Watkins, Evan, *The Critical Act: Criticism and Community*, chapter 5, 'Raymond Williams and Marxist Literary Criticism', New Haven and London, Yale University Press, 1978.

Watkins, Evan, 'Conflict and Consensus in the History of Recent Criticism', *New Literary History* 12 (1981), pp. 345–65.

Williams, Merryn, 'Raymond Williams, 1921–88', *Planet* 68 (April/May 1988), pp. 3–6.

Wollheim, Richard, *Culture and Socialism*, Fabian Tract 331, London, The Fabian Society, 1961

Wollheim, Richard, 'Definitions of Culture', *New Statesman*, 9 June 1961.

Wollheim, Richard, 'The English Dream', *The Spectator*, 10 March 1961, pp. 334–5. Review of *The Long Revolution*.

Woodcock, George, 'Half-Truths on Orwell', *The Nation*, 11 October 1971, pp. 341–2. Review of *Orwell*.

Woodcock, George, 'The Two Faces of Modern Marxism', *Sewanee Review* 86 (1978), pp. 588–94. Review of *Marxism and Literature*.

Zinman, Rosalind, 'Raymond Williams; towards a sociology of culture', Ph.D. dissertation, Concordia University, Montreal, 1984.

Index

'angry young men', 15
Arac, Jonathan, 72–3
Arnold, Matthew, 55
Arts Council, 27–9, 40
Auden, W. H., 6
Austen, Jane, 70–1
authoritarian democracy, 27, 30, 93, 115

Bahro, Rudolf, 31–3
Bakhtin, M. M., 75–7
Barnett, Anthony, 119 n24
Barratt Brown, Michael, 22
Barthes, Roland, 56–7
Begriffsgeschichte, 54
Benjamin, Walter, 114
body, and communication, 107–9, 117, 118 n17, 120
Bourdieu, Pierre, vii, 119 n30
Brecht, Bertolt, 88–9
Brontës, Charlotte and Emily, 73–4
Burchfield, R. W., 53–4
Burke, Edmund, 61

Cambridge Review, 25
Cambridge University, 7, 14, 25–7, 49
Cambridge University Journal, 6
Campaign for Nuclear Disarmament, 14–16, 20, 30, 45
Carpenter, Edward, 31
censorship, 25
Chatto & Windus, 44, 49
childhood, 1–4
Cobbett, William, 61
Collins, Henry, 10–11
communication policy, 13, 15, 18–19,

22, 23, 28–9, 40–1, 125
Communist Party, 7–8, 12, 16, 21, 23
complex seeing, 2–4, 80–1, 87–9
conventions, 84–5, 92, 117
Conviction, 14
Craig, Maurice, 7
Critic, 11
Czechoslovakia, 99, 121

Daily Worker, 7, 25
Dickens, Charles, 70–3, 76
'dramatized society', 90
Dutschke, Rudi, 26–7

Eagleton, Terry, 31, 37 n56, 49
ecology, 31, 108–9, 125
Eliot, George, 74
Eliot, T. S., 50, 57–9, 63, 105
Ellis, John, 97–8
Empson, William, 50–2, 55
European Economic Community, 25
expressionism, individual, 87–8
expressionism, social, 88–9

Fabian socialism, 58
Falklands War, 92–3
Febvre, Lucien, 54
feminism, 30–1, 121, 126
film, 41–2, 87, 108
Fish, Stanley, 59–60
Foot, Michael, 15
form
    Barthes on, 56
    and conventions, notations, 84–5
    dramatic, 80
    essay, 59
    of fiction extended, 77–8

film as cultural, 42
in Ibsen, 3
of literary journalism in *Conviction*,
    14
and montage, 122
novel, 68, 74
as opposed to 'genre', 117–18
pre-emergence of new, 115
television, 92, 94, 121, 122
as 'way of seeing', 104
Forward March of Labour Halted?, 30
Foucault, Michel, 72

gender in writing, 73
General Strike, 29
Goldmann, Lucien, 83, 114
Grierson, John, 41–2
    on film as cultural form, 42
Guardian, 45

Hall, Stuart, 22
Hardy, Thomas, 74
Heath, Stephen, 25
hegemony, 32–3, 77, 99, 106–7,
    114–15, 121–2
Hobsbawm, Eric, 7, 30
Hodgkin, Thomas, 10
Hoggart, Richard, 4 n2, 10, 16
homosexuality, 31
Hulme, T. E., 63
Hume, David, 51, 120

Ibsen, Henrik, 1–4, 80, 90
ideology, 112
Institute for Contemporary Arts, 28
intellectuals, 6–7, 18, 32–3, 58

Jenkins, Hugh, 19, 27

Keynes, John Maynard, 28
keywords
    in *Annales* school, 54
    in *Culture and Society*, 54, 55, 60–2
    in debates about culture, 57
    in debates about nuclear
        disarmament, 49–50
    in Empson, 51

in Hume, 51
in *The Long Revolution*, 103–5
in *Marxism and Literature*, 110
in miners' strike, 126 n11
in *Modern Tragedy*, 81
in Timpanaro, 109
in *Towards 2000*, 124, 125
knowable community
    in anthropology, 78
    in Brecht, lack of, 89
    in the Brontës, 73
    and complex societies, 23
    and *Culture and Society*, 62, 65,
        123
    definition of, 68
    in D. H. Lawrence, 75, 76
    in Dickens, 70–1
    in George Eliot, 74–5
    in Hardy, 74
    in Jane Austen, lack of, 70–1
    main aspects of, 69
    and television, 90
    and *Towards 2000*, 124, 125

Labour Party, 6, 16, 17–22
Lady Chatterley's Lover, 25
language, 110–12, 118–19 n17
Lawrence, D. H., 12, 63–4, 74–5
Leavis, F. R., 9, 12, 25–6, 59, 63, 80
Listener, 44
literary magazines, 41
literature, 8–9, 112, 116

MacCabe, Colin, 27, 85–6
McGovern, George, 99
McGrath, John, 101 n28
majority and minority cultural forms,
    40–6, 70, 80, 94–5, 96
Malinowski, Bronislaw, 57–8
Mankowitz, Wolf, 10–11
Marcus, George, 78
Marcuse, Herbert, 26
Marx, Karl, 71
Marxism, 112–14
Mill, John Stuart, 55
montage, 122–3
Morris, William, 61, 62

National Convention of the Left, 22–3
naturalism in drama, 88, 90
New Left, 16
New Left Review, 45–6
notation(s), 84, 116–17
  film as new type of, 87

O'Casey, Sean, 87–8
Orrom, Michael, 7, 42
Orwell, George, 6, 8, 13, 15, 63–4
Outlook, 7
Owen, Robert, 30–1
Oxford English Dictionary, 53–4

peace, 126
  see also Campaign for Nuclear Disarmament
Penguin Books, 44–5
Politics & Letters (journal), 11–13, 40–1

radio, 43
Raybould, S. G., 10
realism, 85–7
representation, 90–1, 93, 99, 124
Richards, I. A., 50–1, 63
Rossi-Landi, Ferruccio, 110–11

Sanity, 20, 45
Sartre, Jean-Paul, 13, 56–7
Scrivener, Michael, 118–19 n17
Soviet literary controversy, 11–12
Spender, Stephen, 24
structure of feeling, 83–5, 105–6, 114–15
Sunday Citizen, 22

Tawney, R. H., 9, 63
Taylor, Barbara, 30–1
television, 89–99
  commentary in, 98–9, 121
  flow of, 96–8, 122
  Irish, 93, 95
  see also: form, television
Thompson, Edward, 22, 45–6, 49, 105–6

Timpanaro, Sebastiano, 108–9
Toller, Ernst, 88
Tribune 14, 15, 19, 45, 49

Venice, 121–2
Vietnam war, 19, 21, 55, 94, 122
Views, 19, 46
Volosinov, V. N., 111–12

war, 2–4, 7, 8, 49–50, 63, 81, 82–3, 91–2, 97
  in Sean O'Casey, 87
  see also Campaign for Nuclear Disarmament; Falklands War; Vietnam War
Wild Strawberries, 2
Williams, Joy, ix, 17–18, 19
Williams, Merryn, ix
Williams, Raymond
  'Base and superstructure in Marxist cultural theory', 106–7
  book-reviewer for the *Guardian*, 45
  Communications, 8, 9, 10, 18, 125
  The Country and the City, 1, 25
  Culture and Society, 55–65, 123
  'Culture is Ordinary', 14
  'David Hume: Reasoning and Experience', 51
  'Distance', 92–3
  Drama from Ibsen to Brecht, 87–9
  editor of New Thinkers Library, 44
  The English Novel, 25, 68–71, 73–8
  and film, 42–3
  Keywords, 49, 50, 52–4
  Listener, column on television, 120–3
  The Long Revolution, 103–6
  May Day Manifesto, 22–3
  Marxism and Literature, 109–18
  'Means of communication as means of production', 107–8
  Modern Tragedy, 25, 81–3
  on Munich Olympics, 91–2
  The Pelican Book of English Prose, 69
  'The Politics of Nuclear Disarmament', 49

Preface to Film, 84
radio talks for BBC, 43–4
Reading and Criticism, 9
on role of literary magazines, 46
*Television: Technology and Cultural
Form*, 94–7
theory of the state, lack of, 40
Towards 2000, 124, 125
'Towards Many Socialisms', 124
vocation as writer, 1, 3–4
and Wales, 29, 46

Williams, W. E., 44–5
Wilson, Harold, 17, 20–2, 40–1
Wintringham, Tom, 8
Wittgenstein, Ludwig, 111
Workers' Educational Association,
8–10
writing, 60–1, 77, 116–18, 120–1,
123